Melville
The Making of the Poet

HERSHEL PARKER

Melville

The Making of the Poet

NORTHWESTERN UNIVERSITY PRESS

EVANSTON, ILLINOIS

Northwestern University Press
www.nupress.northwestern.edu

Printed in the United States of America

10 9 8 7 6 5 4 3 2 1

Library of Congress Cataloging-in-Publication Data

Parker, Hershel.
   Melville : the making of the poet / Hershel Parker.
      p. cm.
   Includes bibliographical references and index.
   ISBN-13: 978-0-8101-2464-6 (cloth : alk. paper)
   ISBN-10: 0-8101-2464-5 (cloth : alk. paper)
   1. Melville, Herman, 1819–1891—Criticism and interpretation. I. Title.
PS2387.P28 2007
813'.3—dc22

                                                    2007023779

♾ The paper used in this publication meets the minimum requirements of the American National
Standard for Information Sciences—Permanence of Paper for Printed Library Materials, ANSI
Z39.48-1992.

*This book is dedicated
to the great Yale Melville scholars of the 1940s
(the students of Stanley T. Williams)
and to their only peers, Wilson Heflin and Jay Leyda.
It is also dedicated to Robert D. Madison, Dennis C. Marnon,
Scott Norsworthy, Alma MacDougall Reising,
and, not least, Heddy-Ann Richter.*

CONTENTS

ACKNOWLEDGMENTS

My greatest debts are to Jay Leyda, Harrison Hayford, and Merton M. Sealts Jr. I owe special thanks to Dennis C. Marnon and Scott Norsworthy, who handed me their remarkable discoveries about the literary and educational milieux of Lansingburgh and Albany and advised in many other ways. Robert D. Madison repeatedly demonstrated that he had been trained by Hayford. As I said in the second volume of my biography of Melville, it was a blessing to have the Melville scholar Alma MacDougall Reising as copy editor. I am indebted to the most magnanimous of bookmen, William S. Reese. Melville's great-granddaughter Priscilla Osborne Ambrose let me transcribe Melville's marginalia in her set of Edmund Spenser's poetry. Ruth Degenhardt and Kathleen Reilly of the Berkshire Athenaeum again proved exemplary librarians. I am indebted to all the editorial associates and contributing scholars on the Northwestern-Newberry edition of Melville's *Published Poems:* Robert A. Sandberg, Dennis Berthold, Shirley Dettlaff, Brian Higgins, Joyce Deveau Kennedy, Robert D. Madison, Scott Norsworthy, Steven Olsen-Smith, Gordon Poole, Douglas Robillard, and John Wenke. I am also grateful to Lottie Cain Honea, Chris Coughlin, Mary K Bercaw Edwards, Thomas F. Heffernan, James A. Hime, Athel Eugene Gibson, Frederick J. Kennedy, Deborah Norsworthy, Heddy-Ann Richter, Benton Tindall, and Mark Wojnar, and to the remarkably imaginative director and staff at Northwestern University Press.

Portions of some chapters are revisions and expansions of passages in my two-volume biography of Melville (Baltimore: Johns Hopkins University Press, 1996, 2002). The seven-page introduction is a version of parts of the nineteen-page *"The Isle of the Cross* and *Poems:* Lost Melville Books and the Indefinite Afterlife of Error," *Nineteenth-Century Literature* 62 (June 2007): 29–47. The letter from Allan Melvill to Lemuel Shaw quoted at the beginning of chapter 3 is printed with the permission of the Houghton Library, Harvard University.

Melville
The Making of the Poet

Melville's Lost Books and the Trajectory of His Career as Poet

IN THE TWENTY-FIRST CENTURY, AFTER MANY (BUT FAR FROM ALL) old gaps in basic knowledge about Melville's life have been filled and after many often-repeated errors have long been corrected, misconceptions are still carelessly repeated from Raymond Weaver's 1921 biography or from other obdurate sources of errors. Misconceptions about *Pierre,* in particular, and about the whole period from late 1851 up through Melville's finishing his first book of poetry in 1860, have persisted in the face of strong evidence made public for years, or even for many decades. The two most pernicious misconceptions about Melville are that he repudiated fiction writing after *Pierre* (1852) and that he did not start writing poetry in the late 1850s (and have a book of poems ready for publication in 1860). Critics who labor under these intertwined misconceptions have distorted the whole trajectory of Melville's career, in particular his career as a poet.

Harrison Hayford in 1946 began the demonstration that Melville, far from renouncing fiction in 1851 or 1852, had begun a book in 1852 and perhaps had completed it in 1853. In *The Letters of Herman Melville* (1960) Merrell R. Davis and William H. Gilman showed that Melville had in fact completed that book in 1853 and had offered it to the Harpers. Merton M. Sealts Jr. in 1987 reviewed the evidence in full, agreeing with Davis and Gilman and concluding that Melville had finished the book in May 1853 and taken it to the Harpers in June. Then in the same year I discovered the title of the lost book, *The Isle of the Cross,* and something very close to the date of completion, if not the actual date, May 22, as well as a more precise date for Melville's June trip to New York with the manuscript. My presentation of the evidence was published in 1990. In February 1990 Sealts summarized: "Hershel Parker, working with Augusta Melville's correspondence as recently added to the Gansevoort-Lansing Collection, New York Public Library, has established that this work was in fact 'completed under the title of *The Isle of the Cross*'" (9). I put the evidence in a fuller context in volume 2 of *Herman Melville: A Biography* (2002).

Without taking account of the work by Hayford and by Davis and Gilman, Nina Baym in 1979 published an updating of the Weaver theory about Melville's renouncing fiction. By her vigorous arguments and succinct title, "Melville's Quarrel with Fiction," Baym reinforced Weaver's effects on critics, including Richard Brodhead, Andrew Delbanco, and Elizabeth Schultz. These three prominent Melville critics in their 2002 reviews of my second volume deplored what Brodhead (in the *New York Times* for June 23) called "Parker's surmises about works Melville never published that did not survive" (13), *The Isle of the Cross* and the 1860 *Poems*. Delbanco in the September *New Republic* warned that the second volume, like the first, "must be used with caution": "Parker is amazingly certain of his own conclusions. . . . He is sure that immediately after completing *Pierre*, Melville wrote an unpublished novel" (34). Elizabeth Schultz in *The Common Review* declared that "there is only tentative evidence" that *The Isle of the Cross* existed and was submitted to a publisher (45). None of these three critics engaged any of the evidence accumulated over the decades, beginning with Hayford's work in 1946.

In his *New York Times* review Brodhead said this of *Poems:* "Parker is also convinced that Melville prepared a volume of poems in 1860 that failed to be published. If this is so, a stretch that had seemed empty of literary strivings was instead a time of new effort and new failure—a black hole Parker alone has the instruments to detect" (13). Delbanco added that "[Parker] is sure that when Melville traveled by slow boat to San Francisco in 1860, he expected to find waiting for him a finished copy of a book of poems that he had entrusted in manuscript to his brother for transmission to his publishers before leaving the East. (Such a book was never published—and it is a surmise that Melville ever wrote it.) . . . In short, Parker trusts his own intuition completely, and, presenting inferences as facts, he expects his readers to trust it, too" (34). Schultz regretted that "[Parker] reads betrayal and despair into the disappearance of two manuscripts, which he contends Melville completed—a novel, putatively titled *The Isle of the Cross,* and his first collection of poems" (45).

The misconception that Melville did not begin writing poetry (or ambitious poetry) in the late 1850s and did not have a volume of poetry ready for publication in 1860 seems to derive from reliance on Weaver's 1921 biography to the exclusion of all later scholarship. Weaver had not known about *Poems* (1860). His primary source of family information, Melville's granddaughter Eleanor Thomas Metcalf, apparently had not learned about it in time to tell him. The evidence had rested, unread, in the Duyckinck Collection in the New York Public Library until 1922, the year after Weaver's biography appeared, when Meade Minnigerode published *Some Personal Letters of Herman Melville and a Bibliography.* In the standard anthology *Melville: Representative Selections* (1938), Willard Thorp reprinted or summarized this evidence. Thereafter, the fact that Melville had completed a volume of poems in 1860 was familiar to Jay Leyda (who in *The Melville Log* [1951] published additional evidence) and to all Melville scholars and even to many critics who had not worked with Melville documents themselves and who had not seen Minnigerode's book. Melville's "Memoranda for Allan concerning the publication of my verses," twelve specific directions, have been quoted repeatedly as well as printed in Minnigerode, Thorp, the *Letters,* and the Northwestern-Newberry edition of Melville's *Correspondence.*[1] False statements made in conspicuous places have always bedeviled attempts to understand Melville, but the situation is infinitely compounded in the twenty-first century, for the reviews written by Brodhead, Delbanco, and Schultz in 2002 continue to mislead incalculable numbers of readers during their indefinite afterlife on the Internet. The eager new Melvillean who encounters these reviews on the Internet finds them unencumbered by any version of the patented Melvillean warning label, "No Trust."[2] There is, of course, nothing putative about either title, *The Isle of the Cross* or *Poems.* The books are lost, but they existed.

Ignorance about *The Isle of the Cross* and *Poems* has distorted the verifiable stages in Melville's development as a writer. Melville did not renounce writing fiction in 1851 or 1852; he completed *The Isle of the Cross* in 1853 before beginning to write short stories. He did not renounce all writing even after composing his third lecture in 1859, for by that time he was already writing poetry, as he did until his death. Modern critics have been reluctant to, or actually unequipped to, pay thoughtful attention to scholarship, yet more is at work than a climate in which scholarship is ignored. In 1954 Walter E. Bezanson, a great scholar-critic, saw a "contraction" of Melville's "creative powers" in the fact that between 1846 and 1857 he had published ten books and in the five years between 1857 and 1862 had published none (375). Bezanson could not have known for certain about yet another prose work in those extraordinarily creative ten years, *The Isle of the Cross* (Melville's eighth book, if it had been published), but he could have mentioned *Poems* as witness that it was Melville's publishing outlets that had contracted rather than Melville's creative powers. It is hard for any human being, even so fine a critic as Bezanson, to visualize something that does not exist and to make complicated allowances for it.

Yet however strongly the human brain resists taking uncertainty into certain account, critics now must begin to rethink the trajectory of Melville's career in the light of the only partially tangible *The Isle of the Cross* and *Poems*. In volume 2 of *Herman Melville*, I insisted that in the future critics should speculate responsibly about how Melville might have changed (in style, psychology, intellect) in the process of writing the lost *The Isle of the Cross* from mid-December 1852 till late May 1853. Similarly, a responsible critic will take account of how Melville might have developed as a poet in the process of writing the lost *Poems* from 1857 or 1858 until May 1860. No one can think responsibly about *Battle-Pieces* (1866), *Clarel* (1876), *John Marr* (1888), and *Timoleon* (1891)[3] without taking into account that Melville completed a book of poetry in 1860. Critics still refer to *Battle-Pieces* as Melville's first book of poetry instead of his first *published* book of poetry. Critics still write as if *Battle-Pieces* followed *The Confidence-Man* (1857) without any intermediate literary work, or, at best, as if it followed next after the composition of his three lectures in the late 1850s. In 2002, for example, Frank Day described Melville as "a novice poet" (67) in his detailed study of Melville's use of the *Rebellion Record* for twenty poems in *Battle-Pieces*. Criticism is vitiated, if not invalidated, when anything poetically "unconventional" in *Battle-Pieces* is ascribed to Melville's turning directly, however belatedly, from prose to his Civil War poetry. Lawrence Buell says incisively that "Melville published poetry long before turning intensively to it" (138). A more precise statement might be that "Melville turned intensively to poetry (in the late 1850s) long before publishing any of the ambitious poetry he wrote then." The latter formulation would allow us to remember that Melville wrote poetry with high intensity in 1858 through early 1860, perhaps again during intervals in the next two years or so, and again around 1864 or after the fall of Richmond in 1865, whenever he began serious work on *Battle-Pieces*, the first book of poems he was able to publish (1866). The same critic comments that the "unfinished Grandvin-Gentian sketches comprise two major poetic sequences interspersed with prose commentary, a hybrid genre Melville often favored in his late work" (Buell 151). Yet the two poems referred to, the variously titled "Naples" poem and "At the Hostelry," are not late, certainly not from Melville's last decade.[4] One or both of them may well have been in *Poems* (1860), although parts of "At the Hostelry" seem to date from the next year or two, or a little later. The prose pieces written to introduce them, the sketches involving Gentian and Grandvin, date (in their first versions) from the late 1870s. In his last years Melville continued to rework some of the prose parts (and perhaps some of the poetry) and added the new prefatory essay, "The House of the Tragic Poet."

A pervasive and powerful misconception is that any poetry that Melville published in *John Marr* (1888) or *Timoleon* (1891) and any poetry he left unpublished at his death (such as the poems in a "near-final" collection to be called *Weeds and Wildings*) is exclusively "late" poetry, composed late in his life. This misconception has proved almost unshakable because it is so seemingly commonsensical. In fact, a yet-undetermined amount of that poetry must be late, or must have been revised late, while a yet-undetermined amount of it may have been written much earlier. As Thorp suggested in 1938, some early (1857–60) poetry, however much it was later revised, almost surely survives from the lost *Poems* (1860).

In what is less a misconception than an example of hasty misjudgment, the still-influential early twentieth-century biographers were contemptuous of Melville's poetry and assumed that he never took it very seriously. Weaver (1921) said "the inspiration flags throughout" *John Marr* and *Timoleon,* the volumes Melville printed at the end of his life (365). Lewis Mumford (1929) was sure that "Melville rarely achieved form as a poet" in *Battle-Pieces,* and that in *Clarel* Melville "was too frequently the victim of his uncertain taste," so that the "clumsiness in detail adds to the clumsiness of conception: what might have been vivid prose became dull verse" (321). This old disdain survives in the still-prevalent misconception that after the failure of his career as a prose writer Melville took up versifying as a harmless private hobby. By 2005, Delbanco had decided that, after all, Melville had "a small manuscript" of poems in 1860 ("small" being undemonstrated) and that some of the poems survived. In the spirit of Weaver and Mumford, he was sure that reading these poems "is like overhearing a musician who no longer expects to play public recitals but who still practices in private in order to keep his fingers limber" (267). According to this common misconception, the former literary man did not care enough about his hobby to study the poetry by older British poets or his British contemporaries. Self-indulgent and inefficient, Melville did not trouble to analyze poetic techniques and did not struggle to master poetic principles. The misconception that poetry was merely a harmless hobby for Melville was most succinctly, if brusquely, stated by Alfred Kazin in a 1997 forum on Melville at the Barnes and Noble bookstore in Union Square, New York City, where the other participants were Paul Metcalf (one of Melville's great-grandsons) and me. Kazin cautioned: "You have to remember that poetry was just a sideline with Melville; it was never important to him and he was never good at it" (Parker 2:xiii).

Melville's shrewd annotations in dozens of volumes of poetry and books on poetry demonstrate the falseness of this Weaver-Kazin-Delbanco theory. Poetry was anything but a sideline for Melville. He became a poet when he was thirty-nine or forty and remained a poet until he died at seventy-two. He had been a regular writer of prose for publication only for a dozen years, from the end of 1844, when he started *Typee,* until the summer of 1856, when he completed *The Confidence-Man.* He wrote very little prose after that—a lecture in 1857, another in 1858, and a third in 1859, none of which he published. After April 1857 (when *The Confidence-Man* was published), the prose he published, aside from a few letters to newspaper editors, consisted mainly of the notes and the "Supplement" in *Battle-Pieces;* a brief memoir of his uncle Thomas Melvill Jr., which his friend Joseph Smith prevailed upon him to write (after 1872, Smith said) for the 1876 *History of Pittsfield;*[5] and prose headnotes to poems. The Jack Gentian and Marquis de Grandvin prose sketches were from the start attempts to introduce and thereby salvage two longish poems written long before. The story of Billy Budd, which Melville was working on at his death, began as a prose headnote to the ballad of "Billy in the Darbies" and then greatly outgrew its initial purpose. With only a few exceptions, what Melville wrote for publication from around 1858 until his death in September 1891 was poetry. The cyclopedias, Melville warned in 1886, were no more infallible than the pope,[6] and some encyclopedias printed and bound in the twenty-first century as well as some Internet encyclopedias assert, among other errors, that Melville did not write any substantial amount of poetry until late in his life and that only toward the end of his life did he concentrate on writing poetry. The facts need to be repeated for emphasis: Herman Melville was a practicing poet (1857 or 1858–91) for three times as long as he was a professional, publishing writer of prose (1846–57). Poetry was not just a sideline for Melville: it was what he wrote for a third of a century. It was important to him; indeed, it was, for many years of his life, certainly from 1870 into 1875, when he was working on *Clarel* (1876), obsessively important.

Yet much of what we know about Melville and poetry has come to light only in recent decades, mainly from belated study of the "Augusta Papers"[7] discovered in 1983 or from books newly recovered from Melville's library (notably his copies of Wordsworth, Milton, Dante, and Spenser, and his copies of Hazlitt's *Lectures on the English Poets* and Thomas Warton's *History of English Poetry*). With some exceptions, such as Thomas F. Heffernan's 1977 article on Melville's copy of Wordsworth and the second volume of my biography, the new information was slow in being made public. In the chapters that follow, previously published evidence is brought together with bounteous new evidence about basic topics such as Melville's hearing and reading poetry, his buying books of poetry and books containing poetry, his habit of spotting and annotating poetic echoes, his standards for ranking poets, his conscious study of poetic techniques, and his quest for satisfying aesthetic principles. The title of this book identifies a terrain long left unexplored—*Melville: The Making of the Poet.*

CHAPTER ONE

A Poet in Prose: How Critics Prepared
Melville to Think of Himself as a Poet

WHEN HE TOOK UP HIS PEN IN MANHATTAN LATE IN 1844, MELVILLE would never have considered poetry as a medium for telling the once-in-a-lifetime story of his experiences with natives in the interior of one of the Marquesas Islands. He had been a published writer of competent amateurish prose as early as 1839, and prose was faster and easier to write than poetry. Besides that, he had been telling his story on shore and on ship for two years by then, a period when he had the ideal audience for perfecting his ambiguous sexual teasing or bragging—men (many of them young) who at times had long been deprived of sex with women. The more or less autobiographical part of the book would be comparatively easy to put down on paper in acceptable (and for the most part conventional) prose. Yet from the first, beginning at the publication of *Typee* in 1846, two decades before Melville surprised the American reading public by re-emerging into literary life as a poet, some reviewers resorted to "poetic" and its cognates in referring to his books. In some minds "poetic" prose was opposed to moral prose. Low-church Protestants in religious newspapers and magazines called Melville's style in *Typee,* and later in the sequel, *Omoo* (1847), "poetic" in the sense of false, misleading, and even dangerously alluring. This outraged passage is from "*Typee:* The Traducer of Missions," in the New York *Christian Parlor Magazine* (July 1846): "We do not look at the history of the missionary work from the merely enthusiastic or poetic point of view. . . . We shall probably give Typee a glance among the authorities [on Polynesia], as a specimen of that genus of writers whose poetry and poetic feelings lead them to admire only what is savage, and condemn, under assumed pretexts, the ripening fruit of the gospel of Christ."[1] The most vicious of Melville's reviewers, George Washington Peck, in the New York *American Whig Review* for July 1847 stressed the insidious effects of Melville's style: "Omoo is a book one may read once with interest and pleasure, but with *a perpetual recoil.* It is poetically written, but yet carelessly, and in a bad spirit." On July 5, 1849, reviewing the Harper reissue of *Typee,* the New York *Evangelist,* a Presbyterian organ, declared that the book "exhibits a spirit and grace irresistible to most readers, and depicts the loveliest scenery in the world with true poetic genius." The problem was that these graces were put to the service of a "degraded moral tone," in which Melville slanderously attacked "missionary labors and character," so that his writing constituted "unquestionable falsehood from beginning to end." Reviewers in such denominational papers were uneasily sure that Melville through his delightful style was seducing his readers into sinful delights and perhaps even corrupt opinions. Earnest and even vicious as they were, these reviewers constituted a minority, and became almost quiescent during the reception of Melville's next books, *Mardi* (1849), *Redburn* (1849), and *White-Jacket* (1850), but rose up, freshly empowered, to attack *Moby-Dick* brutally late in 1851 and early in 1852.

In some British and American reviews in the secular press, the style of *Typee* and then of *Omoo* was also, and more often, declared "poetic" in the sense that the descriptions were fanciful, highly imaginative, and idealized, as when the Edinburgh *Weekly Register and General Advertiser* for April 14, 1847, called *Omoo* a "work very exquisitely written on an exquisite subject; bursts of what is almost brilliant poetry alternating with the raciest drollery" or when the Boston *Bee* on May 5, 1847, said *Omoo* had "all the attractiveness of a book of travels, abounding in passages of wit, humor, romance and poetry." In a similar spirit the London *Times* (September 24, 1847) came late but happily to *Omoo:* "A better material has not for years fallen into the way of the creator and the poet; a more skilful workman it has been seldom our lot to welcome." This praise of Melville as creator and poet was given very wide circulation in the "Supplement" to the New York *Tribune* of October 30, 1847, in the form of a letter (dated October 4) from its London correspondent, "P." Still later, on November 13, 1847, the *Times* review was touted by Melville's friend Nathaniel Parker Willis in his very popular weekly, the New York *Home Journal,* where Willis reprinted the tribute to Melville as "the creator and the poet."

In keeping with this dominant public opinion was an article by Sarah Jane Clarke, writing as "Grace Greenwood." Her spoof in the Philadelphia *Saturday Evening Post* (October 9, 1847) purported to be a "Letter from the Author of 'Typee.'" Here "H.M." asserted his belief that "*poets* are not properly esteemed and recompensed in our country," as contrasted with the Typee valley, where the "veritable Polynesian Tom Moore," "Clingy Lingy," the finest poet on the island, was indulged in every way, including the granting of sexual privileges: "He was allowed to choose for his bride the prettiest maiden in the valley, and to change his wife every new moon, if so inclined. *The* place of all the world for your Shelleys and Byrons were Typee. . . . I also ascertained that no man was allowed to play critic in Typee, unless himself a poet. The body-servant of the bard was pointed out to me, a poor devil of a fellow, who though of most aristocratic connections, had been degraded to his present position for an impromptu but cutting review, produced upon one of Clingy Lingy's improvisations." After this, Clarke added a fanciful last note from "H.M.": "I should have included this account in my work [*Typee*], but for the fear that on hearing of such a Paradisean state of things, our entire squad of poets would immediately emigrate to Typee." Melville could not have missed this charming supplement to *Typee* on poetry, a subject in which his interest was burgeoning. After his return from England in early February 1850, he would also have been shown the reprinting of this piece in Clarke's *Greenwood Leaves,* published in late November 1849, dated 1850.[2]

In early March 1848 Melville's friend Evert A. Duyckinck, a New York City editor, wrote to his brother George: "Melville the other night brought me a few chapters of his new book, which in the poetry and wildness of the thing will be ahead of Typee & Omoo" (*Log* 273).[3] Melville himself was thinking in just those terms, and may have so expressed himself to Duyckinck. Melville's earliest letters to John Murray, the London publisher of his first two books, focus on the charges in the press that *Typee* was not authentic—not written by the real man named "Herman Melville" and not based on a real experience of that Herman Melville. Still concerned to be believed as a truth-teller, on March 25, 1848, in a letter to Murray he had used the phrase "& it[']s authentic" to describe his manuscript in progress, then changed the wording to "it shall have the right stuff in it." (The manuscript of *Mardi* then presumably stood without any chapters on the contemporary European and American political situation, news of revolution in

Paris having arrived in New York only the week before.) Melville explained that his new book was not, as previously described, "a bona-fide narrative of my adventures in the Pacific, continued from 'Omoo.'" Instead, he was writing "a 'Romance of Polynisian Adventure.'" Partly, he said, he was writing in reaction to "the reiterated imputation of being a romancer in disguise," but also for other reasons, including this: "I have long thought that Polynisia furnished a great deal of rich poetical material that has never been employed hitherto in works of fancy; and which to bring out suitably, required only that play of freedom & invention accorded only to the Romancer & poet." Unexpectedly, he said, he had begun to feel "an invincible distaste" for factual adventure and gone "to work heart & soul at a romance which is now in fair progress." He promised: "It opens like a true narrative like Omoo for example, on ship board & the romance & poetry of the thing thence grow continuously, till it becomes a story wild enough I assure you & with a meaning too." In Melville's usages, the "poet" and the "poetic" are not associated with the metrical activity of verse-making but evoke the Romantic writer's liberated consciousness in bold pursuit of the wild, the strange, the exotic. Romance and poetry were synonymous—they were imaginative, not factual and not commonplace, and they were associated in Melville's mind with a higher form of literature than factual (and partially fictionalized) travel and adventure narrative. In this dodgy, bragging, defensive, confessional letter, Melville proclaimed the supremacy of his literary instincts over fiscal practicality and exulted in the superiority of his new work as a literary achievement. He seriously misapprehended the tastes of his correspondent. Murray had no use for novels, poems, or fictions of any kind. Melville quickly recovered from the rebuff by selling *Mardi* to the British publisher Richard Bentley, who had made overtures to him earlier.

Into the manuscript of *Mardi*, by this time, Melville had introduced (chap. 65 in the American edition) companions for his two voyagers, among them "Yoomy, or the Warbler," whose role is to provide songs when songs are needed or when he needs to sing them. "Grace Greenwood" (Sarah Clarke) had presented her account of the treatment of poets in the Typee valley as if it were a passage Melville had omitted from *Typee* for fear that it would cause a mass exodus of American poets for the Pacific. Her article may have been an unwitting gift to *Mardi*, for Melville may have recognized her depiction of "Clingy Lingy" as too good not to make use of. The name Melville chose for

his poet, Yoomy, may be his respelling of Umi, a character in Hawaiian legends whom he may have encountered in William Ellis's 1826 or
1827 *Narrative.* Yoomy is anything but a self-portrait of a successful
young author suddenly aspiring to poetic greatness:

> A youthful, long-haired, blue-eyed minstrel; all fits and starts; at
> times, absent of mind, and wan of cheek; but always very neat and
> pretty in his apparel; wearing the most becoming of turbans, a Bird
> of Paradise feather its plume, and sporting the gayest of sashes. Most
> given was Yoomy to amorous melodies, and rondos, and roundelays,
> very witching to hear. But at times disdaining the oaten reed, like a
> clarion he burst forth with lusty lays of arms and battle; or, in
> mournful strains, sounded elegies for departed bards and heroes.

The reference to "oaten reed" shows that Melville was familiar with
Virgil (or with his English followers), who in the first *Eclogue* described Pan's gift to shepherds, a pipe made from a reed. He may have
known the song in Shakespeare's *Love's Labor's Lost* in which shepherds
pipe on oaten straws. He probably knew, already, Edmund Spenser's
"Astrophel," the pastoral elegy on Sir Philip Sidney, where Spenser's
conceit is that the shepherds who pipe their poetic "plaints" on oaten
reeds will accept his plaint among their own, as well as the beginning
of *The Faerie Queene,* where Spenser abandons his "Oaten reeds" for a
stern trumpet—abandons the pastoral form for the epic. Thanks to his
invention of "Yoomy," Melville could introduce into his genuinely poetic prose some rhymes of his own composing, the verses safely placed
in the mouth of a minor poetaster, whom Melville's friend Duyckinck
characterized as "a fair type of the class, all sensibility and expression"
(in his New York *Literary World* review, April 21, 1849). Yoomy allowed Melville to try his hand at verse uninhibited by the perils of exposing himself as attempting in his own person to write good poetry.

In 1849 most reviewers of *Mardi* acknowledged that Melville, for
good or ill, had indeed poured romance and poetry into this book, and
his prose was sometimes seen as aspiring, however ineptly, to the status of poetry. On April 19, the Hartford *Republican* decided that the
book was written "in a pleasant, but somewhat exaggerated style,
abounds in fine description, and passages of great poetic beauty, and is
scarcely more romantic in its incidents than the veritable narrative of
'Typee.'" Two days later the Boston *Daily Times* denied that Melville
had great poetic qualities: "His previous works and the first part of
'Mardi,' are founded on facts; or rather they relate to facts altogether,

but because these facts happened to be out of the common course of life, and are given in a graceful and animated style, some critics jumped to the conclusion that Mr. Melville had that quality which renders men great as novelists and poets." *Mardi* would be "saved from oblivion only by the life-like character of its earlier chapters." In its May 1849 issue the New York *Merchants' Magazine* announced: "The matter is truly poetical—philosophical as Plato, yet beautifully imaginative as Moore; the treatment thoroughly dramatic. As a whole, it is a master stroke of genius." In the May 3 New Orleans *Commercial Bulletin* "Croton," the young New York City correspondent A. Oakey Hall (later district attorney and mayor) made a higher claim while punning for his Crescent City readers: *Mardi* was "a regular Mardi-gras of a novel, to judge from the richness of its prose. Prose! It is a poem; and you can pencil out of its pages blank verse enough to set up an hundred newspaper poets, for the balls of bowling critics to roll at." Hall, a protégé of Evert A. Duyckinck, was the first to make such an extravagant claim for Melville as poet. On May 10 in the New York *Tribune,* where Horace Greeley himself had expressed his moral scruples about Melville's first books in 1847, George Ripley defined, even as he deplored, a quality of Melville's new writing: "Even the language of this work is a hybrid between poetry and prose.—Every page abounds in lines which might be dovetailed into a regular poem without any change in the rhythm. It can easily be read aloud so that the nicest ear could not distinguish it from heroic verse." The hybrid was not a success: "Let the author return to the transparent narration of his own adventures, in the pure, imaginative prose, which he handles with such graceful facility, and he will be everywhere welcomed as one of the most delightful of American writers." Yet on the same day the Boston *Daily Chronotype* declared: "There is at times a majestic poetry in this book that reminds us of the old prophets, Isaiah and others."

The reviewer in the London *Sun* (May 29, 1849) called attention to a flaw in the "mixture of the prose and poetic" in *Mardi:* "In this concoction of his literary repast, however, Mr. Melville when he least wishes it makes the intended prose poetical, and the intended poetry prose." The youthful Yoomy, to whom the poetry was ascribed, was "rather a bit of a bore." The reviewer in the *Sun* recognized the quality Oakey Hall responded to, the poetic prose, but mentioned several of the verses given to Yoomy, finding the chorus about the discovery of gold in California so much like "Thomas Hood's memorable chaunt about the leg of Miss Kilmansegge" as to suggest Melville had plagiarized it. The New Bedford *Mercury* of June 8 published a remarkable triple review of *Mardi,* Henry W. Longfellow's prose *Kavanagh: A Romance,* and Arthur Hugh Clough's *The Bothie of Toper na Vuolich,* offering this disclaimer: "We are not sure but that we ought to have entitled this notice—Three new *poems.* They seem to stand on the debateable land between the two realms of poetry and prose, outlaws from the stricter jurisdiction of either. The first, being thickly strewn with little lyrical fragments some of which are exceedingly graceful, is written in that flowing metrical prose which bears the same relation to actual verse that Mr. Melville's previous records of his Polynesian adventures bear to fiction." *Mardi* was "a prose poem in style." The New York *United States Magazine and Democratic Review* (July 1849) began with an elaborate defense:

> We do not despise criticism, nor do we believe that there is much for sale that a man would care to buy; but there are honest men who are petty in their strictures upon works of genius. They do not believe in poetry unless it is fettered with feet, or with rhymes. Like the old lady, they know that "poetry begins with capital letters, and has the lines of a length" and an author who should write a book full of poetic fire, without regard to their rules, is an insubordinate officer, who must be disciplined, or broke, but most likely the latter. To them genius is irregular. It does not curvet according to their patterns, which they assure us are highly ornamental, and very proper. These men would pluck the eagle's quills, and sell them at "a penny a piece," and reduce the royal bird to a respectable barn-yard fowl.

The *Democratic Review* continued with this remarkable tribute to Melville as a man inspired: "We have small respect for authors who are wilful, and cannot be advised; but we reverence a man when God's *must* is upon him, and he does his work in his own and other's spite. Portions of Mardi are written with this divine impulse, and they thrill through every fibre of the reader with an electric force."

On September 29, 1849, the New York *Saroni's Musical Times* declared that style was the "sole redeeming feature" of *Mardi:* "Mr. Melville possesses many of the essentials of poetry—a store of images, a readiness at perceiving analogies and felicitous expressions. Poetic thoughts and turns of phrase occur at every page. Nevertheless, although so poetic in his prose, he is remarkably unfortunate in his verse." The verses in *Mardi* were "not worth quoting." The reviewer launched into a theory that several would-be American versifiers, "who strive for originality of metre, and whose unsaleable works throng the shelves of their publishers," should stop trying to reach poetry: "The English tongue no longer admits of such experiments; its genius has reached its culminating point; it has nothing to do but to remain at its level or descend. To climb higher is impracticable. After the great works of any language have made their appearance, a certain standard is obtained, from which to depart is to sink." The great poetry in English had already been written. The reviewer did not circle back to Melville, but left unelaborated the assertion that he possessed many of the essentials of poetry. For all the contempt showered upon its last two-thirds, *Mardi* apprised British and American readers that Melville was manifesting remarkable if undisciplined literary talents— that he possessed "many of the essentials of poetry."

Early in 1849 Melville found himself prepared to go beyond what had seemed "poetical" to him in 1848, but, after the failure of *Mardi* with most critics and book-buyers, he knew he had to forgo "rich poetical material" for a time. At an astonishing pace he wrote the deliberately more realistic *Redburn* in two months (June–July 1849). Subsequently (in August–September 1849) Melville wrote *White-Jacket,* which also abounds in realism, although the narrator is prone to sudden, intensely rhetorical excursions of the "poetic" sort displayed so prominently in *Mardi*. Reviewers of *Redburn* found nothing poetic, just as Melville had intended when he began the book. In *White-Jacket* Melville gave extended descriptions of the importance of poetry in day-to-day life on an American man-of-war, and reviewers commented not just on the topic of poetry but also on Melville's employment of poetic prose. The London *Athenæum* (February 2, 1850) declared: "Mr. Melville stands as far apart from any past or present marine painter in pen and ink as Turner does from the magnificent artist vilipended by Mr. Ruskin for Turner's sake—Vandervelde. We cannot recall another novelist or sketcher who has given the poetry of the Ship—her voyages and her crew—in a manner at all resembling his." The March 1850 London *Bentley's Miscellany* (Melville's publisher's magazine, granted, but also Cooper's) drew a contrast between him and other sea-writers: "The difference between them may be not inaccurately expressed, as the difference between prose and poetry. The great charm of the marine story in the hands of such writers as Cooper, Marryatt, and [Basil] Hall, is literal truthfulness, shown through just a sufficient haze of imagination, caught from the wide expanse of sky and water, to render it picturesque and effective. But Mr. Melville bathes the scene in the hues of a fanciful and reflective spirit, which gives it the interest of a creation of genius. He is everywhere original, suggestive, and individual. We follow him as if we were passing through an exciting dream." Perhaps taking his cue from the *Athenæum,* Evert A. Duyckinck in the New York *Literary World* on March 16, 1850, contrasted Melville to most other writers: "Your men of choice literature and of educated fancy, your Sternes, Jean Pauls, Southeys, and Longfellows, are not likely to acquire the practical experiences of the tar bucket. The sea of course attracts them with its materials for poetic illustration, but they copy from the descriptions of others. To have the fancy and the fact united is rare in any walk, almost unknown on the sea. Hence to Herman Melville, whose mind swarms with tender, poetic, or humorous fancies, the ship is a new world, now first conquered. No one has so occupied it. . . . We have intimated Herman Melville is a poet, and such he is, though, perhaps, 'lacking the accomplishment of verse.' " What Duyckinck quoted to "prove it" was two paragraphs from chapter 68, the description of the main-mast-man of the *Neversink,* which ended by describing the man's look as "the fadeless, ever infantile immortality within"—phrasing which was a foretaste of passages Melville was to write the next year or two. On March 30, the New York *Two Worlds: A Weekly Journal of American and European Literature, News, Science and the Fine Arts* declared that "a poetic glow" was often thrown over Melville's writings, imparting additional charm to his "flowing and pointed style." By the time the reviews of *White-Jacket* had accumulated, Melville was acknowledged in major papers on both sides of the Atlantic as an extraordinary talent. All this was vague, as *Saroni's* had been the year before, but reviewers were responding to the new "poetic" qualities in the prose—here without the distraction of banal interpolated verses. The praise Melville had wanted to receive for *Mardi* he sometimes received, all unexpectedly, for *White-Jacket.* The praise put him at last where he had longed to be when he wrote Murray that what he was writing had the "right stuff" in it.

After his voyage to England to sell *White-Jacket* and his tentative, frugal excursion onto the Continent, Melville next began a whaling book in which he could be comically realistic yet could reach deeper into the poetical veins he had mined in portions of *Mardi.* Impractical as he had been in following his Romantic and poetical instincts in *Mardi,* he was not so irresponsible as a husband and father as to attempt to write an epic of whaling in poetry. He was ready, in the great burgeoning of his genius, to attempt extraordinary experiments in literary styles, in 1850 and the next years, but in prose, now genuinely poetic, and at times expressed in lines closely akin to Shakespearean blank verse. The British reviewers of *The Whale* recognized this genuinely poetic prose, as when the London *Morning Advertiser* (October 24, 1851) cited "the chapter on the 'whiteness of the whale,' and the scene where Ahab nails the doubloon to the mast" as proof that "we have not overrated his dramatic ability for producing a prose poem." The *Athenæum* (October 25, 1851) in a review fiercely hostile (largely because the "Epilogue" had been left out of the English edition), nevertheless acknowledged "a wild humorous poetry in some of his terrors which distinguishes him from the vulgar herd of fustian-weavers. For instance, his interchapter on 'The Whiteness of the Whale' is full of ghostly suggestions for which a Maturin or a Monk Lewis would have been thankful." This was printed and reprinted in Boston, so Melville and his family could not have escaped it. The London *John Bull* (October 25, 1851) exclaimed at the extraordinary qualities of the book: "Who would have looked for philosophy in whales, or for poetry in blubber? Yet few books which professedly deal in metaphysics, or claim the parentage of the muses, contain as much true philosophy and as much genuine poetry as the tale of the *Pequod*'s whaling expedition." The London *Atlas* (November 1, 1851) acknowledged "that there are fine poetic elements" in the conception of Captain Ahab. The London *Leader* (November 8, 1851) called *The Whale* "a strange, wild, weird book, full of poetry and full of interest."

Melville saw this review, for portions of it were quoted in *Harper's New Monthly Magazine,* and his brother Allan had the whole review, from which he copied other parts into his copy of *Moby-Dick.* Melville probably saw almost no other London reviews, many of which, like that in the London *Weekly News and Chronicle* (November 29, 1851), were filled with extraordinary praise: "This is a wild, weird book, full of strange power and irresistible fascination for those who love to read of the wonders of the deep. The poetry of the great South Seas, the rude lawless adventure of the rough mariners who for years of continuous voyaging peril themselves on its waters; the excitement and the danger of the fishery for the sperm whale, the fiercest and hugest monster 'of all who swim the ocean stream,' combine to make these pages attractive and interesting to many different classes of readers." He may not even have seen his publisher's magazine, *Bentley's Miscellany*

(January 31, 1852): "There are descriptions in this book of almost un-rivalled force, coloured and warmed as they are, by the light and heat of a most poetical imagination, and many passages might be cited of vigorous thought, of earnest and tender sentiment, and of glowing fancy, which would at once suffice to show—contest or dispute about the matter being out of the question—that Herman Melville is a man of the truest and most original genius." Melville never had any idea how many London reviewers had recognized in him a "most poetical imagination."

In the United States few reviewers commented on poetical quali-ties in *Moby-Dick* directly. The New York *Parker's Journal* (November 22, 1851) came near to high praise before retracting: "If any writer of the present day could play with his subject, after this fashion, with impunity, it would be Melville; for his style is a rare mixture of power and sweetness, and, indeed, under the influence of the least excite-ment becomes as truly poetry as if every line were measured for verse, and the fine madness of his soul poured out in lyric flow instead of straightened into prose. But, even his power of expression, and ele-gance of style, will not redeem a book from being prosy after the natural interest of its subject has been exhausted. More than five acts of the best tragedy would be too much for mere mortals to bear." Duyckinck in the *Literary World* (November 22, 1851) and William Allen Butler in the *Washington Intelligencer* (December 16) compared Melville's characters to Shakespeare's, and Butler pronounced the book "a prose Epic on Whaling" and liked his formulation so much that he elaborated it: "a sort of prose epic on whales, whalers, and whaling."

In the fury that greeted *Pierre* in 1852 the rare mentions of any-thing poetic were contemptuous, as when the Boston *Post* (August 4) professed not to know what the book meant: "To save it from almost utter worthlessness, it must be called a prose poem, and even then, it might be supposed to emanate from a lunatic hospital rather than from the quiet retreats of Berkshire." The New York *Evening Mirror* (August 27) said that *Pierre* contained "a good deal of fine writing and poetic feeling," but that the metaphysics were "abominable." Still, the reviewer lingered: "And yet we concede that the book is marked by great intellectual ability; while some of the descriptive portions are transcendently beautiful. It reminds one of a summer day that opens sweetly, glittering with dew-drops, redolent of rose-odors, and melo-dious with the singing of birds; but early clouded with *artificial smoke,* and ending in a terrific display of melo-dramatic lightnings and earth-quakes."

Not until *The Piazza Tales* (1856) did reviewers feel comfortable again with Melville's poetic prose. The scoundrel-journalist Thomas Powell in the New York *News* (May 26, 1856) was rhapsodic:

> The series of beautifully written sketches embraced under the title of the Enchanted Isles exert an indefinable but irresistable sway over the imagination and may be read and dwelt upon again and again, like [the most] gorgeous poem. In fact, if we may use such a comparison and be understood, Mr. Melville's prose, particularly in his magnificent descriptions of scenery, sea and cloud-land, resembles the Tennysonian verse. It possesses all the glowing richness, exquisite coloring and rapid, unexpected turn of phrase that distinguishes the Poet Laureate of our day—Marianna of the Piazza, "the lonely girl, sewing at a lonely window; the pale-cheeked girl and fly-specked window, with wasps about the mended upper panes"—has a distinct and yet not traceable relationship to "Marianna in the Moated Grange."

The "very cadence of the thought—the same heart melody," filled both. In the final paragraph, Powell urged: "Buy this Book, and take it into the country with you, where its hearty, healthy vivacity will gratify and excite as much as its deep undertone of native poetry, inspired by the rural scenes will soothe."[4] The *Republican* of Springfield, Massachusetts (July 9, 1856), praised especially the introductory essay, "The Piazza": "It is a poem—essentially a poem—lacking only rhythm and form." Other reviewers did not use the words *poem* or *poetic,* but the consensus was that Melville had regained his powers as an alluring imaginative writer. Melville would have been inattentive to his critics if he had not, years before, begun to think what it would be like to write poetry instead of only writing poetic prose.

CHAPTER TWO

Melville as Hearer and Reciter of Poetry

MELVILLE EXPERIENCED POETRY IN THE UNBROKEN CONTINUITY between nursery rhymes and songs and rhymes for older children. As the third in a family of eight children, Herman heard not only nursery rhymes from his mother but more complicated poems and songs from his older brother and sister, Gansevoort and Helen. From infancy Herman heard what Gansevoort and Helen were memorizing, as they spoke lines aloud, even if he did not wholly understand the meanings, and from the time he was three or four there were always babies in the house learning the same songs and poems he had already learned, as well as different ones. Poetry was not a passive art for the Melville children: they heard, but as soon as they were able to speak they imitated what they heard, both words and rhythms. As the primary medium for recitation, poetry involved the whole body, since children were trained to fit posture, gesture, and tone of voice to a piece of poetry when "declaiming" it.

As the children grew older they understood that popular songs were considered to be poetry. After all, highly ranked poets from Shakespeare to Lord Byron to Thomas Moore and Joseph Rodman Drake were acknowledged as great songwriters. In the surviving draft manuscript for chapter 14 of *Typee*,[1] Melville declares: "With Captain Macheath in the opera I could have sung 'Thus I lay like a Turk with my doxies around.'" He knew John Gay's *Beggar's Opera*—perhaps from the 1830s, when he may well have derived part of his early image of himself from the song if not from the portrayal of the character onstage. He knew Richard Brinsley Sheridan's "Here's to the maiden of bashful fifteen," a song from *School for Scandal* 3.1, and remembered it in 1862 when he read Abraham Cowley's "The Inconstant," Sheridan's source. The words to popular hymns were often composed by notable religious poets such as Isaac Watts and William Cowper. Melville makes his lank Bildad, for example, sing Watts's "A Prospect of Heaven Makes Death Easy" as he pilots the *Pequod* out of Nantucket in chapter 22 of *Moby-Dick*. Many hymns by Cowper appeared in the 1779 *Olney Hymns* along with some by his friend John Newton, including the one now known as "Amazing Grace," from the poem entitled "Of Faith's Review and Expectation." David H. Battenfeld showed that Melville adapted the hymn in Father Mapple's sermon in *Moby-Dick* from an edition of *The Psalms and Hymns . . . of the Reformed Protestant Dutch Church in North America*. Memorized songs and other poetry were portable, retrievable for private delectation or commiseration and for making a contribution to sociality even in ships or islands at the ends of the earth.

At the time Melville was born and for as long as he lived, spoken poetry was part of people's everyday lives. Even illiterate people memorized poems and songs, and people with even a restricted education memorized long tracts of poetry, which they were often able to retrieve from memory all through their lives. Given the fact that he had a brilliant literary-minded older brother in Gansevoort, and a brilliant older sister in Helen (who rivaled or surpassed Gansevoort in verbal originality), Melville must have heard his parents reading poetry to him and to the two older children long before he could read himself. He probably memorized his first poems by listening to Gansevoort and Helen read and recite. At seven, in 1826, he would have heard Gansevoort memorizing Fitz-Greene Halleck's "Marco Bozzaris" before reciting it at the High School in New York City. After that recitation (which Herman did not witness), Gansevoort was chosen to hold Sir Walter Scott's *The Lady of the Lake* so he could prompt two older lads enacting the scene between Roderick Dhu and Fitz-James—a scene that his mother, Maria Melville, on December 28, 1826, identified so knowingly in a letter to her mother as to show that all the family knew the poem well (*New Log*). At school Herman recited poetry and listened as others recited poetry. After being taken out of the Albany Academy at twelve and a half, he must have memorized some poetry even during his years as a bank clerk and store clerk as well as during his attendance again at the Classical School in Albany around 1835 and at the Albany Academy from September 1836 through February 1837. In 1835 and 1836 he heard Simeon De Witt Bloodgood read or recite many lines from British and American poems (as detailed in the next chapter). At the Lansingburgh Academy during November 1838 through March 1839 he "declaimed" (presumably poetry as well as prose) every two weeks as part of the curriculum, and listened to other students declaim.

Boylike, Herman used some of the poetry he memorized as a weapon for teasing his decorous sisters. On November 27, 1843, when he was in the Pacific, his sister Helen, then in Boston visiting Elizabeth Shaw (later Herman's wife), wrote her sister Augusta of seeing "Macready the tragedian" play *Macbeth* twice, adding: "The witch scenes were admirably got up, and when, dancing about the 'cauldron of hell-broth,' one of the horrid creatures, puts in some terrible contribution; and enjoins it 'to make the gruel thick & slab,' I *could* not help thinking of poor Herman, who made it a favorite quotation, and talked about the 'pilot's thumb, wrecked as homeward he did come,' 'eye of newt, toe of frog,' &c." (Parker 1:107). If the young Herman had made "a favorite quotation" from *Macbeth,* then he also had memorized a good number of other "favorite" quotations with which to regale the family or to delight himself. In 1849 Melville made his young Redburn while away tedious hours at sea by "repeating Lord Byron's Address to the Ocean" (from *Childe Harold's Pilgrimage*), which he "had often spouted on the stage at the High School at home" (chap. 26). Herman probably declaimed poetry of Lord Byron to himself during his checkered early career—farmhand, youthful schoolteacher (near Pittsfield, Massachusetts, and at schools roundabout Albany and Lansingburgh), merchant sailor (on a voyage to Liverpool), whaleman (to the Pacific), and Ordinary Sailor (in the Pacific and on the voyage home). There was a rock south of his uncle Thomas's house where (he told Evert Duyckinck on August 8, 1851) he "used to linger" (probably in 1837) "overlooking the fair plateau on which Pittsfield rears its homes and steeples"—a place that seemed to be created by Nature for reciting Byron. Melville probably satirized himself in chapter 35 of *Moby-Dick:* "Childe Harold not unfrequently perches himself upon the mast-head of some luckless disappointed whale-ship, and in moody phrase ejaculates:—/ 'Roll on, thou deep and dark blue ocean, roll! / Ten thousand blubber-hunters sweep over thee in vain.'" In Melville's early prose narratives the recitation of verse became, as in these examples, a recurrent recreational activity, usually in the form of a sailor giving vent to a sometimes incongruously romanticized poetic temperament. This depiction was based on the reality of Melville's own and other men's recitations.

In the Marquesas in 1842, aboard the *Lucy Ann,* Melville met John Troy, the original of Long Ghost in *Omoo,* and was much in his company at sea and then ashore at Tahiti and Eimeo. Troy may, like Long Ghost, have quoted Virgil and recited poetry by the canto, especially Samuel Butler's *Hudibras.* Whatever Troy recited, Herman heard. In one of Melville's source-books for *White-Jacket,* a "Fore-Top-Man" described a scene on *"Old Ironsides"* in which sailors read aloud novels, mainly, but also poetry: "[J]ust glance your eye along our ships' decks when lying in port; under the break of the poop you may observe a group of mizen-topmen, eagerly listening to some more talented shipmate, who, with voice and effect worthy the subject, is reading aloud passages from one of the splendid and romantic poems of the celebrated Byron."[2] In 1843 and 1844 Melville himself had discovered that some of the sailors on the man-of-war *United States* joyfully read poetry aloud and recited poetry. He made literary friends there, friends selected because they were literary-minded. In particular he admired the Englishman Jack Chase, who "had read all the verses of Byron, and all the romances of Scott" (*White-Jacket,* chap. 4). (In the custom of the time, even those romances by Scott were stuffed with quotations from poetry.) Above all things, White-Jacket says, Chase "was an ardent admirer of Camoens" (chap. 4) and could recite in the original Portuguese parts of the *Lusiad,* the national epic of commerce which anticipated the nineteenth century's obsession with the riches to be gained from what we call the Pacific Rim. Edifying Melville and others with stories of his following "the very track that Camoens sailed" and visiting spots which Camoëns described and where parts of the *Lusiad* were written (chap. 65), Chase was fond of quoting passages from William Julius Mickle's translation (chap. 74), judging from *White-Jacket* (where the accuracy of the quotation may be a testament to Melville's memory but more likely a fair indication that he owned Mickle's translation in 1849).

Among the literary sailors in *White-Jacket* who displayed, like Chase, a taste for the epic form was a poet Melville calls Lemsford. He was based on a seaman named E. Curtiss Hine, who after his return published *The Haunted Barque, and Other Poems* (reviewed February 1848 in the *American Whig Review*), as well as a novel called *Orlando Melville or Victims of the Press-Gang* (1848). According to the narrator of *White-Jacket,* Lemsford knew "the truth of the saying, that *poetry is its own exceeding great reward,*" and dashed off "whole epics, sonnets, ballads, and acrostics," some of which he read to the narrator (chap. 11,

"The Pursuit of Poetry under Difficulties"). The "saying," more than a little blasphemous since it echoed Genesis 15:1, was from Coleridge's preface to the 1797 *Poems*. Melville may have read the whole preface, but the saying was widely quoted, and identified as Coleridge's, in, for example, the *Southern Literary Messenger* (November 1834), the *United States Democratic Review* (October 1848), and the *American Whig Review* (February 1852). Literary dicta were available in the popular press, and might even be quoted by a literary-minded companion who had not gained access to the original source.

The following passage from *White-Jacket* (chap. 11) may be greatly fictionalized, but it suggests the kind of literary society Melville experienced while he was in the navy, when Chase acted as a patron to Lemsford:

> My noble Captain, Jack Chase, rather patronized Lemsford, and he would stoutly take his part against scores of adversaries. Frequently, inviting him up aloft into his top, he would beg him to recite some of his verses; to which he would pay the most heedful attention, like Mecænas listening to Virgil, with a book of the Æneid in his hand. Taking the liberty of a well-wisher, he would sometimes gently criticise the piece, suggesting a few immaterial alterations. And upon my word, noble Jack, with his native-born good sense, taste, and humanity, was not ill qualified to play the true part of a *Quarterly Review;*—which is, to give quarter at last, however severe the critique.

A whaleship may have been Melville's Yale College and his Harvard, as Ishmael says in *Moby-Dick* (chap. 24, "The Advocate"), but a frigate was his Scriblerus Club and his Ambrose's Tavern. In the intervals between his watches Melville was a member of an ongoing symposium in which poetry was its own exceeding great reward. From then onward throughout Melville's lifetime, poetry was an essential part of the lives of men and women in all the social classes he lived among, whether they were his brothers in New York City and his mother and sisters in Lansingburgh, literary New Yorkers he met through Evert and George Duyckinck, fellow breakfasters in the poet-banker Samuel Rogers's house in London, intellectuals in Dr. John W. Francis's Bond Street house in New York, or fellow customs-officers in New York City (one of whom was the poet Richard H. Stoddard). In Melville's time, no confirmation was needed that it was manly to love poetry. If any such confirmation had been needed, Jack Chase had supplied it bountifully.

Given his admiration for the art of recitation as practiced by Jack Chase and other proficients, Melville had much to endure when poetry was read by someone lacking "voice and effect." During an excursion to Monument Mountain on August 5, 1850, Melville and Hawthorne, both excited about meeting each other and eager to continue their conversation, were forced to listen to Cornelius Mathews read aloud all of the poem he had brought with him, William Cullen Bryant's "Monument Mountain" (*Log* 384). In an expansive mood Melville may have attended the dedication of the new Pittsfield Cemetery on September 9, 1850, where original odes "by John C. Hoadley, Mrs. Emily P. Dodge and Mrs. J. R. Morewood were sung by a choir" (*Log* 394). (Both Hoadley and Sarah Morewood later became important in Melville's life, and he gave them both volumes of poetry—Chatterton to Hoadley, Dryden to Sarah Morewood.) On September 20, 1850, Hoadley, a Pittsfield manufacturer, wrote (or copied out) a poem on the vulgar saying, "A man should never weep." It began, "It may be manliness to boast / Thy cheek was never wet / With tears of sorrow or remorse, / Of pity or regret," and culminated in the shortest verse in the Bible: "[W]hen thou call'st it manliness, / Remember, JESUS WEPT!" Augusta Melville copied out that poem on October 7, 1850, just as the Melvilles moved into Arrowhead (*New Log*). Is it possible that Herman Melville was never favored with a recital of it by its author? In 1851 Hoadley read his own poetry aloud in Pittsfield at the Fourth of July celebration (again with Melville's neighbor, Sarah Morewood); and later, in 1854, in Lawrence, after he had become Melville's brother-in-law, he read aloud to his family all of Longfellow's *The Golden Legend*. Eloquent reading of dreary poetry could be hilarious, as Melville showed on August 7, 1851, when he read aloud "On Onota's Graceful Shore / A Ballad of the Times that Tried Men's Souls," in the presence of the author, J. E. A. Smith—"the mad poet," Evert Duyckinck called him. Deftly managing not to let Smith gain an inkling that he was being satirized, Melville read the patriotic lines "with emphasis" and interrupted his performance "with such phrases as 'great glorious' 'By Jove that's tremendous &c.'"[3] Melville's tolerance had limits. In early October 1852, while crushed by the reviews of *Pierre,* he went to hear the Albany poet Alfred Billings Street (a neighbor of his uncle Peter Gansevoort) read at the Pittsfield Young Ladies' Institute ("And then the loved one changes to the wife. / Home is a bower of roses to his life") but afterward could not bring himself to speak to Street and invite him out to Arrowhead. His rudeness greatly distressed the poet, who complained to Peter Gansevoort when he returned to Albany (*Log* 461). (Hoadley, always diplomatic as well as less burdened by discriminating taste, on occasion exchanged poems with Street [*Log* 477].)

Melville at Arrowhead, even as he had done as a youth, continued to go about the house and grounds reciting bits of poetry. We know because in 1854 one of his sisters mentioned his repeating his favorite lines about "little breezes" and "little zephyrs"—lines still unidentified (Parker 2:215). In his first lecture, in 1857, Melville quoted both Burns's "To a Mountain Daisy, On turning one down with the plough, in April 1786" and Byron's *Childe Harold's Pilgrimage*.[4] At the funeral of his Unitarian father-in-law in 1861 Melville listened to the Unitarian Orville Dewey (whose account of his visit to Wordsworth had been famous for many years) recite the ending of "Thanatopsis" by the Unitarian William Cullen Bryant. During the composition of *Clarel* Melville tried out lines in his house in New York within hearing of his younger daughter, Frances, who well into the twentieth century "derided" his performance, perhaps seeing it as too stagy, perhaps simply as immodest and self-indulgent, since she had long known from the newspapers that his poetry was very bad.

Melville's last, and sympathetic, audience was his wife, Lizzie, after they were living in New York City alone except for their unmarried daughter, Bessie. Poetry, at the end, drew Melville and his wife closer together as she helped him prepare his poetic manuscripts for publication. At this time, even though his energies were failing, Melville would probably have read some of his poems aloud to Lizzie as they prepared for the press *John Marr and Other Sailors* and *Timoleon and Other Ventures in Minor Verse*. And surely he read aloud to Lizzie some of the poems that were to become part of *Weeds and Wildings*, a volume designed specifically to honor her. He would have especially enjoyed reading to her the poems he wrote to commemorate shared memories of their years at Arrowhead. In the dedication addressed to her, "To Winnefred," he summons thoughts, memories, and feelings about a flower that was, to them both, "one of the dearest of the flowers of the field"—the red clover.[5] Writing of this flower, he was reminded of their "bridal month" more than forty-four years past, as well as one October afternoon when he had brought into her warm "chamber" a red clover bouquet. "Tears of the happy," she had said, seeing the melting snowflakes roll off the flower petals. Many of these poems, especially those of "Part I – The Year," are simple yet vivid evocations of rural, family-centered scenes and events from the Melvilles' years at Arrowhead: "Butterfly Ditty," "The Blue-Bird," "A Way-side Weed," and "Stockings in the Farm-house Chimney." At the end of his life as at the beginning, Melville lived nourished and blessed by the sound of poetry spoken aloud, even if he himself was the speaker he most often heard.

CHAPTER THREE

The Omnipresence of Poetry, 1820s–1848

AS A MEMBER OF A HIGHLY LITERATE BOSTON SOCIETY, MELVILLE'S father, Allan Melvill, frequently quoted poetry or alluded to poems.[1] On May 28, 1804, in a letter to Lemuel Shaw (later Herman's father-in-law) Allan elaborately proclaimed that he held himself aloof from partisan politics (just then emerging in the new republic), then broke into blank verse: "*I was a Politician once, but late I've lost the relish for the work, discovering that fair play is seldom used, to effect the end desired, leaving the path of honest argument, & shunning truth, patriots of modern days, 'WHO LOVE GOOD PLACES, AT THEIR HEARTS,' yet give the tongue a licence, descend to scurrilous abuse, and deal out loathsome ribaldry, till Falsehood foul coadjutor, is fairly tired*—this much for blank verse—blank indeed you will say, & perhaps exclaim with the Irishman, behold the *footsteps* of a Dabbler's *hand.*" (Characteristically, he embodied in his poetry a quotation from a poem, Cowper's *Table Talk,* clearly assuming that Shaw would recognize it and relish it.) Books of poetry that Allan owned were auctioned off in the late 1820s, so Herman Melville was denied the complex experience of reading many of the great English poets in books owned by his father. Melville did in fact read Spenser in the eight-in-four edition his father had owned (but not marked) since January 1803.[2] Melville's first reading of *The Faerie Queene* may have occurred as early as in the "cholera summer" of 1832, when, after work at the New York State Bank, his long evenings were his own for the first time in his life, with his mother and her other children in Pittsfield. That timing would fit an autobiographical reading of the description (written late in 1851) of Pierre's reading his own dead father's copy of *The Faerie Queene,* when aesthetic responses to lusciously sensual passages occur simultaneously with and hardly distinguishable from pubescent stirrings, creating an intense, bewildering confusion.

In the Melville house also was the copy of William Tennant's *Anster Fair* (Edinburgh: Cockburn, 1812; Sealts 500a) that the Reverend Robert Swan had inscribed to Allan Melvill on May 20, 1818, at St. Monans, during Allan's visit to Scotland. This mock-heroic poem in ottava rima was commonly said to have influenced John Hookham Frere's 1817 *The Monks and the Giants* (published as by William and Robert Whistlecraft), then, directly or indirectly, Byron's *Beppo* (1818) and *Don Juan* (which started publication in 1819). The Melville brothers may have delighted in Tennant's account of the revenge the lovelorn and temporarily noseless Charlie Melvil took on his tormenters, but that passage is unmarked. Apparently as late as 1875 Melville noted across from the title page: "This poem gave the hint of style to Frere in the 'Monks & Giants' (Whistlecraft) which suggested to Lord Byron the style and stanza of Don Juan— acknowledged by the last named poet."[3] In the invocation to the god of poetry he checked "Why scorch me ev'n to death with fiery inspiration?"—the poet's plea to Phoebus to give him a more moderate spark of poetic fire. Just possibly, the book was so precious a reminder of her husband that Maria Melville kept it away from the children.

From childhood Melville knew Sir Walter Scott as a poet before he knew him as a novelist, and in the 1830s he became fascinated by the younger Scottish poet George Gordon, Lord Byron. In 1834 Herman's older brother, Gansevoort, perforce the man of the family at nineteen, the proprietor of a cap and fur store, and too poor to seek a bride of his own, was delighted by a sensuous description in Byron:

> Slept in the store, before going to bed read part of the bride of Abydos, and was particularly pleased with the 10th. 11th. 12th. & 13th stanzas especially the lines immediately following "My love thou surely knewest before" in the 13th the character of Zuleika as pourtrayed by Byron in the bride of Abydos, is the most sweetly beautiful female character that I have ever met with in Poetry, so gentle, affectionate, amiable, & ingenuous in disposition, so simply beautiful in her ideas, and so happy in expressing them, and appearing to possess every quality of heart and mind, calculated to make those around her happy, joined with a person, which would realize all the ideas that the Mahometan has of the beauty of the Houris, those

dark eyed girls of Paradise, all conspire to make a woman as near perfection, as it is possible for her to attain. (Parker 1:92)

Tellingly, Gansevoort expected to meet characters in poetry, which often meant in the narrative poems of Scott and Byron, not lyric poetry. On November 9, 1843, the year before Herman returned from the Pacific, Gansevoort cried out to "the Friends of Ireland" at Washington Hall in New York City that the "enemies of Ireland and of Liberty shall be taught that 'Freedom's battle once begun, / Bequeathed from bleeding sire to son, / Though baffled oft, is ever won'" (New York *Tribune,* November 10, 1843). He counted on his audience to know its Byron and to recognize in the quotation from *The Giaour* a parallel between still-oppressed Ireland and formerly enslaved Greece. Gansevoort's specific responses to poetry are not an invariable indicator of Herman's, but in the 1830s both brothers read all the Byron they could get hands on—satires, love poetry, plays, and certainly the great narrative poems. Before Herman could have dared to aspire to a literary life, Gansevoort, his notes show, was thinking of authorship as an ultimate career choice, alone or in conjunction with the law.

Scornful of conventional values, self-dramatizing, world-wandering, startlingly beautiful, uninhibited in sensuality, unrestrainable in poetic output, self-involved yet heroically self-sacrificial in the cause of freedom, Lord Byron became the embodiment of the ideal poet for Herman, not least because he was himself a Scot of noble blood. Probably by the mid-1830s, Melville was especially familiar with *Manfred* and *Childe Harold's Pilgrimage,* if not *Don Juan.* For Herman, *Childe Harold's Pilgrimage* was eminently quotable from lofty vantage points on land and sea—and as late as 1857 and 1858 he quoted it from the moderate elevation of lecture stages. Before and just after his years at sea Herman could not have missed, nor could he have failed to admire, the Byronic aspects of his brother's own character and the infused, poetic energy of the rhetorical declamations that in 1844 led one admirer to call Gansevoort (as the third Melville brother, Allan, wrote Herman in October 1844), "the orator of the human race." After his death at the age of thirty in 1846, Gansevoort seemed to Herman more Byronic than ever—heroically burnt out by his both fervored and painstaking pursuit of impossible goals. And Herman just at that time saw himself as Byronic when he self-consciously echoed the poet's declaration that he had awakened to find himself famous (in his letter to William B. Sprague, July 24, 1846). In his fiction Melville seized on Byron's life and poetry as embodying quintessentially poetic qualities, all that was inherently antipathetic to commonplace conventionalities, all the profoundly reckless and irrepressibly creative powers that would lead the unimaginative, uncomprehending lawyer-narrator of "Bartleby" (1853) to try to tame Byron patronizingly as merely a "mettlesome poet." Byron was an alter ego whose example proclaimed that a great poet could live triumphantly, if tragically, during Melville's own lifetime. In his hints about the earlier life of one of the most alluring characters in *Clarel,* the mysterious Vine, Melville evoked the mythic story of Admetus, the king of Thessaly, whom the god Apollo had served, for a time, as his humble shepherd (pt. 1, canto 29). Melville had himself been Apollo laboring as a shepherd to Francis Bloodgood, the Admetus of the New York State Bank, or laboring for Gansevoort Melville, the Admetus of the cap and fur store, or whaling under the command of Captain Valentine Pease, the Admetus of the *Acushnet*—an unrecognized poetic genius held as hireling to a succession of masters until his discharge from the navy in October 1844. Melville by the 1850s knew Percy Bysshe Shelley's *Prometheus Unbound,* the modern drama of a freed Greek god; Lord Byron, in the 1830s and 1840s, had been a poetic god, alive in Melville's own lifetime, an Apollo Unbound.

In the 1830s even for impoverished young men and youths like Gansevoort and Herman Melville, for whom captivating recent poetry was as near as a copy of Scott or Byron, Albany itself was far from a backwoods or backwater outpost, literarily speaking. Never the equal of New York City for literary publishing, Albany as the political capital was the home of expert printers of the state documents. For local readers (Albanians, they sometimes called themselves) and for politicians from the rest of the state in temporary residence, Albany printers competently supplied, a few weeks late, the most recent quarterlies and monthlies from Scotland and England, in full or in selections chosen for their readers. Then, as all through Melville's life, in the absence of an international copyright law, reprints of even the best British magazines and books could be purchased cheaply—although often in wretchedly small type—because American printers paid no royalties and turned a profit as soon as they recouped their printing costs. Albany bookstores also stocked foreign and domestic periodicals shipped up from New York City and, less often, Philadelphia or Boston. The British magazines that reviewed volumes of poetry invariably printed long quotations, carefully selected, whether to capture the best of the verse or to illustrate some challenging argument of the reviewer. Local printers sometimes offered cheap reprints of British poetry, and booksellers stocked poetry reprinted in New York City and elsewhere. A printer in any upstate New York or inland New England town might publish hundreds of copies of a rhetoric or elocution textbook that contained advice on reading poetry aloud. The Erie Canal made it easy to ship such books to Albany from Utica, for instance, and textbooks from Andover, Massachusetts, reached Albany even before a railroad linked the Hudson River valley and Boston in the early 1840s.

Albany had literary people of its own, notable among whom was Francis Bloodgood's son, Simeon De Witt Bloodgood (1799–1866), whose wife was a Van Schaick, a fourth cousin of Gansevoort and Herman Melville (whose Gansevoort grandmother had been a Van Schaick), and who were connected in other ways, as were all the old Dutch families. As Janette Currie and Scott Norsworthy have shown, Simeon De Witt Bloodgood played a remarkable role in bringing contemporary British writings to Albany. After Sir Walter Scott's death in 1832 Americans were avid for anecdotes about the great poet and novelist. Knowing that James Hogg, world-famous as "the Ettrick Shepherd," had anticipated this appetite with his "First Interview with Sir Walter Scott" in 1829, Bloodgood wrote directly to Hogg requesting "something original or anecdotes about Sir Walter," as Hogg explained to Scott's son-in-law, John Gibson Lockhart, in 1833 (Currie 1). Lockhart was then trying to block the publication of Hogg's *Anecdotes of Scott* in Great Britain, so Hogg sent Bloodgood "Familiar Anecdotes of Sir Walter Scott," which Bloodgood placed with the Harpers (1834), prefaced with his own "A Sketch of the Life of the Shepherd." For all his hardships at this period, Hogg was proud, as he wrote in 1833, to hear from different parts of the United States that he was "more read there, and oftener reprinted, than any other living author" (Currie 2). Janette Currie found in the Albany *Daily Advertiser* of April 27, 1833, this item headed "THE ETTRICK SHEPHERD":

> We had the pleasure to receive a few days since, a long letter from James Hogg, the Ettrick Shepherd, in relation to the publication of some of his works in the United States. He is about writing a series of ten or twelve volumes. We regret to learn from his own pen, that though "a poor shepherd half a century ago," he is, notwithstanding a life of industry, "a poor shepherd to this day." He writes that he has heard of the "splendid city of Albany on the Hudson," "at his own cottage in Yarrow," and that his poems have been extensively

read in the United States. The fame and fate of Burns seem almost that of Hogg. When he is no more, we shall probably hear of anniversary dinners on his birthday, and a monument to his memory "in Edinboro' town", but it would be much more honorable to the British public to place him in comfort and independence at once, rather than expend their tardy benevolence in building him a grave.

The *Advertiser* was printed and published by yet another family connection of the Melvilles, J. B. Van Schaick and Company, who also printed and published the Albany *Gazette.*

Although his earliest known reference to the poems of the "Ettrick Shepherd" comes as late as 1866, in the "Supplement" to *Battle-Pieces,* Melville knew James Hogg's poetry in his youth, when the Shepherd was almost as popular a Scottish poet as Robert Burns and Sir Walter Scott. Much of Hogg's work printed in the United States was prose, but some of his poems were reprinted as well, and his prose anecdotes sent readers back both to Scott's poetry and Hogg's own. In Philadelphia Adam Waldie rivaled Bloodgood in reprinting Hogg's prose, and Waldie also reprinted some of Hogg's poetry in the *Port Folio, and Companion to the Circulating Library* and the *Museum of Foreign Literature, Science and Art.* (Gansevoort Melville pored over the volumes of the *Circulating Library* in 1837, making notes from them in his *Index Rerum,* a popular device for the instant retrieval of useful information, described below.) In January 1834 Hogg promised Bloodgood that he would send a tale or one or two ballads for a new eclectic Albany magazine called *The Zodiac: A Monthly Periodical Devoted to Science, Literature and the Arts.* Several remarkably intimate pieces of prose by and about Hogg were printed there between July 1835 and June 1836, including (in August 1835) "A Letter from Professor Wilson" written to Hogg in September 1815, in which John Wilson commented sardonically on Wordsworth's *White Doe of Rylstone,* Robert Southey's "Roderick, the Last of the Goths," and Scott's "Field of Waterloo." The *Zodiac* was treating Albanians to rich gossip sure to appeal to literary-minded youths hungry for news of the great contemporary British writers, in this case gossip printed in Albany almost three decades, it seems, before it was printed in Edinburgh in 1862. In October 1835 the *Zodiac* printed Hogg's "The Moon was A-Wanin'"; in February 1836 "Verses to the Comet"; and in March 1836 "A Father's Lament." The *Zodiac* regularly acknowledged its sources in British periodicals available in Albany: "Walter the Witless" was from the London *Athenæum;* "Literary Remunerations" from

Chambers' Edinburgh Journal; Thomas Carlyle's "State of German Literature" from the *Edinburgh Review;* the Reverend J. Moultrie's "Stanzas" from the *Etonian* ("In many a strain of grief and joy, / My youthful spirit sang to thee; / But I am now no more a boy, / And there's a gulf 'twixt thee and me"); "To A Sleeping Child. From the French of Victor Hugo" from the *Foreign Quarterly Review;* and from the same magazine "To Luigia Pallavicini, On her Recovery from Sickness. From the Italian of *Ugo Foscolo.*" The *Zodiac* printed Coleridge's "An Ode to the Rain" in November 1836 and quoted that poet in "Literary Fashions" from *Chambers' Edinburgh Journal.*

The *Zodiac* of July 1836 reprinted from Park Benjamin's *American Monthly Magazine* an editorial on German literature (not specifically on poetry) that seems to have made a lasting impression on Melville. The writer rejoiced that growing interest in German literature would be beneficial in counterpoising the American emphasis on materialism, on "internal improvements" (like canals) that are purely external: "Let us not forget that there are internal improvements of another sort very proper to immortal beings; and beware, lest in a contented ignorance we turn our backs upon what is elegant, refined, and imaginative, because it will do nothing either for steamboat or rail-road, and is therefore stigmatized as not being 'practical.'" In Melville's own criticism of the United States at the end of his lecture on "Statues in Rome" (1857) he calls the locomotive a symbol of modernity in contrast to the Apollo Belvedere and immediately thereafter complains that the "world has taken a practical turn." Besides this editorial, the *Zodiac* printed some translations from German, including in October 1836 an unsigned translation of Johann Christoph Friedrich von Schiller's "The Song of the Bell." The lines "When with the strong, the delicate, / When with the bold, the mild we mate, / Then melodious is the song" (as Norsworthy pointed out to me privately in 2005) may have stuck in Herman Melville's head for many years before it informed the imagery and rhythms of his poem "Art."

Gansevoort and Herman were not the only members of the family eager to read the latest *Zodiac.* One of Augusta Melville's teachers at the Albany Female Academy, A. D. Woodbridge, whose family home was in Stockbridge, Massachusetts, was a frequent contributor of poetry to that paper.[4] The September 1835 *Zodiac* contained a poem by Woodbridge to Catharine Sedgwick, "To the author of 'Redwood,' 'Hope Leslie,' etc. on her return to this her native village, July, 1835" (at a time when Helen Melville was a student at Elizabeth Dwight

Sedgwick's school, conducted in the house in Lenox where the novelist summered). Of special interest to Augusta would have been the September 1836 issue, with Woodbridge's "My Parting Gift" ("Lines addressed by a teacher, at the close of a term, to different members of her class, who at the commencement of a new term were to enter a higher department"); Woodbridge copied out this all-purpose memento for Augusta, who retained it all her life. Poetry was something that students wrote about in their composition classes: on January 15, 1837, Augusta submitted an appreciative essay at the Albany Female Academy on Felicia Hemans's poetry.

Gansevoort had the advantage of extra years of schooling, and was therefore better equipped to make up for gaps in his education, but Herman also did the best he could. Out of school since October 1831, Herman attended the Albany Classical Institute for a time in 1835–36, where his teacher, Charles E. West, had been a Union College classmate of Gansevoort's friend and mentor, Alexander W. Bradford. Then Herman attended the Albany Academy from September 1, 1836, to March 1, 1837. At both schools he probably encountered much poetry, but the textbooks have not been identified. A splendid Albany resource was the Young Men's Association for Mutual Improvement, a quintessentially American institution designed for ambitious young men, most often those denied higher education but eager to improve their minds. It was anything but a boys' club. In the Albany YMA members could develop skills ranging from polite conversation to formal debating to delivering public orations. On March 9, 1837, the Albany *Evening Journal* published a report on the association and its 736 members. In the reading room were 1,400 volumes, 26 daily newspapers, 5 triweekly papers, 7 semiweekly papers, 41 weekly papers, and some 30 monthly and quarterly reviews (magazines). Most of the magazines were Scottish or English—not imported sets, for the most part, but volumes reprinted in Albany or New York City or Philadelphia. Eager to garner and retain full runs of periodicals, the YMA in the Albany *Argus* on January 1, 1835, requested all readers to check any of their "broken sets" of *Brewster's Edinburgh Encyclopedia* to see if they could spare one of the numbers the YMA listed as needed to complete its set. The YMA library nurtured Herman's lifelong love of the older British quarterlies and monthlies—volumes that almost invariably contained much poetry. The earliest catalogue of the YMA library yet discovered, published in 1837, contains all the books available to Herman except perhaps some of the most recent acquisitions; an 1843 catalogue shows that the YMA continued to make regular additions to its library. In 1837 the YMA possessed, mostly in the form of American publications printed well after the War of 1812 but before Herman became a member, an enormous library of British and American poetry, some classical poetry, many books on the lives of poets, and many volumes containing shrewd, knowledgeable literary criticism on the greatest British poetry of the previous decades.

When Herman joined the Albany Young Men's Association for Mutual Improvement in January 1835, Gansevoort was already flourishing as a member. On September 21, 1835, Gansevoort was elected to the Executive Committee of the YMA. The next year, on January 23, 1836, Gansevoort was elected president of the Debating Society of the YMA, and that Fourth of July he read aloud the Declaration of Independence as part of the YMA's procession and celebration. Herman managed to keep paying his membership dues for two and a half years. He joined in time to hear Westerlo Woodworth speak on "American Poetry" on March 6, 1835 (a lecture announced in the Albany *Argus*). More important, he was in time to benefit from a pioneering series of lectures on American literature given at the YMA by their cousin-by-marriage Simeon De Witt Bloodgood, beginning on February 10, 1835. Documentation proving Gansevoort Melville's association with Bloodgood survives fortuitously from a decade later when, as Secretary to the American Legation in London, Gansevoort regularly sent newspapers home to Bloodgood. Given his character, his prominence in the YMA, and the family connection, it is possible that Gansevoort had something to do with a "request"—that Bloodgood give "A Series of Lectures on American Literature, Delivered by Request before the Young Men's Association, in the City of Albany, New York, by S. De Witt Bloodgood." Reaching a wider audience, and allowing the young men of the association to ponder them in type, Bloodgood's lectures were printed in the monthly Albany *Zodiac* beginning in the August 1835 issue. The *Zodiac* for July 1836 (the month Gansevoort read Jefferson's Declaration aloud) contained the lecture by Bloodgood devoted to the third president. The publication of the lectures, if not Bloodgood's delivery of them, terminated abruptly in October 1836. Herman remained a member of the YMA into 1837. On April 26, 1837, after failing in business during the financial panic of that year, Gansevoort resigned from the Executive Committee and soon left for New York City, in the hope of starting a career as a lawyer, and in June Herman went off to Pittsfield to work his uncle Thomas's farm for a few months before teaching school in the hills nearby.

A safe assumption, given the Melville brothers' connection to Bloodgood and to the YMA, and given their zeal for learning, is that both of them attended all or most of his lectures and that they read them all in the *Zodiac*. Bloodgood began his "Introductory Remarks" (printed in August 1835) with a tribute to earnest, ambitious young men denied a formal higher education, the men who had created the Young Men's Association for Mutual Improvement: "Felicitous in its design, and successful in its progress, this Association may become illustrious in its career. Who can say what noble traits of character, what heaven born energies may not yet be developed through its influence? Who can tell what pre[e]minence may not be obtained through its means by some who hitherto were unaided in their efforts, solitary in their reflections, and diffident of themselves, though conscious of something within them 'struggling to be free'" (*Hamlet* 3.3). That "Who can say" ranks as one of the most prophetic questions young Herman Melville heard or read. What Bloodgood said in the lecture was already conventional but nevertheless inspiring: "[T]he history of a nation is inseparably connected with, if not absolutely dependent upon its cultivation of literature." He cited Timothy Dwight's asking how long there had been an England before England had a well-written book—a rejoinder to the British who had scoffed at the meagerness of American literary productions. Bloodgood declared that England owed "her fame to three individuals more than any others" including its kings and queens—three poets, Spenser, Shakespeare, and Milton. He named three later British poets as of particular interest because they wrote about the American colonies or the new country: James Thomson (in "Liberty" 5.2.638–46); Thomas Campbell (in *Gertrude of Wyoming*); and Thomas Moore (in "The Lake of the Dismal Swamp" and other poems), although he chastised Moore for mingling "ridicule of the country with his praise."

In his survey of American literature from the Pilgrims to the present Bloodgood quoted many British poems. He quoted nine lines from Byron's *Childe Harold's Pilgrimage* (2.88) on Greece as a "shrine of departed greatness" and twelve lines from Byron's "By the Rivers of Babylon We Sat Down and Wept," one of the "Hebrew Melodies." Bloodgood warned that great writers may die in poverty: "Antiquity is full of impressive examples, but even in modern times we see Cervantes begging his bread, Camoens perishing in a hospital, Tasso borrowing a crown from a companion to save himself from starvation, Corneille dying of hunger, the author of the Fairy Queen perishing of hope deferred,—he who knew, by sad experience, what it was, in spite of his genius, 'To fawn, to crouch, to wait, to ride, to run, / To speed, to give, to want, to be undone.'" These lines were familiar, Bloodgood assumed, from the passage on suitors at court in Spenser's *Mother Hubbard's Tale,* especially since the passage only recently had been brought to the attention of the English-reading world in Sir Walter Scott's *The Fortunes of Nigel* (chap. 9). Bloodgood quoted a line on Bishop Berkeley from Pope's *Essay on Man,* the "Epilogue to the Satires, Dialogue 2." He quoted ten satirical lines from Cowper's *The Task* (bk. 4, "The Winter Evening") about the arrival of the newspaper and its perusal ("Cat'racts of declamation thunder there, / There, forests of no meaning spread the page, / In which all comprehension wanders lost"). He quoted a long passage from Sir William Jones's "Ode in Imitation of Alcaeus" ("What constitutes a state?"). Jones the poet was also the great linguist whom Melville cited in chapter 79 of *Moby-Dick.*

In the course of describing and quoting many American poems Bloodgood took for granted that his auditors all knew at least a few of them. One was Timothy Dwight's "Columbia, Columbia, to glory Arise!" of which he quoted the two last stanzas as "familiar to every American school boy." He quoted sixteen lines from John Pierpont's "The Pilgrim Fathers." He quoted an American version of one of the Psalms, which he acknowledged was wretched in comparison with Byron's. He quoted Henry Ware Jr.'s "The Vision of Liberty" ("let the blessings thou [great Heaven] hast freely given, / Freely on all men shine, / Till equal rights be equally enjoyed, / And human power for human good employed"). He quoted some lines from Mrs. Warren, whom he identified as the daughter of James Otis (Mercy Otis Warren, really the sister of the patriot James Otis). He elaborately introduced a long passage from near the end of canto 3 of John Trumbull's *M'Fingal: A Modern Epic Poem* (first published in full in 1782),[5] dually inspired by Butler's *Hudibras* and James Macpherson's *Fingal,* and quoted lengthy passages from Trumbull's "Destruction of Babylon." Bloodgood quoted a kinswoman of Mrs. Bloodgood's, Eliza Bleecker, apologizing a little: "We have been more minute perhaps, than we should have been, had not a peculiar interest attached to the circumstance of her former residence in our vicinity."[6] Bloodgood ran together passages from James Gates Percival's "The Graves of the Patriots" before paying tribute to Samuel Adams, an intimate friend of the Melville brothers' Boston grandfather. He quoted Charles Sprague's "The Centennial Ode," a tribute to the Pilgrims, as recited in September 1830 in Boston.

In treating Joel Barlow in the fourth lecture Bloodgood dismissed the ambitious efforts at writing an American epic and praised a trifling work: "He is principally remarkable in his literary career for his Columbiad, which nobody reads, and his poem of Hasty Pudding, which every one reads." In the fifth lecture Bloodgood quoted eighteen lines from the opening of "Hasty Pudding" ("I sing the sweets I know, the charms I feel, / My morning incense, and my evening meal! / The sweets of Hasty Pudding!"), declaring that the "whole poem is kept up with equal spirit, and a humor not to be found in any other of his poems." Bloodgood liked the early *Vision of Columbus* (1787) no better than the later *Columbiad* (1807): "His longer poems can not be expected to retain a lasting place in our literature." In fairness he quoted thirty lines from the *Vision of Columbus,* a "contrast between a northern and southern climate," as being in Barlow's "graver manner" and as having been "selected by competent judges as a fair specimen of his poetic talent." Bloodgood took occasion to inveigh against the *Quarterly Review* for scorning American literature ("There is, or was, a Mr. Dwight, who wrote some poems, his baptismal name was Timothy"). He meant Sydney Smith's notorious article in the 1818 *Edinburgh Review,* but some of what he quotes suggests that he may also have been thinking about a slur by Southey that the first plaything given to an American child was a rattlesnake tail. From "Greenfield Hill" Bloodgood cited enough to vindicate his (Dwight's) "poetic powers" against any foreign criticism. As evidence that Dwight was entitled to "a place in the front rank of letters" Bloodgood quoted eighteen lines from "The Destruction of the Pequods" ("And soon man's Demon Chiefs from memory fade"). Bloodgood in his sixth lecture quoted from Francis Hopkinson a song to "fair Rosina" and some twenty satirical lines addressed to medical students in Philadelphia. He noted that Colonel David Humphreys (spelled Humphrey in the *Zodiac*), a friend of Dwight and Trumbull, wrote the well-received "An Address to the Armies of America," and he mentioned also Humphreys's "The Happiness of America" and "American Industry." Deciding that Humphreys's "poetic powers" never "soar to any uncommon height" but rarely "fall below mediocrity," Bloodgood acknowledged that "great popularity" had attended Humphreys's efforts, and quoted from the "Address to the Armies of America" three stanzas on the departure of the British fleet from American shores ("E'en now from half the threaten'd horrors freed, / See from our shores the lessening sails recede").

Superficial as they were, Bloodgood's lectures, read from the stage and later printed, gave Herman Melville what was then a rarity, a course in American literature, one he could supplement with knowledge acquired elsewhere. For instance, from his youth Herman must have known from his uncle Thomas Melvill something of Joel Barlow the man because his father and uncle were Americans in Paris when Barlow was. According to a letter from Melville's uncle Thomas to Lemuel Shaw on February 3, 1834 (Parker 1963, 54), Barlow had recommended him to Thomas Jefferson as the best-qualified American in Paris to take over the American consulate when the incumbent, Fulwar Skipwith, resigned—possibly in 1796, when Skipwith resigned as consul general, but perhaps in 1808, when he resigned as commercial agent. Although Bloodgood dismissed the importance of Barlow's *The Vision of Columbus* and *The Columbiad,* Melville at the start of *The Confidence-Man* may have drawn on one or both of them for his mention of Manco Capac. Bloodgood seems not to have mentioned either William Emmons or Richard Emmons, poetical brothers. In the late 1820s during visits to Boston Melville would have seen the poet-orator William Emmons on the Common. From a booth there, Emmons alternately sold copies of his orations and cups of a delicious beverage, egg-pop, the source of the sobriquet "Pop" Emmons. Given his grandfather's role in the raising of the monument across the Charles River, Melville may have encountered *The Battle of Bunker Hill, or The Temple of Liberty; an Historical Poem in Four Cantos* (1839), identified on the title page as by "Col. William Emmons." The poem, in which several of Melville's family names appear as heroic colonists, concludes with the address "forwarded by those patriots who composed the Continental Congress, 10th May, 1775, to the oppressed people of Ireland," to whom the Congress offered "a safe asylum from poverty, and in time from oppression also," an asylum, the address continued, already sought by thousands of Irishmen. In his oration "An Address Commemorative of the Battle of Bunker Hill, June 17, 1775," William Emmons quoted extensively from his yet-unpublished poem on that subject; the epic poet and former president John Quincy Adams paid for the publication of this oration.[7]

During the 1820s and 1840s, and afterward, writers (novelists, essayists, orators who printed their speeches, as Ralph Waldo Emerson sometimes did) punctuated their prose pages with tags from poetry, the conventions of the time allowing them to strew phrases from Shakespeare and other writers with or often without much regard to their original context. But readers recognized contexts that are now quite elusive. On November 25, 1851, the Edinburgh *Evening Courant* in its review of *The Whale* assessed Ahab's resolve: "The interests of his employers, the safety of his crew, and every other consideration gave way to this. 'No love-lorn swain, in lady's bower, / E'er panted for the appointed hour' as did Captain Ahab to fall in with Moby Dick." Many readers in 1851 would instantly have recognized the martial nature of the wished-for confrontation in Scott's *The Lady of the Lake.* To read a novel was often to encounter dozens of passages of poetry. Many popular novelists besides Scott (James Fenimore Cooper was one) quoted lines of poetry as mottoes to chapters. Gansevoort owned the edition of Scott published in Boston by Parker, and he and Herman were reading Cooper in 1837. Growing up when he did, Melville saw many bits of poetry, couplets, stanzas, in many prose books that he encountered, very often before seeing the whole poems. Any literate American in books, magazines, and newspapers had ready access to lavish quotations from old poetry and new poetry without necessarily being put to the expense of buying a recent book; for example, as explained below, Melville apparently knew something about an imaginary dialogue between Petrarch and Boccaccio, a discussion of Dante, in Walter Savage Landor's *Pentameron and Pentalogia* (1837) before the book was published in the United States. The convention of interspersing poetry into prose may well have influenced Melville's practice in *Mardi* of interrupting the narrator's prose with pieces of Yoomy's light verse.

In America in the 1830s and 1840s many studious young men availed themselves of John Todd's invention, the *Index Rerum,* already referred to, which transformed the venerable commonplace book into an instant retrieval system, the poor man's self-made index to "things," the equivalent of a personalized Internet browser. Henry David Thoreau used an *Index Rerum* at Harvard. More often, the *Index Rerum* was used by young men looking to improve themselves without the benefits of enrolling in a college, and often without the benefits of a mutual improvement association. The purpose was to guarantee that striking passages (on authorship, say) which one encountered in reading would not be lost but would be instantly available thereafter for use in public speeches or in any sort of writing. Just how dedicated Gansevoort was to self-improvement (and to making best use of his reading) is manifest in his surviving volumes of the *Index Rerum* for 1837 and 1840 (both of which contain notes made in other years).[8] No such evidence as an *Index Rerum* remains for Herman's self-improvement efforts. Some indications suggest that he was never as devotedly systematic as Gansevoort, but he may have made up in intensity of focus and capaciousness of memory what he seemed to lack in drudging application. We know from letters Gansevoort wrote the next younger brother, Allan, and the youngest, Tom, that he considered himself very much in the place of a father in recommending courses of study, so he undoubtedly encouraged Herman by passing him books as well as (something we have record of) newspapers: Gansevoort demonstrably sent Herman newspapers from New York when Herman was in or around Lansingburgh. Even though the strongest evidence for Herman's education and self-education in poetry comes in literary allusions in his writings, beginning in 1839, much can be learned by mustering evidence like that of Bloodgood's lectures.

Much can also be learned by examining Gansevoort's surviving volumes of his *Index Rerum.* In the course of 1837, at the start of which he and Herman were in the same house in Albany, and during the rest of which he was in New York while Herman was in Pittsfield, Gansevoort filled thirty-seven pages of the "Appendix" of his *Index Rerum* with quotations from his reading, including poetry in novels by Sir Water Scott. Pretty clearly, most of the books Gansevoort took notes on were borrowed from the Young Men's Association. He noted a passage on German language and poetry in Basil Hall's *Schloss Hainfield;* three stanzas of "Life" by "the Hon: R. H. Wilde, of Georgia"; and two lines on weariness ("And weary day, and weary week / And wearier month went lagging by—"). From Lord Chesterfield's *Letters to his Son* (which Herman also read about the same time), he copied down (on the topic of "Stooping to Conquer") two vulgarly applied lines from Dryden: "The prostrate lover, when he lowest lies, / But stoops to conquer & but kneels to rise." He also copied Chesterfield's two lines from Congreve on critics: "Rules for good writing, they with pains indite / Then show us what is bad, by what they write." Perhaps from Scott's *Fair Maid of Perth,* Gansevoort took a quotation from Dryden on country girls ("A country lip may have the velvet touch / Though she's no lady, she may please as much"); and from some unlocated source a quotation from Coleridge's "Genevieve" on "Woman's feelings"

("Hopes, and fears that kindle hope"). (He meant the poem about Genevieve called "Love.")

For many weeks in 1837 Gansevoort was enthralled by Washington Irving's *The Sketch-Book,* at least one copy of which was in the YMA library. Irving's book was exceptionally peppered with poetry, for he not only used poetic mottoes for chapters but also quoted poetry within many of the articles. He was such an open and enthusiastic quoter that at one point he thought in print about crowding some of his pages "with extracts from the older British poets" on one particular topic, burial customs. Irving gave poetic passages from Thomson; William Roscoe (the Liverpool poet whom Allan Melvill had met in 1818); Thomas Middleton (one on "the concealed comforts of a man / Lock'd up in woman's love"); William Cartwright; Cowper; Thomas Moore; John Fletcher; Roger L'Estrange; James I of Scotland; Henry Howard, Earl of Surrey; Marlowe; Drummond of Hawthornden; Shakespeare (*Cymbeline, Hamlet, As You Like It,* and *The Winter's Tale*); Robert Herrick (quoted half a dozen times); Beaumont and Fletcher's *The Maid's Tragedy* (quoted more than once); "Corydon's Doleful Knell"; Thomas Stanley; and Christolero's Epigrams, by "T. B." (i.e., *Chrestolero: Seven Bookes of Epigrams,* by Thomas Bastard). He quoted from songs in *Poor Robin's Almanack* (1684), from Cartwright, George Withers, Sir John Suckling, Garrick on the Avon, Shakespeare's epitaph, Sir H. Wooton, and Chaucer ("Belle Dame sans Mercie"). Irving referred to the "monumental bronze" tint of Outalissi in Campbell's *Gertrude of Wyoming,* the "good Indian" to whom Melville casually alluded in his 1849 review of *The Oregon and California Trail,* "Mr Parkman's Tour." ("Wyoming" then applied only to a part of northeast Pennsylvania, the site of Campbell's poem, and another area in western New York State.) Irving's quotations from Herrick were substantial enough to work as a little anthology, and he quoted in full one famous Moore poem, "She is far from the land where her young hero sleeps." Strewing poetic tags through a work could be merely pedantic bragging, but writers like the antiquarian Irving intended the quoted passages to open remote periods of literature to their readers so that their awareness of their poetic heritage might be expanded. Gansevoort was impressed enough to write down in his *Index Rerum* some of the poetry quoted in *The Sketch-Book,* "The Wife" from Middleton and a passage from Cowper on the pleasures of rural domestic life. Gansevoort very likely passed *The Sketch-Book* on to Herman. Whenever he got hold of it, Herman fell under its spell. This fact has been obscured by the vehemence of his essay on Hawthorne's *Mosses from an Old Manse,* written in August 1850, where he scorned Irving as merely imitative, content to be the "American Goldsmith."[9] By that time Melville had already plundered *The Sketch-Book* for *Redburn;* in the mid-1850s he paid it the high homage of loving imitation in "The Paradise of Bachelors and the Tartarus of Maids" (1855); and later in life he wrote a poem, "Rip Van Winkle's Lilacs," on the long-classic piece in *The Sketch-Book.* Irving helped teach Melville to write prose, but he also exposed him to dozens of lines of poetry, and probably from a wider range of English poets than he had yet encountered elsewhere.

In 1837, probably using the copy listed in the Young Men's Association catalogue of that year, Gansevoort worked through the second edition of J. H. Dwyer's *An Essay on Elocution; with Elucidatory Passages from Various Authors to which are added Remarks on Reading Prose and Verse, with Suggestions to Instructors of the Art* (New York: G. & C. Carville, & E. Bliss, 1828). Gansevoort made notes on the "Character of a Libertine," on Lord Chatham, on Charles Phillips's praise of his late friend John Philpot Curran in a speech at Cheltenham in 1819 to the Gloucester Missionary Society, and on Phillips's after-dinner remarks on Irish gratitude toward the United States. Already, long before 1843, when he became famous as a Repealer (demanding the repeal of the 1800 Act of Union between England—and Scotland—and Ireland, as the United Kingdom), Gansevoort was saturating himself in stories of heroic Irishmen who had resisted Union. Herman would have found in Dwyer some useful advice as a reader of poetry and as a teacher. In "Remarks on Reading Prose and Verse" (that is, on reading aloud) Dwyer offered the sensible advice that "reading and speaking are precisely the same thing, save that in reciting we have a greater intimacy with the subject, and are enabled to give a little more energy and action. The tones, emphasis, accent, and sense, are the same, whether we speak or read." Far from inculcating artificial techniques of declamation, Dwyer coolly advised: "The material difference between reading prose and rhyming verse, rests in giving more time between each word and sentence in verse than in prose; reading with very little reference to the jingle, or rhyme, but with great attention to the sense; using the same inflections as in prose, and rather avoiding than encouraging that measured tone, improperly called musical; for if the harmony of that author's verse, to whose sense we do justice, do not distinctly speak for itself, his claims to poetry must rest on a very slight foundation indeed."

Breaking down his topic for the benefit of teachers as much as for students, Dwyer listed these aspects of elocution: *Articulation; Accent; Emphasis* (a topic he exemplified by poetic passages from Joseph Addison's *Cato* and Portia's "quality of mercy" speech from *The Merchant of Venice*); *Pronunciation; Climax* (exemplified by passages from *The Tempest,* James Thomson, W. W. Dimond, and *Hamlet*); *Suspension* (a bit of Edward Young's *The Revenge,* and Portia on mercy); *Parenthesis* (John Home's *Douglas,* Addison's *Cato,* and the "long farewell to all my greatness!" from the collaborative *Henry VIII*); *Antithesis; Monotony,* or *Monotone* (the "to be or not to be" soliloquy from *Hamlet,* but commencing late, at "For who would bear the whips and scorns o' the time" [*sic*], and "Satan exalted sat" from the opening of book 2 of Milton's *Paradise Lost*—the passage illustrated in Melville's print that hung in the dining room at Arrowhead during his occupancy and for decades afterward); *Modulation* (two pages from book 4 of *Paradise Lost,* more than three pages from Dryden's *Alexander's Feast,* a page from Campbell's "Hohenlinden," and almost three pages from William Collins's *The Passions*); *Enumeration* or *Amplification* (four lines from Thomson's *The Seasons* and Othello's "Farewell" speech); *Pauses* (bits from *King Lear* and *Othello*); *Irony* (bits from *Othello* and *The Merchant of Venice*); *Alliteration* (snippets from Byron's *Childe Harold's Pilgrimage,* cantos 2 and 3); *Interrogation; Iteration* or *Repetition,* by some called *Echo* (a line from *Othello* and the "With thee conversing" passage from book 4 of *Paradise Lost*); *Personation* (defined as "the representation by a single reader or speaker of the words, manner, and actions of one person, or of many individuals, as if he or they were themselves reading or speaking; in effect 'giving form to fancy, and embodying thought'" and exemplified by a long passage from canto 6 of Scott's *Marmion,* Hotspur's popinjay speech from *Henry IV, Part 1,* Mercutio's Queen Mab speech from *Romeo and Juliet* [cautiously stopping short of the lines about teaching maids good carriage], Jaques' "seven ages" speech from *As You Like It,* and Campbell's "Lochiel's Warning"); *Metaphor* (a passage from John Home, newly famous for being quoted in chapter 28 of Scott's *Woodstock,* and a line from Campbell's *Pleasures of Hope,* part 1); *Comparison* (bits from Goldsmith's *The Deserted Village* and book 3 of *Fingal*); *Personification* or *Prosopopoeia* (book 5 of *Paradise Lost* ["These are thy glorious works"]); *Apostrophe;* and *Action.* Dwyer also quoted several prose passages in exemplifying these topics.

Dwyer thus included several soliloquies and other extended purple passages suitable for memorizing, though he did not describe them that way. Curiously, he did not instruct teachers or students as to the best ways of using the "Poetic Pieces" he appended at the end of the book, following the samples of oratory that caught Gansevoort's eye. These poems included S. Osborne's "Time"; Charles Woolf's "The Burial of Sir John Moore" (listed in the table of contents as by "Anonymous"); Ambrose Philips's "Winter at Copenhagen"; and Scott's "The Interview between Fitzjames and the Lady of the Lake." Then followed several selections from Campbell: "The Sacking of Prague," "The Pilot," "The Soldier of Hope," "On Woman," "The Sceptic," "The Rose of the Wilderness," "The Last Man," and "The Rainbow." From N. P. Willis (who was to become a friend of Gansevoort's, and then of Herman's) he included "The Sacrifice of Abraham." Several pieces from Lord Byron followed: "Night before and Battle of Waterloo," "Venice," "Rome," "The Ocean," "Greece," and "The Corse." Then came Moore's "Paradise and the Peri" and an exercise in maudlinity, Dimond's "The Sailor Boy's Dream." The author identifications, notably, were made only in a "Contents" page at the back of the book, not along with each of the "Poetic Pieces." The function of the selections in teaching elocution was valued over acknowledgment of authorship; what counted was not who wrote a passage but what a teacher could do with it. So far, it has not been proven that Herman ever held Dwyer's book, but Gansevoort used it, and chances are that in 1837 or later Herman had occasion to read it as a student, even if an autodidact, and as a teacher. The Melville family certainly knew in their entirety many of the poems quoted by Dwyer, although the evidence may be fortuitous, as with the allusion to Thomson's *The Seasons* in Augusta Melville's record, discovered in 1983, of the Berkshire excursions of 1852.

Herman, like Gansevoort, earnestly worked to improve his skill in elocution by becoming a debater. Evidence is strong that young men's debates were laced with quotations from poetry, as were surviving orations from this time when oratory was an integral part of belles lettres. During his term at the Albany Academy between September 1836 and March 1837 Herman joined the Ciceronian Debating Society. His behavior there and in the successor organization, the Philo Logos Society, earned him a public reprimand by "R." in the Albany *Microscope* on April 15, 1837, two months before he left Albany to manage his uncle's farm near Pittsfield. Returning early in 1838, after teaching in the Berkshires in the fall, Melville convened the inactive Philo Logos Society at a meeting in which he was elected president.

Controversy over the validity of the election and his behavior in the previous year was played out in the *Microscope* in what is now known as the "Philo Logos Letters."[10] How serious these letters were, how much they are exercises in vituperation, in imitation of British political philippics, is not clear. However, they demonstrate that as a debater and as a polemicist Melville did indeed gain additional exposure to poetry, even though no poetic tags have been identified in his own letters to the *Microscope.* In his letter in April 1837 "R." had lamented the difficulty of getting "rid" of Melville: "He, like a wary pettifogger, never considers 'this side right, and that stark naught,' or in other words, has no fixed principles." The allusion is to a popular poem (printed in the Quebec *Gazette* of November 9, 1775, for example, and sometimes casually attributed to Benjamin Franklin) on "Paper," built on the analogy of blank paper and tabula rasa, where these lines occur: "The retail Politician's anxious thought / Deems *this* side always right, and *that* stark naught." On March 10, 1838, Charles Van Loon, the deposed president of the Philo Logos Society, repeated R.'s epithet "Ciceronian baboon" and accused Melville of playing "fantastic tricks" (words from *Measure for Measure,* a passage from which was on Gansevoort's mind as he was dying in London in 1846). Van Loon called Herman's "abusive language" in a February 28 letter to the *Microscope* "the raving of an unmasked hypocrite, the 'wincing, of a gall'd jade'" (*Hamlet*) and announced himself ready to punish Melville by lashing the "rascal naked through the world" (*Othello*). "To Herman Melville—Sir,—," Van Loon continued in the March 31 *Microscope,* "the sensible Hudibras has well observed, that, there is no kind of argument like matter of fact" (*Hudibras* 2.3.192). On April 7, attacking Melville for convening the special meeting at which Melville was elected president, Van Loon declared (carelessly, if we are to believe "Americus" in the same issue of the *Microscope*), "there is something rotten about Denmark." In the April 14 *Microscope* Van Loon had the last word: "[A]lthough silly prejudice may condemn me for publishing in the Microscope, I shall enjoy my 'exceeding great reward'"— the phrase from Genesis 15:1 given new currency by Coleridge's assertion in the 1797 preface that poetry is its own exceeding great reward. All Melville's early life poetry was, as the "Philo Logos Letters" show, inescapable in public speech, especially formal speech, and inescapable in print—not just in magazines and newspapers and in books of poetry but in many other sorts of books, including the newly popular literary gift-books or annuals.

While he taught school near Pittsfield in late 1837 and the first weeks of 1838, Herman would have used poetry as a tool for teaching elocution and literary devices, even if he did not "teach" poetry in the modern sense. From mid-November 1838 through the first few days of April 1839 Herman was back in school, enrolled at the Lansingburgh Academy, his mother having moved her family to Lansingburgh, on the east side of the Hudson, just north of Troy, in May 1838. While Herman was at the Lansingburgh Academy, Gansevoort was also there (after a period in New York City), bedridden, so that Herman had to carry him from bed to fireplace, but surrounded by books which he read and abstracted into the first, second, and then third volumes of his *Index Rerum.* Herman was casually or purposefully exposed to all the books Gansevoort was reading and many he had been reading. There in February 1839, and probably earlier in Albany, Herman was expected to write verse for Valentine's Day, for a youth of either sex was required to strive for proficiency if not high originality in the composition of light verse. The recorded family comment comes late but applies to earlier years: on February 15, 1847, in Lansingburgh Helen wrote to her younger sister Augusta, who was away in Albany: "We received Fanny's letter yesterday, and also Kate's Valentine written by the same hand & Pen. What geese, Cuyler [Van Vechten, an Albany cousin] & Fanny [the youngest of the Melville sisters] were to send note paper with his own initials stamped thereon, and then get it written in such a well-known hand.—We opened one directed to Herman [away on a trip to Washington], quite a pretty one, from some fair lady in the village" (NYPL-GL). A young man would not only write facile, flirtatious poetry but would also read aloud seductive new poems from England. William H. Gilman (104) recorded an unconfirmed report that Herman used poems by Tennyson in a youthful courtship on the riverbank at Lansingburgh—in the summer of 1838, possibly, or the spring of 1839 or 1840.

Even though he was taking the course that was to prepare him as a surveyor on the Erie Canal, Herman was required to write an original composition and to "declaim" every two weeks, a stipulation spelled out in the 1839 Catalogue of the Lansingburgh Academy (discovered by Dennis Marnon in 2005). He may have been able to consult a copy of Dwyer's *Elocution,* although the copy Gansevoort had read in 1837 may have been the YMA's. In the Catalogue of the Lansingburgh Academy the textbooks for rhetoric are Lord Kames's *Elements of Criticism,* Hugh Blair's *Lectures on Rhetoric and Belles Lettres,* and

Samuel P. Newman's *A Practical System of Rhetorick, or The Principles and Rules of Style, Inferred from Examples of Writing; to which is added a Historical Dissertation on English Style,* all three in unspecified American reprints. The text by Newman, a professor of rhetoric at Bowdoin College, was pedestrian in comparison to the two by the Scots, and Herman would not willingly have settled for using it if there was a choice, despite the passages of literature by Byron, Goldsmith, Hemans, Irving, Scott, Butler, Milton, Mark Akenside, Thomson, Cowper, Shakespeare, and extensive use of *The Sketch-Book.* (Newman also quoted Daniel Webster's Bunker Hill address more than once—probably an oration already familiar to Herman.) Blair in his *Lectures* was very much a "D.D." ("One of the Ministers of the High Church," said the title page on the 1817 edition published in New York City by Evert Duyckinck, the father of Melville's editorial friend of the same name) and a fervent Scottish nationalist. Blair was particularly good in providing an introduction to pastoral poetry, quoting English translations of Virgil's "Eclogues" (by Thomas Warton, in particular). Blair's judgments were self-assured: he seconded Dr. Johnson's praise of Thomson; Blair himself praised Thomas Parnell's "The Hermit" (a poem whose popularity requires a readjustment of values in the twenty-first century, being singularly apt to disturb modern sensibilities); he praised Milton's "Il Penseroso"; but his religious and grammarian's scruples spoiled Shakespeare for him. His lectures on epic poetry made a good guide to classic epics as well as later examples, among them Tasso's *Jerusalem,* Camöens's *Lusiad,* Fénelon's *Telemachus,* Voltaire's *Henriade,* and Milton's *Paradise Lost.* Blair had already published his *A Critical Dissertation on the Poems of Ossian, the Son of Fingal* (1763), and spoke here of the works of Ossian as abounding "with examples of the sublime" and as manifesting the mastery of poetic description.

The great textbook at the Lansingburgh Academy was Lord Kames's *Elements of Criticism,* a remarkable introduction to aesthetic issues that relied for illustrations upon hundreds of brief quotations mainly from classical and from British poetry. Since his literary illustrations were chosen to make specific rhetorical points, attention was directed to them sharply—out of context, but in such a way that they would be remembered when encountered again in context. These passages from literature were used to exemplify both lofty aesthetic concepts and rough-and-ready problems in such matters as personification, hyperbole, metaphor, and other figures of speech, as well as practical advice on how to order material effectively. Anyone using this text was introduced to many characters of Shakespeare (notably Othello and Hotspur) in specific problematical situations; to much praise of *Fingal* (including an endorsement of Blair's "delicious morsel of criticism," his book on Ossian); to much Pope, particularly *The Rape of the Lock* (often mined for bad examples); Butler's *Hudibras;* Edmund Waller; Cowley; Milton's *Paradise Lost;* Battista Guarini's *Pastor Fido (The Faithful Shepherd,* which Melville bought long afterward in the 1647 Richard Fanshawe translation); Thomson's *Seasons;* and many quotations from Congreve's *The Mourning Bride.* Kames offered serious disquisitions on many topics, including versification, and in a chapter on "Narration and Description" gave wise advice about starting an epic modestly (as Melville was to do in *Clarel*). Kames's *Elements of Criticism* was a very great introduction to poetry. To read Kames was to take a master's class in theoretical poetics and the practical reading of poetry. The exposure to such critical strictures, while it did not make Melville a poet in his teens and twenties, may have provided materials for the foundation on which he was later to construct his poetics and his artistic credo.

One slight reason for thinking that Melville had Kames as a text rather than Newman or Blair is his own quoting from *The Mourning Bride* just after he left the academy. In his "Fragments from a Writing Desk" (printed in the Lansingburgh *Democratic Press* in May 1839) Melville wrote allusively, just as his models did. In the "Fragments" Melville quoted Chesterfield's *Letters,* which he and Gansevoort had shared, as well as poetic passages from Campbell's "The Pleasures of Hope" (ten lines!), from Shakespeare's *Hamlet* and *Romeo and Juliet,* from Congreve's *The Mourning Bride,* Byron's *Childe Harold's Pilgrimage,* Milton's "L'Allegro," Akenside's *The Pleasures of Imagination,* and the "gentle" Coleridge's "Genevieve." (Melville would have seen in the March 1836 *Zodiac* John Wilson's praise of "Genevieve" as a poem "known to all readers of poetry.") In his own voice (or Ishmael's) Melville claims in *Moby-Dick* (chap. 42) that he had not read "The Rime of the Ancient Mariner" when he first experienced a profound mystical thrill at the sight of an albatross: "For neither had I then read the Rhyme, nor knew the bird to be an albatross. Yet, in saying this, I do but indirectly burnish a little brighter the noble merit of the poem and the poet." He certainly knew some of Coleridge's poetry early in life. Failing to gain a job on the Erie Canal, Melville left on June 1, 1839, for New York City and Liverpool. After his voyage to Liverpool,

Melville would have taught with poetry again in the fall at Greenbush, across the river from Albany, then again in the spring of 1840 at Brunswick, near Lansingburgh, and somewhere near Lansingburgh, yet again, for a short time in the late summer and early fall of 1840, before he left for New York City.

Together or apart, Gansevoort shared poems with his younger brothers.[11] In a letter from Lansingburgh on June 26, 1841, to Allan in New York City, Gansevoort quoted Burns's "Elegy on Captain Matthew Henderson," with "Robin" instead of the usual "Matthew": "If thou art staunch without a stain, / Like the unchanging blue, man, / He was a kinsman o' thy ain / For Robin was *a true man*." From Bridgeport on September 2, 1842, Gansevoort wrote Allan, identifying himself with "Old Ironsides," the ship in the most famous poem by Oliver Wendell Holmes, who had satirized their heroic paternal grandfather in "The Last Leaf": "As for your amiable brother, his old hulk seems to be so much shattered that it will not bear refitting— and yet the governing spirit of that old hulk is determined as ever to 'Set every threadbare sail, and give her / To the GOD of storms, the battle and the gale.'" Gansevoort must have sent similar messages to Herman when he sent newspapers from New York City to Herman in or around Lansingburgh, probably including some of the papers he made note of in his *Index Rerum.*

It is clear from his notes that throughout 1840 while Gansevoort Melville was pursuing his legal studies (despite being tempted by the possibilities of becoming a political orator) he was also still weighing an alternative route to fame, a literary career. Some of his entries recorded poetry and popular songs. In 1840 he cross-referenced his now lost *Index Rerum* 3.106: "Anacreon, rivalled by Willis." In March or later he noted an article on "The English Language" in that month's *Knickerbocker Magazine.* On April 9 or later he copied a sonnet, "A poetical fragment—N Yk Courier & Enquirer April 9, 1840, being a satire on Benj F. Butler, now District Attorney of the Southern District of N Yk occasioned by his conspicuous opposition to the registry law lately passed." Perhaps in early September he copied part of a poem addressed to "Nat Willis" by "Straws," in the New Orleans *Picayune:*

> "The curse of Genus"
> Oh, Nat! it's true vot people says
> About "the curse of genus?",
> For me I'm cursin' all the time,

> In a vay vot's wery heinous! . . .
> For ev'ry pop'lar genus now
> Is of the genus loafer.

On the last two lines Gansevoort commented: "Popular geniuses nowadays." Perhaps in September he copied from that month's *Ladies Companion* lines from Rufus Dawes's poem "Lift Your Hearts &c." (Dawes [1803–59] was a justice on the Massachusetts Supreme Court, under Lemuel Shaw, and a novelist and a poet—a model as a man with a legal and a literary career.) Around September Gansevoort copied lines by Mrs. Lydia H. Sigourney, "On Parting with a Pupil." From *Brother Jonathan* of September 12, 1840, Gansevoort copied part of a poem on "The Deluge" (possibly Mary Ann Carter's 1838 *The Deluge, the General Resurrection, and Other Poems*). While at Galway, New York, after September 19 Gansevoort Melville copied "The Schwitzers War Song" from *Brother Jonathan.* Perhaps this was "War-Song of the Royal Edinburgh Light Dragoons," in which Sir Walter Scott bitterly criticized the Swiss for not avenging the Swiss Guards slaughtered in the August 1792 attack on the Tuileries ("Switzers," however spelled, being the term familiar from *Hamlet*). Gansevoort also copied part of a song, "The Next Presidency," from the New York *Herald* of September 22. On September 25 from Galway he wrote his brother Allan: "The news from Maine looks rather lowering, & seems to discourage our friends in this part of the country: 'But shall we go mourn for that, my dear / But shall we go mourn for that?' "—a line Sir Walter Scott copied into his journal from Joanna Baillie's *Orra.*

Once he sailed on a whaler in 1841, Herman Melville found that almost all sailors knew many hymns (which could be sung straight or parodied) and many popular songs (in this era, it bears repeating, when honored poets often wrote popular songs). His casual quoting of Allan Cunningham's "A Wet Sheet and a Flowing Sea" in *The Confidence-Man* (chap. 22), for instance, may indicate a long knowledge of this and other pieces in *Poems of Scotland.* Probably many sailors had left home knowing poems which they could recite. Perhaps a few carried printed poetry they could read, memorize, and lend to any other sailors they found to be literary-minded, but whale-ship libraries (in those ships that had libraries at all) were not stocked with poetry, judging from the inventory of the books taken aboard the *Charles and Henry,* Melville's third whaler (Heflin 11–17). The library on the *United States* did contain poetry, notably William Cullen Bryant's 1840 *Selections from American Poets,* where more than seventy-five poets were sampled, including the compiler. Of the seventy-eight poets represented in Bryant's anthology, only a few are poets Melville is known to have read. The library on the *United States* may well have contained poetic dramas, judging from the books Melville gives the *Neversink* in *White-Jacket* (chap. 41): "some odd volumes of plays, each of which was a precious casket of jewels of good things, shaming the trash nowadays passed off for dramas, containing 'The Jew of Malta,' 'Old Fortunatus,' 'The City Madam,' 'Volpone,' 'The Alchymist,' and other glorious old dramas of the age of Marlow and Johnson, and that literary Damon and Pythias, the magnificent, mellow old Beaumont and Fletcher."

While at sea Melville may well have read some of Richard Emmons's American epic, *The Fredoniad.* In the South Pacific on November 27, 1843, the *United States,* with Melville aboard, hoisted its colors at half mast in memory of "the late Commodore Porter," only recently dead, and at noon fired thirteen minute guns in tribute to his memory. This would have been the time for someone to produce the four-volume *The Fredoniad: or, Independence Preserved. An Epick Poem of the Late War of 1812,* and turn to canto 11, "Cruise of Captain Porter," and especially the exalted conclusion of canto 12, "Porter's Defence of the Essex." Set there, in the stretch of the Pacific the *United States* was then sailing, this passage depicts Fredonia herself streaming down the heavens and calling bright angels down with her trumpet as she cries: "Earth! list to the decree! Porter shall live, / Whilst Fame immortal, has a breath to give!" In the right mood, driven to a temporary rhetorical excess of patriotism, a literary nationalist among the tars might have sounded much like the Virginian vacationing in Vermont in Melville's essay on Hawthorne's *Mosses from an Old Manse.* There the "Virginian" declares that Americans should "first praise mediocrity even," in her own poets, before praising merit in foreigners: "I was much pleased with a hot-headed Carolina cousin of mine, who once said,—'If there were no other American to stand by, in Literature,— why, then, I would stand by Pop Emmons and his 'Fredoniad,' and till a better epic came along, swear it was not very far behind the Iliad.' Take away the words, and in spirit he was sound." Melville did not often praise mediocrity, but his chauvinism was at its most intense point because of the grandeur of what he was writing, *Moby-Dick,* and the war which guaranteed the independence of the United States was still very close. Others could rise in at least tongue-in-cheek praise of Emmons, among them Park Benjamin, quoted earlier.

William Falconer's *The Shipwreck* (1762) might have been circulated aboard the *United States,* for in chapter 65 of *White-Jacket* Melville has Jack Chase declare that the "'Shipwreck' will never founder, though he himself [the author], poor fellow, was lost at sea in the Aurora frigate." Melville quotes a bit of it in "Extracts" in *Moby-Dick,* and recalls it in a poem first published in *Timoleon.* Melville's continuing interest in Falconer, after 1862 if not much earlier, was heightened by a passage in Thomas Moore's biography in which Byron explained his own preferences among sea-poets: "In what does the infinite superiority of 'Falconer's Shipwreck' over all other shipwrecks consist? In his admirable application of the terms of his art; in a poet-sailor's description of the sailor's fate." In *White-Jacket* Melville casually alludes to Byron's verses on his cousin Peter Parker, the ruthless raider of the Chesapeake: "There is a tear for all who die, / A mourner o'er the humblest grave" (chap. 52). By the time he returned from the Pacific in 1844 Melville knew many poems by Scott, Byron, and others that only the most learned Romantic specialist knows today. *Hudibras* had figured in a Philo Logos letter, and in 1846 as he wrote *Omoo,* he recalled the sound of *Hudibras* being recited in the South Seas. Into chapter 46 of *Omoo* Melville worked two provocatively appropriate lines from Pope's epistle "To a Lady," in the wrong order: "A sad good Christian at the heart— / A very heathen in the carnal part." In chapter 65 of *White-Jacket,* Jack Chase, the idolator of Camöens, honors the translator Mickle as himself a poet, deducing from one of Scott's own footnotes that Mickle's ballad of Cumnor Hall "gave Sir Walter Scott the hint of Kenilworth." Few admirers of Camöens were devoted enough to make pilgrimages to remote waters and shores he described in the *Lusiad,* but by the 1840s several poets, including Felicia Hemans, had addressed poems of praise to Camöens. Many of the British critics of the previous century (such as Hugh Blair) and poets of Melville's youth became ardent admirers of Camöens through Mickle's translation or in the original Portuguese. (In Melville's time neoclassic treatment still governed epic discourse, as is clear in the translations selected for Melville's Harper's Classical Library, which he purchased early in 1849 [Sealts 147]. The Renaissance era of translation that had begun with Chapman and merged into the neoclassical translations of Dryden, Pope, and others was still highly regarded among professional critics and poets throughout the first half of the nineteenth century.)

Home from the Pacific, Melville was exposed again to a great deal of poetry in the newspapers and magazines as well as books of poetry and anthologies. His brother Allan had saved many newspapers containing Gansevoort's speeches, so Melville may have seen the great Jackson Day speech of March 15, 1844, in which Gansevoort had quoted Halleck's "Alnwick Castle" ("And died, the sword in his red hand, / On the holiest spot of that blessed land" ["mailed hand," he may have said]). Gansevoort also quoted Joseph Rodman Drake's "The American Flag" ("Flag of the free heart's only home, / By angel hands to valor given, / Thy stars have lit the welkin dome, / And all thy hues were born in Heaven"). He quoted Halleck's "beautiful lines to the memory of Burns," followed by two passages from Byron's *Marino Faliero*.[12] Winding up his speech, Gansevoort appealed for unity in words from Whittier's "Ritner" on "Forgetting the feuds and the strife of past time" and "Counting coldness, injustice, and silence a crime." All of these passages were probably equally familiar to both Gansevoort and Herman.

After late 1847, when the Melvilles moved to New York City (mother, four daughters, Herman and his bride, Elizabeth Shaw, and Allan and his bride, Sophia Thurston), Melville began to have access to private and public libraries, but he still could encounter poetry in the household, for at any time two, three, or more of the young women kept commonplace books into which they copied poems. Particular poems available in the Melville household, known by others in the family if not Melville himself, are cited here to show the pervasive availability of poetry—whether great, good, indifferent, or downright wretched. As elsewhere in this chapter, the listing of poems is at times minute, but even the poems his late brother Gansevoort had noted in his *Index Rerum* or his sister Augusta now copied into her commonplace book, *Orient Pearls at Random Strung,* are only representative. Some of Gansevoort's volumes of *Index Rerum* are lost, as are the commonplace books of Melville's wife and his sister Catherine, and probably of his other sisters as well. Probably around 1842, after eight or nine years of writing weekly compositions, Frances (Fanny) Melville, the youngest sister, wrote in "Myself" that "nothing as the poet truly says, 'is so bad as getting familiar with sorrow' "—the poet being the English songwriter Thomas Haynes Bayly (1797–1839) and the poem the look-on-the-bright-side "Never Look Sad," not Melville's own view of life. In early 1848 the first poem that his sister Augusta copied into her *Orient Pearls* was from "A Persian Song of Hafiz,"[13] by the linguist admired by Melville, Sir William Jones (1746–94); Herman learned enough about Hafiz to feel certain that William Davenant had caught "a fine Persian tone" in a "Song" ("The Lark Now Leaves").[14]

In late 1847 and 1848 Melville was working too hard on *Mardi* to pay full attention to the mutual admiration society of American literary chauvinists constituted by Evert Duyckinck and Cornelius Mathews and a few others. A problem for chest-beating nationalists like Mathews was that they were hopelessly Anglophiliac, would-be literary chauvinists trapped as hapless idolators of almost all things British and poetic. Mathews and Duyckinck had been devoted advocates of the poetry of Elizabeth Barrett since one or the other of them reviewed her *The Seraphim, and Other Poems* (1838) in the February 1841 issue of their magazine, *Arcturus*. In December of that year Cornelius Mathews began a correspondence with her with a fan letter along with the February magazine. She replied in kind, with letters and copies of her works, some in her own hand, and hid her amusement in 1842 after the egregious Mathews appointed himself to what she called "the office of *trustee for the further extension of my reputation in America.*" Year by year Barrett and Mathews both adeptly played the half-cynical, half-sincere game of reciprocity, here scratching a shoulder, there massaging a neck. Mathews was privileged early in 1847 to have a letter from Pisa in which the poet informed him of her marriage and her change "from the long seclusion in one room, to liberty and Italy's sunshine"; duped by Anglophilia, he imprudently shared it with an English confidence man two years later (Powell 150).

It is not known when Melville first became friends with Henry T. Tuckerman, the essayist and poet, but it was probably well before they both attended Anne Lynch's Valentine's Day party in 1848. They may have met at the house on Bond Street of the great obstetrician and genial repository of all there was to know about Manhattan, Dr. John W. Francis. Melville had been on good terms with Dr. Francis since September 22, 1847, at the latest, when the doctor was a guest at Allan Melville's wedding to a Bond Street girl, Sophia Thurston. Melville considered Dr. Francis an intimate friend all through the 1850s, a time when Dr. Francis in public addresses and writing spoke admiringly of Melville and Tuckerman in the same breath. Both men were regulars at Dr. Francis's Sunday evenings, whenever Melville and Tuckerman were in New York. By January

1850 and again in 1852 Tuckerman praised Melville's narrative powers in *Typee*. Tuckerman in person showed toughness of mind that rarely manifested itself in his prose, so Melville may well have read Tuckerman's essays, and even some of his poems, in a way more kindly than some of them merited. A man who longed to see Italy himself, Melville seems to have read Tuckerman's *Sicily* in the 1839 text (*Isabel, or Sicily a Pilgrimage*), for the section on Syracuse is the only source yet identified for his treatment of the Arethusa fountain in *Moby-Dick*. In all likelihood Melville looked through Tuckerman's *Thoughts on the Poets* (1846)—more than two dozen poets, several of the eighteenth-century British poets Melville had known since childhood, all of the great Romantic poets as well as Campbell, Samuel Rogers, Hemans, two Italians (Petrarch and Alfieri), the younger English poets Tennyson and Elizabeth Barrett, and two Americans (Joseph Rodman Drake and Bryant). For the most part, Tuckerman was a friendly guide over familiar poetic territory, but it was perhaps through him that Melville developed an intense interest in Alfieri. (Melville had a nodding personal acquaintance with William Cullen Bryant, who had fiercely resented Gansevoort Melville because he had helped gain the nomination for Polk in 1844; later Melville's wife, like Bryant a member of the Unitarian All Souls Church, felt entirely free to call at the Bryant house to see the Bryants' visitor, Orville Dewey.)

Poetry was not just something that eminent foreigners and eminent American citizens wrote. Many people the Melvilles knew wrote and published—and not just Augusta's Miss Woodbridge. Everyone might write valentines and have valentines addressed to them in youth, and poetry about people they knew, and even about family members, could be printed. In 1848 Anne Lynch assigned young Bayard Taylor the task of writing a public valentine to Herman Melville as well as to several other celebrities, and N. P. Willis (that "rival of Anacreon," as Gansevoort had noted) promptly published the results in his *Home Journal*. Herman, unlike most people, became the subject of poetry other than valentines. On February 8, 1847, Maria Melville relayed to Augusta news from Washington: "Herman writes that he was shewn a very pretty volume of Poetry by Mr W E Chan[n]ing of Boston they are now published for the first time, one is called the 'The Island of Nukeheva.' It is poetically descriptive of Tipee and is very pretty" (Parker 1:487). This poem (written after Ellery Channing and Henry David Thoreau had shared their ideas about *Typee,* if not sharing a single copy) begins:

> It is upon the far-off deep South Seas,
> The island Nukuheva, its degrees
> In vain—I may not reckon, but the bold
> Adventurous Melville there by chance was rolled,
> And for four months in its delights did dwell,
> And of this Island writ what I may tell.
> So far away, it is a Paradise.

In July 1850 the London *Town and Country Miscellany* printed this stanza of Albert Smith's "A Dream of the Grand Exposition": "Quite hard at work, Herman (I don't mean the German / Who conjures, but Melville the sailor—the sailor) / Was showing a few how a Typee ragout / Could be made from the crew of a whaler—a whaler." Later poems inspired by Melville or written directly to him range from Robert Buchanan's "Socrates in Camden" (1885) to W. Henry Canoll's "Melville" (1886) and Buchanan's *The Outcast* (1891).

Melville knew many poems written by his personal friends such as Nathaniel Parker Willis as well as poems in which some of his acquaintances figured, notably James Russell Lowell's *A Fable for Critics* (1848), which satirized Evert Duyckinck and Cornelius Mathews. Despite Melville's growing popularity as a subject for poetry, all through the century the most famous poem anyone ever wrote about anyone in the family was Holmes's "The Last Leaf" (1831), a cheeky caricature of the old Major Melvill.

Some of what Melville learned about poetry and poets was gossip. Americans heard and read stories of famous poets from American travelers, and not only literary people, who had made pilgrimages to British authors, casually intruding themselves upon poets. James Hogg was pestered in his last years by dozens of callers a day. Orville Dewey, who preached Melville's father-in-law Judge Shaw's funeral service in 1861 and baptized three of Melville's children in 1863, had published in 1836 an account, quickly famous, of the way Wordsworth had received him at Rydal Mount in 1833. The tendency of British poets to gossip to travelers is clear in *Haps and Mishaps of a Tour in Europe* (1853), by "Grace Greenwood" (Sarah Jane Clarke), the admirer of Melville, who recalled her encounter with "Barry Cornwall,—born Procter," the songwriter Melville had met at Samuel Rogers's in 1849. She wrote: "It gave me quite a new sensation to hear personal recollections of such men as Byron, Moore, Wordsworth, Keats, Coleridge, and Charles Lamb. Of the latter, Mr. Procter related some new anecdotes, giving his peculiar delicious drolleries in a manner surely not unworthy of Elia himself." Melville too contributed to the spread of such anecdotes when he regaled his brother Allan by mail with a description of dining with the poet-novelist Sir Walter Scott's cold fish son-in-law, John Gibson Lockhart, himself a poet, in London in 1849, for Allan promptly put the gossip into further circulation so that it quickly reached as far as Long Island.[15]

The hard evidence that Melville read a particular poet may consist of a single known comment in his marginalia or his literary works, and sometimes that evidence may not be as hard as it looks. Into a copy of Dante, Melville copied this from Landor's *Pentameron and Pentalogia:* "What execrations! What hatred against the human race! What exultation and merriment at eternal sufferings!"[16] Melville may have taken these words secondhand from Leigh Hunt's *Stories from the Italian Poets* (1846) or another source. Similarly, Melville may well have known poems by Jonathan Swift (as he definitely knew poems by Swift's friends), but his few known references to "the Dean" do not indicate a specific knowledge of his poetry (nor for that matter of *Gulliver's Travels,* commonly available in expurgated texts). Very often, only a dubious reference or two proves (or strongly suggests) that Melville knew the poetry of a famous contemporary (Robert Browning being the most conspicuous example). In the manuscript of his essay on Hawthorne's *Mosses* Melville held up for national pride N. P. Willis's "The Belfry Pigeon," yet this is his only known reference to Willis's poems. (A further twist in the fortuitous survival of evidence is that if Willis had not published a passage from a letter Melville wrote to him from London in 1849 we would not know for sure that the two men had ever been on confidential terms.[17])

But the pervasiveness of poetry in Melville's time is further manifest in its common function as an acceptable award or gift. A courtship gift from Melville's father to his mother was a New York 1813 Akenside's *The Pleasures of Imagination.* In 1831 the Albany Academy awarded young Herman *The London Carcanet. Containing Select Passages from the Most Distinguished Writers,* which included poems by Scott, Moore, and Byron (Sealts 331). Herman is said to have given an early (1830 or so) edition of Tennyson's *Poems* to Mary Parmalee, at Lansingburgh, around 1838 or 1839 (Gilman 104). At some time (1840?) the *London Carcanet* passed out of Herman's possession (to Mary L. Day? Harriet M. Day, Harriet Fly?—all names that are now in the volume), but not before he had inscribed in three very different samples of penmanship three sensual stanzas from Gay's *The Beggar's*

Opera, where young Melville identified himself with Macheath. On December 19, 1844, Mrs. R. M. Blatchford gave Augusta the 1842 two-volume Ticknor edition of Tennyson's *Poems,* which Augusta surely shared with her newly returned brother Herman during his visits to Lansingburgh and later, when they lived in the same house. In this edition was a poem that caught Herman's imagination, "Will Waterproof's Lyrical Monologue" (as evidenced by his sightseeing in London in late 1849; see chap. 4 below). A gift from Gansevoort to their sister Fanny in 1845, as he left for London, was Longfellow's *Voices of the Night.* Oliver Wendell Holmes gave his *Urania* (1846) to Judge Lemuel Shaw, whose daughter Elizabeth married Melville the next year. Melville's mother-in-law, Hope Savage Shaw, in 1848 gave him Longfellow's *Evangeline, a Tale of Acadie.* In April 1849 Evert A. Duyckinck gave Augusta Melville (when she was in Melville's New York City household) a "most acceptable gift," Leigh Hunt's new two-volume *A Book for a Corner; or, Selections in Prose and Verse.* On Wednesday the eleventh in 1849 (either April or July), Augusta thanked Evert Duyckinck for "volumes" on (meaning by?) Leigh Hunt— perhaps including one already mentioned, *Stories from the Italian Poets.* (In October 1861 Melville acquired Hunt's *Rimini and Other Poems* [Boston: Ticknor & Fields, 1844; Sealts 290a], the title poem of which was a treatment of Dante's story of Paolo and Francesca so important in Landor's *Pentameron* and in Melville's own *Pierre.*) The first volume of *A Book for a Corner* contained William Shenstone's "The Schoolmistress" and Pope's "Ode on Solitude." The second volume contained Thomson's "The Enchantments of the Wizard" and "Indolence" from *The Castle of Indolence;* Parnell's "The Hermit"; Thomas Gray's "Ode on a Distant Prospect of Eton College" and "A Long Story"; Cowley's "Thoughts on a Garden, from a letter to Evelyn" (mostly verse); Lady Winchilsea's "Petition for an Absolute Retreat"; Warton's "Two Sonnets" and "Inscription over a Calm and Clear Spring"; and Gray's "Elegy in a Country Churchyard."[18]

As far as we know, Melville bought few volumes of poetry before 1849, one being Philip Pendleton Cooke's *Froissart Ballads, and Other Poems,* which he bought on December 2, 1847 (Philadelphia: Carey & Hart, 1847; Sealts 158), another important one being Macpherson's *Fingal, an Ancient Epic Poem,* in 1848 (London: Becket & De Hondt, 1762; Sealts 343). In his middle and later years the proportion of books Melville purchased shifted from prose to poetry. From 1849 on, and especially from the late 1850s on, he bought more and more poetry or books about poetry and art books that dealt with issues in aesthetics. In the late 1860s and 1870s he continued to buy prose books by and about Hawthorne and research books for *Clarel,* for instance, but fewer miscellaneous prose volumes.

It is clear that from his childhood and his youth Melville was steeped in English poetry of the Renaissance, Restoration, and eighteenth century, and of the great generation of Scottish and English poets born around 1770. By his young manhood he knew poetry by Edmund Spenser (c.1552–99), William Shakespeare (1564–1616), Ben Jonson (1572–1637), Edmund Waller (1606–87), John Milton (1608–74), Samuel Butler (1613–80), Abraham Cowley (1618–67), Andrew Marvell (1621–78), John Dryden (1631–1700), Matthew Prior (1664–1721), Alexander Pope (1688–1744), and John Gay (1685–1732), among others. He knew especially well the poets of his grandparents' and parents' childhoods and early lives, among them James Thomson (1700–1748), Samuel Johnson (1709–84), William Shenstone (1714–63), Thomas Gray (1716–71), William Collins (1721–59), Mark Akenside (1721–70), Oliver Goldsmith (?1730–74), William Cowper (1731–1800), James Macpherson (1736–96), Thomas Chatterton (1752–70), George Crabbe (1754–1832), Robert Burns (1759–96), Samuel Rogers (1763–1855), and the more recent poets such as William Wordsworth (1770–1850), James Hogg (1770–1835), Sir Walter Scott (1771–1832), Samuel Taylor Coleridge (1772–1834), Robert Southey (1774–1843), Walter Savage Landor (1775–1864), Thomas Campbell (1777–1844), Thomas Moore (1779–1852), Leigh Hunt (1784–1859), Barry Cornwall (the pseudonym of Bryan Waller Procter, 1787–1874), and Lord Byron (1788–1824).

William H. Gilman (see p. 51) recorded the Lansingburgh rumor that Melville in his youth knew poetry by Alfred Tennyson (1809–92). It is possible, however, that Melville knew little or nothing of Tennyson or, for that matter, of Percy Bysshe Shelley (1792–1822) and John Keats (1795–1821), until after his return from the Pacific in 1844. The early catalogs of the Albany Young Men's Association list no separate volume under the name of Shelley, Keats, or Tennyson. Exigencies of publishing (such as Tennyson's silence through much of the 1830s) and of American republishing seem to have retarded the American reputations of all three poets.

From childhood Melville also knew some American poems and in his youth heard and read lectures that focused on specifically

American literature, including poetry. By youth or early manhood he had at least sampled several ambitious American poems. The YMA had a fine collection of classical literature in translation. In adult life Melville's purchase of the thirty-seven-volume Classical Library from Harpers in 1849 provided him with translations of Virgil, Horace, Ovid, Homer, and Pindar. Earlier, he knew something of Italian poets of the Renaissance. Melville bought the Cary translation of Dante in the 1847 Bohn edition entitled *The Vision; or Hell, Purgatory, and Paradise* on June 22, 1848 (Sealts 174), and, as Merrell R. Davis suggested (85), soon wrote "Babbalanja relates to them a Vision" (*Mardi,* chap. 188). The next year, 1849, may be when Melville wrote Ariosto's and Tasso's names beside Milton's invocation at the beginning of *Paradise Lost*—clear evidence that he knew something about their own invocations.[19] He knew some of Virgil's *Eclogues* in translation, and probably by this time knew the *Aeneid,* in Dryden's translation. Early in life, he knew some poetry of Goethe and Schiller, in translation, and had, before his later reading of Heine and Staël, at least a general sense of recent German poetry, what one could learn from Carlyle's essays in magazines and the remarkable essay in the *Zodiac* taken from the *American Monthly Magazine.* Long before he manifested any longing to become a poet himself, Herman Melville was familiar with many thousands of lines of poetry and could probably quote hundreds of them at will. In this he was not greatly unlike many of his contemporaries, but in this he was quite unlike most educated persons of the twentieth or twenty-first century including even most academic specialists in British and American poetry.

CHAPTER FOUR

The Renewed Power of Poetry in Melville's Life, 1849–1856

AT SEA, ESPECIALLY ON WHALERS, WHERE BOOKS WERE SCARCE, vulnerable, and the supply rarely replenished, any man whose head was stuffed with poetry, as Melville's was when he went to sea, was in demand. (By the end of 1842 Melville was also in demand as a man who had stories to tell—or teasingly to withhold—about his and others' sexual adventures in whaleships and on Pacific islands.) At home, while he was writing *Typee* and *Omoo,* Melville read mainly prose works by voyagers which he could plunder for his own narrative. *Mardi* (1849) was the book in which Melville declared his literary independence, although he was not to win it until *White-Jacket* (1850) or, arguably, not until *Moby-Dick* (1851). When he began *Mardi* in May 1847, Melville turned to nautical books for sources, then as he underwent sudden intellectual growth from late 1847 through 1848 he turned to books by philosophical and psychological writers— Robert Burton, Rabelais, Sir Thomas Browne, Bishop Berkeley, Lord Chesterfield, Dr. Johnson, Edmund Burke, and many other prose writers. For the most part, he read poetry when it impinged on his daily life, as Channing's "The Island of Nukuheva" did early in 1847 and Longfellow's *Evangeline* did later, or as *A Fable for Critics* did late in 1848, when Evert Duyckinck and Cornelius Mathews were stung by Lowell's satire. Chances are that not until early 1849 did poetry again mean more to Melville than prose, as it had in his youth and early manhood when he had been under the spell of Lord Byron.

Most of Melville's allusions to poetry in *Mardi* are casual. Early he calls Dante "grim" (chap. 3), echoing Lord Byron (*Don Juan* 10.27), but perhaps also knowing that "grim Dante" was in the 1833 text of

Tennyson's "The Palace of Art." In *Mardi* are references to "Manfred-like" behavior (chap. 4); borrowings from the marginal glosses of "The Ancient Mariner" (as in the title of chap. 16); echoes from Tennyson's "Mariana at the Moated Grange" (chap. 31); references to two of Shakespeare's more gnarled characters (Richard III, chap. 84, and Timon of Athens, chap. 174); a reference (chap. 174) to the impossibility of disentangling collaborative passages by Beaumont from those by Fletcher; and (in chap. 177) a portrayal as Marko of Fitz-Greene Halleck (the writer of the 1820s international war cry, "Marco Bozzaris," who had descended from shining poet to prosaic clerk for John Jacob Astor). The book also contains some spoof titles of typical books of poetry: "Suffusions of a Lily in a Shower," "Sonnet on the last Breath of an Ephemera," and "The Gad-fly, and Other Poems" (chap. 123).[1]

Melville's interest in putative Norse or Gaelic heroic poems is manifest in his buying, in 1848, the *Froissart Ballads* (Sealts 158), which consisted of "versified transcripts from Froissart" as well as new imitations of Froissart; in borrowing *Frithiof's Saga* from Evert A. Duyckinck early that year (London: Hookham, 1838; Sealts 500); and in buying sometime that year James Macpherson's *Fingal, an Ancient Epic Poem, in Six Books: Together with Several Other Poems, Composed by Ossian the Son of Fingal* (Sealts 343). From his months at the Lansingburgh Academy, Melville probably remembered that Lord Kames, respectful of Hugh Blair's "dissertation," had drawn repeatedly on *Fingal* for illustrations in *Elements of Criticism*. Technically *Fingal* was in prose, purportedly translated from the Gaelic poet, but admirers thought of the language as if it were like that of the book of Job and other Hebrew poetry in the King James translation. The Dantean title of chapter 185 of *Mardi* (from *Purgatory*) showed he was freshly and powerfully influenced by the edition he bought in 1848, and in chapter 188 he borrowed Babbalanja's vision from *Paradise*. The most important poetic influences on *Mardi* seem to be Ossian and, in some late-written chapters, Dante.

In *Mardi* Melville (as far as we know) first tried his hand at writing poems he was willing to publish, but the verses were not as ambitious and powerful as many of the sections of prose. Indeed, by putting verses into the mouth of Yoomy, the warbler, Melville defined them as examples of a lower order of verse. Chapter 119 sets forth Melville's rankings: "Like a grand, ground swell, Homer's old organ rolls its vast volumes under the light frothy wave-crests of Anacreon and Hafiz; and high over my ocean, sweet Shakespeare soars, like all the larks of the spring. Throned on my sea-side, like Canute, bearded Ossian smites his hoar harp, wreathed with wild-flowers, in which warble my Wallers; blind Milton sings bass to my Petrarchs and Priors, and laureats crown me with bays." (The laureates in Melville's time were Southey, until 1843, then Wordsworth until 1850, then Tennyson.) Seeing the world of poetry as capacious, Melville acknowledged the grandeur of Homer while being protective of the lesser and more vulnerable poets such as Anacreon and Hafiz. Ossian looms over poets like Petrarch and Matthew Prior, but the Petrarchs and Priors are also true poets. In his comments in book 17 of *Pierre* on poets of the first, second, and third degree, Melville made much the same distinctions when he asserted that, as a reader, his young hero Pierre had "freely and comprehendingly ranged" among "the beautiful imaginings of the second and third degree of poets"—not the first degree— not Homer, Shakespeare, Ossian, Milton, and (judging from some passages late in *Mardi,* then in *Moby-Dick, Pierre,* and elsewhere) not Dante. Yoomy was, at best, a Waller.

At the beginning of 1849 Melville was open for profound new experiences—fatherhood, first of all, but also intellectual and aesthetic growth. He had finished the ambitious book by which he hoped to win a high general literary reputation, not just additional fame as a writer of South Sea adventure; he had completed an intense self-education in the profound thinkers (as he would have said) of Western civilization, including classical writers and modern foreign writers in translation. He had realized that it was time for him not only to engage weighty ideas involving history, religion, philosophy, psychology, and political theory, but also to clarify in his own mind the terms in which the best critics of his time had been talking about literature. His attempts to temporize about *Mardi* to John Murray may have been enough to make him confront serious deficiencies in his own aesthetic vocabulary. He found literary criticism in his *Penny Cyclopædia,* enough to make him discontented with the casual criticism he had seen accompanying poetry in magazines or newspapers, or introducing poetry in any of the new annual gift-books, or criticism quoted in or promulgated in books on poets, such as his friend Tuckerman's *Thoughts on the Poets.*

The best literary criticism, Melville knew, was to be found in the great British quarterlies. From his father, long before he could read the quarterlies for himself, he knew the name of Francis Jeffrey, who had entertained Allan Melvill in 1818 and from whose garden in

Edinburgh Allan had plucked a rose as a keepsake for his wife. Melville would have known that Byron had castigated Jeffrey in "English Bards and Scotch Reviewers," even to the point of comparing him to another Jeffrey, the George Jeffrey of the Bloody Assizes in James II's time, a period familiar from Macaulay's history, and Melville would have understood the basis for Byron's attacks on Southey and Wordsworth, in particular. A high point in his erratic education had been the time he was free to read the British periodicals in the library of the Young Men's Association in Albany.

At the end of 1848 or the first weeks of 1849 Melville ordered *The Modern British Essayists* (Philadelphia: Carey & Hart, 1847–48; Sealts 359), a widely advertised new compendium which dealt with religion, history, philosophy, political science, and other subjects but which in most volumes gave much space to poetry. On February 16, 1849, the New York City publisher and bookseller John Wiley charged Melville's account $18 for the set. No scholar has reported seeing it, but it presumably consisted of eight volumes, as Merton M. Sealts Jr. explained in his *Melville's Reading* (no. 359):

> The "set" . . . included eight numbered volumes: v. 1 (1847 *or* 1849): Thomas Babington Macaulay, 1st Baron Macaulay. Essays, Critical and Miscellaneous . . . v. 2 (1847): Sir Archibald Alison, Bart. Miscellaneous Essays . . . v. 3 (1848): Sydney Smith. The Works . . . v. 4 (1848): John Wilson. The Recreations of Christopher North [pseud.] . . . v. 5 (1848): Thomas Carlyle. Critical and Miscellaneous Essays . . . v. 6 (1848): Francis Jeffrey, Lord Jeffrey. Contributions to the Edinburgh Review . . . v. 7 (1848): Sir James Stephen. Critical and Miscellaneous Essays . . . Sir Thomas Noon Talfourd. Critical and Miscellaneous Writings . . . With Additional Articles Never Before Published in This Country . . . v. 8 (1848): Sir James Mackintosh. The Miscellaneous Works . . . In addition, an unnumbered volume published by Carey & Hart in 1841 was advertised in some catalogues as part of the set: Sir Walter Scott, Bart. Critical and Miscellaneous Essays . . . Collected by Himself . . .[2]

The 1841 Scott volume cited by Sealts may well have been (or have been *intended as*) the source for the Scott volume advertised as "in press" under its new title *The Critical Writings of Sir Walter Scott* about the time Melville would have ordered his set. The book advertised with this title may never have been printed. One three-volume set of Scott has been located with the series title *Modern British Essayists* on the spine, in what seems to be the publisher's binding, but unlike the other volumes just named the Scott is not in double columns, and is printed on better paper. What came into Melville's hands are probably the eight volumes enumerated by Sealts (and not a Scott volume, although some of Scott's critical writings may have been in the Melville house already).

However ready Melville was for a profound shift in his life as a literary man, a shift in which he would ponder the great British reviewers of the previous half century, chance had a featuring blow at events. In Boston in February 1849, awaiting the birth of his and Lizzie's first child, and then staying on during her recovery, Melville found a seven-volume set of Shakespeare, locally printed by Hilliard, Gray (1837; Sealts 460) in what he called "glorious great type," easy enough for him to read with his already weak eyes. On February 24, 1849, a week after Malcolm was born, Melville wrote to Evert A. Duyckinck:

> I have been passing my time very pleasurably here. But chiefly in lounging on a sofa (a la the poet Grey) & reading Shakspeare. It is an edition in glorious great type, every letter whereof is a soldier, & the top of every "t" like a musket barrel. Dolt & ass that I am I have lived more than 29 years, & until a few days ago, never made close acquaintance with the divine William. Ah, he's full of sermons-on-the-mount, and gentle, aye, almost as Jesus. I take such men to be inspired. I fancy that this moment Shakspeare in heaven ranks with Gabriel Raphael and Michael. And if another Messiah ever comes twill be in Shakespere's person.——I am mad to think how minute a cause has prevented me hitherto from reading Shakspeare. But until now, every copy that was come-atable to me, happened to be in a vile small print unendurable to my eyes which are tender as young sparrows. But chancing to fall in with this glorious edition, I now exult over it, page after page.——

What Duyckinck wrote in response was designed to dash this irreverent exuberance, particularly any linking of Shakespeare with the archangels (toward whom Duyckinck felt fiercely protective). On March 3, Melville rejected any implication that he was ready to join the bard-idolators, the snobs (in the now obsolete sense of sycophants) "who burn their tuns of rancid fat at his shrine." Melville would instead "stand afar off & alone, & burn some pure Palm oil, the product of some overtopping trunk." And he would look to Shakespeare, at first, for ideas, not for "poetical" qualities such as diction and sound. His theory now was that in Elizabeth's time all men wore muzzles on their souls, even Shakespeare: "For I hold it a verity, that even Shak-speare, was not a frank man to the uttermost. And, indeed, who in this intolerant Universe is, or can be? But the Declaration of Independence makes a difference." Melville fondly hoped at this moment that he might be frank in the books he would write. Duyckinck's own review of *Moby-Dick* less than three years later (*Literary World,* November 22, 1851), where he protested at Melville's dislodging "from heaven, with contumely, 'long-pampered Gabriel, Michael and Raphael,'" would have served, all alone, to disillusion him. Whatever specifically aes-thetic qualities he recognized in Shakespeare then or later, Melville first articulated his awe of Shakespeare as thinker ("Here is forcibly shown the great Montaignism of Hamlet"), a man with profound ideas.[3] That he did not single out for comment anything about Shake-speare's astonishing language may simply indicate that he felt ill-equipped to talk in such terms, though within two years he was able to imitate that language magnificently in *Moby-Dick.*

It was while Melville was reveling in Shakespeare in Boston that the set of *Modern British Essayists* arrived in New York. Some of the volumes (likely the Macaulay, Wilson, and Jeffrey) included a bound-in aggressively worded late 1848 Carey and Hart advertisement de-claring this "a new, revised, and very cheap edition." Carey and Hart confidently promised: "The series will contain all the most able papers that have ever appeared in *The Edinburgh Review, The London Quarterly Review,* and *Blackwood's Magazine,* and may indeed be called the cream of those publications." It announced volumes by Robert Southey, J. G. Lockhart, William Gifford, and J. Wilson Crocker (i.e., Croker) that apparently were never printed. Carey and Hart then itemized poten-tial customers: heads of families (wanting models of style for their children); managers of book societies and book clubs; school inspec-tors, schoolmasters, and tutors (wanting suitable prizes or additions to school libraries); travelers (the publishers thinking the hefty volumes suitable "to fill a corner in a portmanteau or carpet-bag"); passengers on board a ship; officers in the army and navy, and all "Economists in space or pocket," who need to lay up "a *concentrated Library,* at a mod-erate cost"; and those who need to send gifts to friends in distant countries. Judging from his letter to Richard Bentley on July 20, 1851 ("This country & nearly all its affairs are governed by sturdy backwoodsmen—noble fellows enough, but not at all literary"), Melville would particularly have delighted in the next paragraph of the Carey and Hart ad: "The Modern Essayists will yield to the Settler in the Backwoods of America, the most valuable and interesting writings of all the most distinguished authors of our time, at less than one quarter the price they could be obtained in any other form." The last buyer was envisioned as the "Student and Lover of Literature at Home, who has hitherto been compelled to wade through volumes of Reviews for a single article," who "may now become possessed of *every article worth reading* for little more than *the cost of the Annual subscription*" (presumably not a subscription to a British periodical but to an American reprint).

Here in one set, as advertised, were hundreds of articles from the great British quarterlies that enlightened the age, especially the Whig *Edinburgh Review,* founded in 1802 by Sydney Smith (1771–1845), Francis Jeffrey (1773–1850), and Henry Peter Brougham (1778–1868). Here also were an abundance of articles from the great magazine's two Tory rivals, the London *Quarterly Review* (founded in 1809) and *Blackwood's Edinburgh Magazine* (founded in 1817), as well as others. In the preface of his volume, Smith itemized his and his friends' Whig grievances against the state and church:

> To appreciate the value of the Edinburgh Review, the state of England at the period when that journal began should be had in remembrance. The Catholics were not emancipated—the Corporation and Test Acts were unrepealed—the Game Laws were horribly oppressive—Steel Traps and Spring Guns were set all over the country—Prisoners tried for their Lives could have no Counsel—Lord Eldon and the Court of Chancery pressed heavily upon mankind—Libel was punished by the most cruel and vindictive imprisonments—the principles of Political Economy were little understood—the Law of Debt and of Conspiracy were upon the worse possible footing—the enormous wickedness of the Slave Trade was tolerated—a thousand evils were in existence, which the talents of good and able men have since lessened or removed; and these effects have been not a little assisted by the honest boldness of the Edinburgh Review.

The Tory *Quarterly Review,* stoutly defending Church and Crown, was founded by William Gifford (1756–1826), the first editor; among the contributors were George Canning (1770–1827), John Hookham Frere (1769–1846), Sir Walter Scott (1771–1832), and Robert Southey (1774–1843). William Hazlitt (1778–1830) chastized Gifford in *The Spirit of the Age* (1825) for his hostile recasting of Charles Lamb's essay on Wordsworth's *The Excursion* and for his publishing the virulent attack by John Wilson Croker (1780–1857) on Keats's *Endymion*. The *Quarterly Review* was no friend to the followers of the Romantics, either, particularly Tennyson, whose 1832 book Croker had savaged in what became a notorious review, said to have kept the poet from publishing for a decade. The Tory *Blackwood's Edinburgh Magazine* soon after its founding came into the hands of John Gibson Lockhart (1794–1854), John Wilson (1785–1854), and James Hogg (1770–1835), the poet known to Melville as the "Ettrick Shepherd."

Melville may have picked up his *Modern British Essayists* as early as March 3, when he made a brief trip back home to Manhattan. If so, being a man who traveled light, he would have left the volumes off at his house on Fourth Avenue rather than hauling them to Boston. The insides of the volumes were never handsome, despite the Carey and Hart claims. The paper used was of inferior quality, and the texts were in double columns, with tight gutters and skimpy margins, even when the edges had not been cut in rebinding. Worst of all, the tiny print was torturous even to eyes not "as tender as young sparrows," although Melville could read small print when he needed to, at least in the daylight, if he paced himself. These were bulky volumes, but with the series title "THE / MODERN / BRITISH / ESSAYISTS" and the volume author's name (or probably in one instance two authors' names) in gold stamping on the spine, Melville's set would have looked handsome enough ranged on a shelf. There would be scant authority for thinking of volumes sold together by Carey and Hart as constituting a "set," bibliographically speaking, but presumably any shipping clerk would have put together Melville's set in one color of cloth, either red or brown. One modern assemblage of these volumes, variously bound, stretches to some thirteen linear inches on the shelf and stands roughly nine and a half inches tall by six inches deep. *Modern British Essayists* may have remained in Melville's library for the rest of his life, but, perhaps because no one has found in his writings a specific reference to the set or to a volume in it by title, his use of *Modern British Essayists* has gone virtually unexplored, except for brief references in my two-volume biography of Melville. *Modern British Essayists* played a significant role in Melville's self-education, particularly about British poetry. Pretty clearly, he looked through the set right away, for his next book, *Redburn,* bears marks of familiarity with at least the Smith and the Wilson volumes.

For Melville the volumes were all valuable but far from equally so as far as poetry was concerned. The Stephen volume did not contain essays on poetry. The essays by Sir James Mackintosh (1765–1832) for the most part had been published in the *Edinburgh Review*. In an "Advertisement to the London Edition" the editor explained that he has in general arranged the pieces in order, moving from the "more purely Philosophical, and proceeding through Literature to Politics." Melville might have been attracted to a review of Samuel Rogers's *Poems* (especially after meeting the author late in 1849) and Staël's *De L'Allemagne*. In the Carlyle volume Melville had the review of Lockhart's biographies of Burns and of Scott along with a great deal on contemporary German writers, including a review of a biography of Jean Paul Friedrich Richter, and a good deal on Goethe, but this volume did not contain the great Carlyle, with whom Melville became acquainted elsewhere. The bulk of the Macaulay volume consisted of essays from the *Edinburgh Review* in roughly their order of publication, beginning with an essay on Milton (1825), one on Machiavelli (1827), and one on Dryden (1828). The volume contained several other essays likely to attract Melville's eye, such as one from 1831 on "Moore's Life of Lord Byron" and an undated essay on "Cowley and Milton" (following an 1840 essay). In Melville's volume the 1847 additions to an earlier Carey and Hart volume began with an "Appendix" on 569, two poems, "Pompeii" (source not identified) and "The Battle of Ivry," from *Knight's Quarterly Magazine* (1824), followed by ten essays from the *Edinburgh Review* (these out of chronological order). Melville quickly would have tired of Macaulay's pomposity, pedantry, and vacuity, as in this definition in an essay on an inherently fascinating topic, "Milton": "By poetry we mean, the art of employing words in such a manner as to produce an illusion on the imagination: the art of doing by means of words what the painter does by means of colour." The other volumes were more to the purpose when Melville began studying poetry again, now as a famous prose writer himself.

Archibald Alison (1792–1867) was the son of the Archibald Alison (1757–1839) famous for *Essays on the Nature and Principles of Taste* (1790). (In the sixth volume of the set Melville could read Francis Jeffrey's extensive review of the father's book, "Alison on Taste.") The term "master-spirits," which Melville used in his essay on Hawthorne, derived ultimately from *Julius Caesar,* but his use of it may have been suggested by the younger Alison's applying it in "The Copyright Question" to great geniuses who are too profound to be appreciated by their own times. All profound writers experienced the pressure "to exchange deep writing for agreeable writing," Alison said. No "metaphysics, no

conic-sections, nothing but cakes & ale," Melville reassured Richard
Bentley on June 5, 1849, about his work in progress, *Redburn;* "nothing weighty," he reassured George P. Putnam on June 7, 1854, about
Israel Potter (1855). The last essay in the Alison volume, "Homer,
Dante, and Michael Angelo," from the January 1845 *Blackwood's,* concluded that great subjects remain untreated: "Nature is inexhaustible;
the events of men are unceasing, their variety is endless. . . . Rely
upon it, subjects for genius are not wanting; genius itself, steadily and
perseveringly directed, is the thing required. But genius and energy
alone are not sufficient; COURAGE and disinterestedness are needed
more than all." All this would have been heartening to Melville.

The volume by Sydney Smith consisted of contributions to the
Edinburgh Review followed by some speeches. From his citation of it in
his essay on Hawthorne, we know that Smith's 1820 query in "America" rankled in Melville, as in many Americans: "In the four quarters
of the globe, who reads an American book? or goes to an American
play? or looks at an American picture or statue?" In his 1818 essay on
"America" (also reprinted in the *Modern British Essayists* volume)
Smith had been more particular:

> Literature the Americans have none—no native literature, we mean.
> It is all imported. They had a Franklin, indeed; and may afford to
> live for half a century on his fame. There is, or was a Mr. Dwight,
> who wrote some poems; and his baptismal name was Timothy.
> There is also a small account of Virginia by Jefferson, and an epic by
> Joel Barlow; and some pieces of pleasantry by Mr. Irving. But why
> should the Americans write books, when a six weeks' passage brings
> them, in their own tongue, our sense, science and genius, in bales
> and hogsheads? Prairies, steam-boats, grist-mills, are their natural
> objects for centuries to come. Then, when they have got to the Pa-
> cific Ocean—epic poems, plays, pleasures of memory and all the el-
> egant gratifications of an ancient people who have tamed the wild
> earth, and set down to amuse themselves.—This is the natural
> march of human affairs.

Smith was incendiary, as Melville remembered from one of Simeon De
Witt Bloodgood's lectures at the Albany Young Men's Association for
Mutual Improvement. But you never knew what would catch
Melville's eye. The 1821 essay on "Man Traps and Spring Guns"
(227–32) seems a likely source for the "frightful announcement" the
young hero encounters in chapter 43 of *Redburn,* the book Melville
wrote the summer after buying the collection.

The volume by T. Noon Talfourd (1795–1854) is made up primarily of essays from the *New Monthly Magazine,* the *Retrospective Review,* and the *London Magazine.* Several public addresses conclude the volume, the most interesting to literary people being the one delivered "in the Court of Queen's Bench, June 23, 1841," where Talfourd defends Moxon, the publisher of Shelley's works. This was Edward Moxon (1801–58), the cold, stiff man Melville managed to thaw during his interview late in 1849. One of the literary essays, "On the Genius and Writings of Wordsworth," reprinted from the *New Monthly Magazine,* was just the sort of loving guide to poems that Melville could benefit from. Toward the end of it, Talfourd appealed to his readers to take up Wordsworth for themselves rather than being kept away by "base or ignorant criticism":

> Not only Coleridge, Lloyd, Southey, Wilson, and Lamb—with whom his name has been usually connected—but almost all the living poets have paid eloquent homage to his genius. He is loved by Montgomery, Cornwall, and Rogers—revered by the author of Waverley—ridiculed and pillaged by Lord Byron! Jeffrey, if he begins an article on his greatest work with the pithy sentence *"this will never do,"* glows even while he criticises, and before he closes, though he came like Balaam to curse, like him "blesses altogether."

Here was exemplified the riches of the *Modern British Essayists,* for Talfourd was referring to the November 1815 article on *The Excursion; being a Portion of the Recluse, a Poem,* which began: "This will never do!"—an essay Melville now possessed in the Jeffrey volume of the same set.

John Wilson (1785–1854), the author of the volume entitled in this Carey and Hart set *The Recreations of Christopher North,* was a glamorous figure in Melville's early life, famous not only for his writing but for his striking physique and long blond hair and for his exploits as a sportsman. Melville remembered him from the Albany *Zodiac.* In his twenties, after graduation from Oxford, Wilson had bought an estate at Windermere called Elleray, and while there became a friend of Wordsworth, Coleridge, Southey, and De Quincey. Melville found in the Wilson volume primarily reprints from *Blackwood's Magazine* (later *Blackwood's Edinburgh Magazine*), original publication dates not given, but all dating from before or during 1842, when the collection was first published. This volume was immediately useful at the end of May or early June 1849, for Redburn's shooting jacket may have derived from the frontispiece illustration. Scanning the "Christopher North" volume, Melville would have remembered his reading of Wilson's letter to Hogg in the *Zodiac* long before. Wilson himself then became the renewed object of interest for his comments on *Mardi* in the August 1849 *Blackwood's* review of Mayo's *Kaloolah*. (On August 21, 1849, the Boston *Evening Transcript* spread the news that in North's review *Mardi* was "spoken of as having been 'closed with a yawn, a day or two after its publication!' ") In early September 1849, Thomas Powell (discussed later in this chapter) wrote Evert Duyckinck about "that old humbug Christopher North" in relation to this review (*Log* 311–12). Knowing that the curmudgeonly John Wilson had deigned to pontificate about him may well have heightened Melville's interest in the volume over the next years. He would have found challenging Wilson's question of whether there was a great English poem (answer: only *Paradise Lost*). In the volume Melville found many comments on Wordsworth, and could read, with hostility, Wilson's praise of doctrinally correct sacred poetry. The long-term importance of the *Recreations* for Melville is that it afforded him intimate glimpses into the Wordsworthian milieu of the Lake District through several of the pieces: "A Day at Windemere [*sic*]," "Stroll to Grassmere" ("First Saunter" and "Second Saunter"), in particular. Wordsworth is quoted and expounded in other essays, including "Morning Monologue," "An Hour's Talk about Poetry," "Sacred Poetry" (which contained Wilson's conclusions about religion in Wordsworth's poetry), and "A Few Words on Thomson." "Go, read the EXCURSION," Christopher North commanded in the prologue to "The Moors." Melville did read it, and other poems by Wordsworth, carefully, aided by Wilson's sympathetic, intimate guidance. In this volume Melville probably experienced his first encounter with many passages by Wordsworth which would strike him sharply when he read them later, in their contexts.

The volume by Francis Jeffrey (1773–1850) was probably even more important to Melville than the Wilson, beginning with the preface, which contained this explicit statement: "The Edinburgh Review, it is well known, aimed high from the beginning:—And, refusing to confine itself to the humble task of pronouncing on the mere literary merits of the works that came before it, professed to go deeply into *the Principles* on which its judgments were to be rested; as well as to take large and original views of all the important questions to which those works might relate." In modern terminology, the quarterly, from the first, aspired to address theoretical issues, issues involving aesthetic principles. What would have caught Melville's attention in this volume, after the preface, were reviews of the great Romantic poems that Jeffrey had published in the *Edinburgh Review* as the poems were appearing. *Lyrical Ballads* pre-dated the establishment of the magazine, but the poetry section of the volume contained Jeffrey's reviews of Campbell's *Specimens of the British Poets;* Byron's *Sardanapalus* and *Manfred;* R. H. Cromek's *Reliques of Robert Burns;* Campbell's *Gertrude of Wyoming* and *Theodoric;* Scott's *The Lay of the Last Minstrel* and *The Lady of the Lake;* Crabbe's *Poems, The Borough, Tales,* and *Tales of the Hall;* Keats's *Endymion, Lamia, Isabella,* and *The Eve of St. Agnes;* Rogers's *Human Life;* Southey's *Roderick: The Last of the Goths;* Byron's *Childe Harold's Pilgrimage* and *The Prisoner of Chillon;* Moore's *Lalla Rookh;* Wordsworth's *The Excursion* and *The White Doe of Rylstone;* and Hemans's *Records of Women* and *The Forest Sanctuary.* However little of this poetry we ourselves are familiar with, we would be wise to assume that Melville knew almost all of it, even if the best evidence for his knowing, say, *Gertrude of Wyoming,* is the offhand reference to the "good Indian" Outalissi in his 1849 review of Francis Parkman's *The Oregon and California Trail.* Here Melville possessed an extraordinary cache of classic practical criticism, Jeffrey's brilliant tutorials in how to read *The Excursion* or *White Doe of Rylstone,* for two examples. These reviews embodied Jeffrey's determination to write criticism from aesthetic principles, so that, self-taught in the theory of literature, Melville found in Jeffrey, no matter how belatedly, one of his best teachers. As late as 1862 he copied out aesthetic hints from Jeffrey's essay on the Italian dramatist Victor Alfieri.

Having passed 1848 frugally by borrowing books from Evert Duyckinck (the Dante he purchased in June was an exception), Melville had embarked on a satisfying buying spree on the strength of his expectations for *Mardi.* Besides the seven-volume *Shakespeare* (bought very early in February) and *Modern British Essayists,* Melville's other purchases early in 1849 included the two-volume *Poetical Works of John Milton* (Boston: Hilliard, Gray, 1836; Sealts 358b), in typography a companion to the Shakespeare. He dated the set New York 1849, but the "N.Y." was probably his notation of his home city, not the place of purchase, and he may have bought it late in February or in March, for early in the summer he showed that he had been re-reading Milton. For many years critics tended not to consider poetical influences on Melville if they did not have his own marked copies, thereby sometimes slighting his knowledge of Spenser, Milton, Wordsworth, Tennyson, Elizabeth Barrett Browning, Robert Browning, and others. (An exception is an acute early book on Melville and Milton by Henry Pommer, based largely on verbal echoes of Milton in Melville—a study vindicated by Melville's markings when his two-volume set of Milton's poems came to light.) Melville's copy of Wordsworth first turned up in the 1970s, his Milton in the 1980s, his Spenser in the 1990s. Melville may have bought his *The Complete Poetical Works of William Wordsworth* (Philadelphia, 1839 [Sealts 563a]) soon after seeing how largely the poet figured in *Modern British Essayists* and before he realized how little money *Mardi* would bring in.

On March 19 Melville bought the thirty-seven-volume Harper's Classical Library (Sealts 147), which included in translation the major Greek and Roman historians and orators, the Greek tragedians and Roman satirists, and abundant classical poetry: Anacreon and Pindar (who gave their names to forms of verse, Anacreontics and Pindarics), Virgil's *Eclogues* (translated by Francis Wrangham) and *Georgics* (translated by William Sotheby), Dryden's translation of the *Aeneid,* Pope's translation of Homer, Philip Francis's of Horace, and Ovid translated by Dryden, Pope, Congreve, Addison, and others. Cicero and Demosthenes were included in the set as "orators." In Boston, in late March or the first day or so of April, he bought the four-volume (or more) Pierre Bayle's *An Historical and Critical Dictionary* (London: Harper, 1710; Sealts 51). Melville looked forward, he wrote to Duyckinck on April 5, to continuing his course of reading, when he could lay his "great old folios side by side & go to sleep on them thro' the summer, with the Phaedon in one hand & Tom Brown in the other." The *Phaedrus* he possessed in the Classical Library (not a folio set), but his *Phaedon* is unlocated. *Plato's Phaedrus: A Dialogue Concerning Beauty and Love* was in fact available in a thin London folio (Edward Jeffrey, 1792), and Sir Thomas Browne could be found in more than one folio edition, including the one he had borrowed from Duyckinck in 1848. It was December before Melville bought his known folio of Sir Thomas Browne. The folio *Phaedon* may have been a flight of wish-fulfillment, named as an evocative companion for the tangible volumes of the Bayle dictionary.

Melville's intense encounter with Shakespeare alone seems enough to call 1849 the year Melville became a serious student of poetry. But that year he also re-encountered Milton. He was of course sensitive to aesthetic qualities, as shown by his copying out Cowper's tribute to the music of *Paradise Lost* and, still more clearly, by his astonishing re-call of Milton's vivid words when he came across echoes of them in later English poetry. Yet Melville seems to have read Milton in large part for poetic expression of ideas, particularly theological doctrine. Before long he began paying attention to Wordsworth, if only, for a time, through the lavish quotations in his *Modern British Essayists,* from which he could have fashioned his comment that August or Sep-tember, in *White-Jacket,* on the "gentle and sequestered Wordsworth" at "placid Rydal Mount" (chap. 11). He also started reading the poetry in the Harper's Classical Library. In 1849 he bought Schiller's *Poems* in the Tauchnitz edition (Leipzig, 1844; Sealts 439), probably picking it up at the Astor House in the shop of Rudolph Garrigue, "Foreign Bookseller," for thirty-seven and a half cents. (The Tauchnitz Burns, Byron, Moore, Ossian, Pope, and others were for sale at the same price.) In London in December he bought Thomas Chatterton's *Poeti-cal Works* (Cambridge: Grant, 1842; Sealts 137).

Melville's fantasy about a summer's luxuriant reading (which surely would have included poetry) collapsed as it became clear that *Mardi* would be a commercial and critical failure both in England and the United States. Guilty, and making amends, Melville wrote *Red-burn* in June and July; then he wrote *White-Jacket* in August and Sep-tember. Late that spring Melville had ill-advisedly meddled in the explosive matter of the warring actors, William Charles Macready and Edwin Forrest (perhaps without seeing either production of *Macbeth*), thereby playing a small part in the Astor Place riots, from which he could conclude that literary people were better off reading Shake-speare in the closet than seeing him mangled on the "tricky stage" (as Melville said in August 1850 in his essay on Hawthorne). Then even as he absorbed himself in writing *Redburn* he was drawn into the edges of another British-American sensation, the eruption into the Duyc-kinck literary circle of Thomas Powell, a genuine London literary man as well as a forger of commercial and literary documents. Powell came bearing British poetry and intimate tales of the living British poets and other literary people.

In London, Powell had used one poet as the means to approach an-other, and he sealed his new intimacies in two ways: by gifts (the more ready since Powell paid for them with stolen money, which also subsi-dized the publication of his own plays and poems from year to year) and by flattering comments on his new acquaintances' literary pro-ductions. He had made the acquaintance of Wordsworth by 1836. By

1839 his dear friend Southwood Smith had introduced him to Leigh Hunt, to whom he gave financial advice. By the winter of 1839–40 Powell had some hand in *The Poems of Geoffrey Chaucer, Modernized* (1841), being "edited" by R. H. Horne in loose collaboration with Wordsworth, Hunt, Elizabeth Barrett, and Powell's brother-in-law, Leonahard Schmitz (Dickens 3:578). On July 18, 1841, Elizabeth Barrett cited Powell to Mary Russell Mitford as not only a friend of R. H. Horne but "a very dear friend also of Wordsworth's." She went on: "Mr Powell has written to me two or three times, & sent me his poems, which are marked by poetical sentiment & pure devotional feeling, but by no remarkable power. You know we had him with us in the Chaucer" (Kelley and Hudson 5:81–82). Through Thomas Talfourd, Powell met Robert Browning and soon became "a constant visitor" at his house at Peckham; in 1842 Browning "took pity on him and helped his verses into a little grammar and sense" (Dickens 3:578) and gave him his manuscript of act 1 of *Colombe's Birthday* (Dickens 3:578). As Elvan Kinter says, "Browning was completely taken in; he introduced Powell to the 'Colloquials,' and, most telling of all, apparently confided to him the secret of *Pauline,* which was carefully withheld from everyone else where possible" (Kinter 1097). In 1843 Powell dedicated a play, *The Blind Wife,* to Browning (Dickens 3:578), and proved so charming that Browning's father violated his son's privacy by giving Powell some of Robert's juvenilia (unless Powell forged these documents). Powell added Charles Dickens to his list of friends, and by April 16, 1844, Dickens was inviting him to dinner.

In 1846 Powell's London literary career unraveled. Robert Browning on January 11, 1846, denounced him to Elizabeth Barrett in a letter that testifies to Powell's extraordinary power of insinuating himself into the good graces of writers much superior to himself and testifies even more clearly to Powell's genius for producing complicated states of outrage in people who had found him out. Browning continued to sputter out his outrage to Barrett, as in the letter of June 8, 1846, denouncing Powell's "impudence and brazen insensibility" (Kinter 766). Powell was annoying and persistent, "dreadful to encounter beyond all belief," a gnat-like Nemesis all the rest of Browning's life. Impudence and brazen insensibility in literary and social matters were one thing, embezzlement another. The story of Powell's defrauding Thomas Chapman broke in June or July 1846. From Lausanne, Dickens wrote, "It is terrible to think of his wife and children." Shortly after this, Powell took laudanum in what passed as a suicide attempt. For the sake of his family, Chapman did not prosecute him (Dickens 4:575n. 2). By late in 1848, Powell was again in trouble with the law, accused of "obtaining money by means of false checks" (*Times* [London], January 10, 1849) and was arrested and committed to an insane asylum, Miles's Lunatic Asylum, at Hoxton. The magistrates were highly indignant, according to the same report, suspecting that Powell's insanity "had been produced by artificial means—by the excessive use of opium, and resorting to the expedient of igniting charcoal in his bedroom—the object being to produce a temporary state of delirium, in the expectation by that means to evade justice." Early in 1849 Powell fled with his wife and children to the New World.

Powell arrived in Manhattan, forty years old (Poe's age), a few months before the term "Confidence Man" was coined in that city to identify the modus operandi of a kindred spirit, a native rogue. Already a portly embodiment of John Bull, Powell lightly resumed his career of crime, finding it good to be shifty on a new island. He cashed forged letters of credit at a local banking house even as he burst into the Anglophiliac New York literary world with a brilliantly contrived gift to the chief editor of the weekly *Literary World,* Evert A. Duyckinck (co-owner of the magazine with his brother George)—not a forged Browning association copy this time but something his American recipient would value more highly: "You take such good care of a book that I feel a double pleasure in begging your acceptance of the accompanying copy of 'Tennyson'—it contains some alterations in his own hand—Tho' trifling I thought you would prize it—."[4] It would not have occurred to the enthralled Anglophile Duyckinck to wonder whether the alterations were in Tennyson's hand or Powell's own. At least Powell truthfully claimed to be (or once to have been) on friendly terms with almost anybody who was anybody in the London literary milieu. His intimate anecdotes of literary London continued for many weeks to charm Evert and George Duyckinck and their friend Cornelius Mathews (in effect a co-editor of the *Literary World*); and their hard-writing associate Herman Melville was impressed enough with Powell to give him a copy of his new book, *Mardi.* On September 8, 1849, the *Literary World* under the heading "Unique Poems" printed as its lead article Powell's headnote to a recent poem by Robert Browning, there entitled "The Duke's Interview with the Envoy," then the poem itself, the text marred by Powell's italicizing many of its "characteristic" lines. His headnote began: "The genius of Browning is as peculiar and *provoking,* as it is *undoubted:* he enjoys the singular merit of being the most wilful and impracticable poet of the present time. He delights in putting the reader into the difficult position of either believing himself or the poet to be at fault. . . . He is the antithesis to Common-place—but while he avoids the old route he often gets shipwrecked on the rocks of the unintelligible; he compresses everything; as in some system of shorthand, he begins by leaving out the musical vowels, and then cuts down the consonants, till a few letters alone remain, which he insists upon doing the work of the whole Alphabet." Busy as he was with *White-Jacket,* Melville surely read this poem and Powell's literary criticism on it, only the first of the poems by Browning that Powell would soon help bring to Melville's attention.

With Duyckinck having boosted him into the pages of the *Literary World,* Powell soon gained a contract with G. P. Putnam (the eminent publisher of the greatest American writers, Cooper and Irving) for a two-volume survey of contemporary English and American writers. Sensing danger somehow, Putnam broke the contract, but by September (despite being arrested early in the month for forgery) Powell had a book in press at the respectable house of Appleton's—the scurrilously gossipy anecdotal *Living Authors of England,* which he had produced by copying out lengthy quotations from literary works of his quondam acquaintances and preceding them or tagging onto them magisterial-sounding off-the-cuff commentary. Powell's method of rushing his book-making along (all the while bemoaning the heat and humidity of a Manhattan summer) meant that Americans got a good sampling of British poetry (and prose passages) along with their gossip. Two features of *Living Authors of England* proved explosive. First, Powell gratuitously dragged Washington Irving into discussion only to slur him, an act of irreverence which evoked ferocious hostility, notably a denunciation from the Transcendentalist George Ripley in Horace Greeley's influential New York *Tribune.* Anyone who wants to comprehend the depth and intensity of American reverence for Irving at mid-century need only read these documents. Second, Powell included an impudent chapter on Dickens's personal habits in which he flattered Cornelius Mathews with an extended comparison between the New York novelist (who liked to be known as "the American Dickens") and the London novelist—just possibly a devious strategy for setting Mathews up as a comic butt. The comparisons were so absurd that William Cullen Bryant's *Evening Post* omitted all mention of Mathews when it offered a prepublication sample from the Dickens chapter in September. A copy of the *Post* article reached Dickens fast. All afroth with outrage, Dickens exposed Powell in a letter to a New York acquaintance who had given a dinner for him in February 1842, Lewis Gaylord Clark, the editor of the *Knickerbocker.* Since Dickens wrote on the basis of the excerpt in the *Evening Post,* he had no idea that Powell had compared him to Mathews. Dickens probably did not know (and wouldn't have cared if he had known), but Clark was the bitterest enemy of the Duyckinck-Mathews clique. In writing to a literary man who had befriended him Dickens was innocently blundering into the hornets' nests of the publishing world of lower Manhattan. This storm broke while Melville was away.

Before, during, and after Melville's voyage to England in 1849–50 Tennyson was the contemporary British poet he was most aware of. Tennyson had not been famous enough to be collected by the Young Men's Association of Albany, judging from the catalogues of 1837 and 1843. If Melville really possessed a volume of Tennyson's poetry and gave it away in the late 1830s, as William H. Gilman was told (104), he gave away an uncommon book. A few years later, in 1842, the Ticknor reprint of the new London two-volume edition became widely available. Augusta's friend Mary Blatchford's mother gave Augusta this set just before Christmas, 1844, so Melville could have seen it during his stays at Lansingburgh, where he finished *Typee* in 1845. Among the poems in it were "Mariana," which Melville may have alluded to in *Mardi,* and a poem that caught his fancy, the boozy tribute to the Cock Tavern, "Will Waterproof's Lyrical Monologue." In the next years after his return from the Pacific, Melville saw Tennyson commented upon in the press as a good second-rate poet, a delicate lyricist, but not serious, not hefty like Wordsworth, even (as Edward Bulwer-Lytton notoriously charged in 1846 in the first edition of his poem *The New Timon*) effeminate, the "School-miss Alfred." Too full of eccentric compound words said another, listing them scornfully the way G. W. Peck later listed Melville's coinages in *Pierre.* Melville at this time would have formed a long-lived view of Tennyson as a thin substitute for the too-early-lost Shelley and Keats—softly sensuous like Keats but lacking Keats's acute powers of observation, and aspiring like Shelley but lacking Shelley's fearless outspokenness on specific political abuses and remedies. Aside from aesthetic and intellectual qualities, Tennyson may already have struck Melville as too melancholy a poet to be endured in sustained doses. Nevertheless, it was flattering to be compared to him, as in this 1846 piece on *Typee* in the

London *New Quarterly Review:* "There is something very striking in
Mr. Melville's account of the approach of the vessel to the land of
promise. The mild influence of the climate spread a 'delightful lazy
languor' over the ship's company. We are reminded of the fine passage
in Tennyson's 'Lotos Eaters': 'In the afternoon they came unto a
land, / In which it seemed always afternoon; / All round the coast the
languid air did swoon, / Breathing like one that hath a weary dream.' "
In his attack on *Omoo* in the July 1847 *Whig Review* (a long review
characterized by unintended revelation of his own weird sexual
twists), Peck linked Melville and Tennyson as objects of disdain: "The
manliness of our light literature is curdling into licentiousness on the
one hand and imbecility on the other; witness such books as Omoo,
and the namby-pamby Tennysonian poetry we have of late so much
of." Melville was licentious, Tennyson imbecilic.

The Duyckinck circle followed Tennyson's career more tolerantly
than Peck and others, especially after Powell arrived bearing that veritable volume by Tennyson that purported to contain a few changes in
the poet's own hand. On September 22, 1849, just before Melville
sailed for England, the *Literary World* in its review of Lieutenant Frederick Walpole's *Four Years in the Pacific* pointed out "coincidences" between that book and *Typee,* quoting as authority the London *Examiner.*
The *Literary World* elaborated on "other coincidences still more remarkable": "Like Melville in Typee, Lieut. Walpole became lame and
disabled in the Sandwich Islands, and found similar careful nurture in
a domestic household with a gentle Fayaway in the person of the
graceful little Elekeke." Then the *Literary World* printed a poem it entitled "Lieut. Walpole's 'Fayaway' ": "So innocent-arch, so cunning-
simple. / From beneath her gathered wimple. / Glancing with black
beaded eyes, / Till the lightning laughters dimple, / The baby-roses in
her cheeks; / Then away she flies." This was signed "Tennyson"—and
indeed the lines were Tennyson's, but from the early poem "Lilian."
Melville sailed for England with many readers of the *Literary World*
duped into thinking that Tennyson had written about the heroine of
Typee, Fayaway, as young Channing had in fact done. On the voyage
Melville may have anticipated some literary tavern-crawling, and a
week and a half later he went to " 'the Dr Johnson Tavern' " (November 16).[5] Having steeped himself in "Will Waterproof's Lyrical Monologue," Melville the same day made his way to the "Cock Tavern,"
identifying it as "Tennyson's." The poet was nowhere near as great as
Byron, say, but the man Tennyson, saturated with tobacco and steeped

in port, was well worth following about in London. Two days later Melville made his way "to the Rainbow tavern—(Tennyson's)," no matter that the Cock, celebrated by the boozy Will, was by far Tennyson's favorite haunt. (On his return visit at the end of April 1857 Melville recorded: "Lay a sort of waterlogged in London.—Reverie at the 'Cock'"—in a Tennysonian mood, he meant, but no longer waterproofed, no longer proof against typhoons or mere spring rains.)

On his voyage home from England in January 1850 Melville may have sampled some of the poetic Elizabethan and Jacobean dramas he had purchased, but his longing to saturate himself in the poetic dramatists contemporary with Shakespeare was lifelong and probably never wholly satisfied because other interests intruded—in 1850 his starting *Moby-Dick* (after he asked to borrow a set of Elizabethan dramatists from Duyckinck in 1862, he was deflected into many weeks of reading books that helped him articulate an aesthetic credo). On New Year's Day, 1850, early in the voyage home, he read in his copy of Davenant's *Works* (London: Printed by T. N. for Henry Herringman, 1673; Sealts 176), marking this passage in the preface to *Gondibert:* "For a wise Poet, like a wise General, will not show his strengths till they are in exact Government and order; which are not the postures of chance, but proceed from Vigilance and labor." Melville had been cagey enough in *Mardi* when he published poems appropriate to his young Yoomy, but not to a writer as ambitious as Melville had himself been in 1848. His "strengths," although he may not have recognized it, had been in the poetic prose of some of the earlier chapters such as 19, "Who Goes There?" Perhaps he also looked through his new volume of Chatterton's poems. Bridling at the editor's bland confidence in the introduction that "Shakspere must ever remain unapproachable," Melville called this "Cant" and retorted that no man "must ever remain unapproachable," an opinion that would break out a few months later in his essay on Hawthorne's *Mosses from an Old Manse.*

The Powell scandal had followed Melville to London in November 1849, for Allan sent newspapers to him; "the Powell Papers," Melville called them (in a December 13 journal entry). Even while Melville was still in England, sympathizing with the "poor devel" (December 17), Powell in a new manuscript treacherously linked Melville with Irving as the two worst enemies of the American mind (for allegedly hogging the money British publishers paid to Americans), and thereafter pursued his attack on Melville with information from a November

14 letter of Melville's from London that N. P. Willis had incautiously quoted in his *Home Journal* on January 12. Upon his arrival in New York on the last day of January 1850 Melville was confronted by some of the damage Powell had done already, particularly the ugly charge in *Living Authors of America* that the Duyckincks quoted in the *Literary World* two days later, on February 2—that Melville and Irving were the worst enemies of the American mind. (Powell had dropped this calumny into his chapter on Edgar Allan Poe, who had died just at the time Melville was leaving for England.) Then Melville was assaulted by Powell's new diatribe against him and Irving in the *Herald* on the sixth. By good fortune, he never, even during the most vituperative stages of the Powell scandal or the ongoing slinging match between N. P. Willis and the *Literary World* group, became tarred by Lewis Gaylord Clark or others as a mere member of the Duyckinck-Mathews "Mutual Admiration Society," and Powell's personal attacks on him faded away.

Nevertheless, in February 1850 Melville must have looked through both *Living Authors of England* (published in late October, while he was bound for England) and *Living Authors of America* (published while he was on his long voyage home). The furor had died down by the time Melville saw *Living Authors of England,* so he could focus on any value the lengthy quotations from poetry might have for him—verse by Wordsworth, Landor, Rogers, Barry Cornwall, Moore, Hunt, Tennyson, Robert Browning, Arthur A. Clough, R. H. Horne, Elizabeth Barrett Browning, Henry Taylor, Coventry Patmore, Alfred Domett, and others. The quotations from poems were so extensive as to form little anthologies—of Tennyson, in particular, where lines were quoted about many women: Claribel, Lilian, Madeline, Adeline, Oriana (the name Melville had adopted for his Lizzie), and Eleanore. Powell intermixed quotations from "The Two Voices" (Tennyson's "greatest poem") with lengthy explication. He quoted "The Sisters," "Margaret," the "opening to 'Oenone [printed as Æone],'" "Locksley Hall," "The Lotus-Eaters," and "Choric Song." He ended with an economical introduction to the recent "The Princess: A Medley" as "a pleasing banter on the rights of women."

Mathews had imprudently entrusted Powell with his letters from Elizabeth Barrett written before and after her marriage, and Powell had stuffed them into the end of his chapter on her in *Living Authors of England.* Here in this tawdry setting she was made to hope that Mathews's *Wakondah* "may attain his full 'bulk' as a worthy national poem, and be recognised as such on either side of the Atlantic," then she was exposed as continuing with a cliché borrowed from American chauvinists, the notion that grandeur of natural scenery produces great poetry:

> When American poets write, as they too often do, English poems, must not the sad reason be that they draw their inspiration from the English poets, rather than from the grand omnipresence of nature; must not both cause and result partake of a certain wrongness? I fear so. And all should be hope, and nothing fear, in America! You have room there for whole choruses of poets—Autochthones— singing out of the ground. *You,* with your Niagara for a Hippocrene, and your silent cities of the woods, too old for ruins, and your present liberties, and your aspirations filling the future.

Entrusting Powell with Barrett's letters was an act of insolent vainglory on Mathews's part. Now they were published, and however specious they were as literary theory, her ideas had gone into Melville's thinking before he burst out in August 1850 with his own rhapsodic literary nationalism, apparently soon after he had borrowed from Evert Duyckinck "Miss Barrett's Poems" in the 1844 two-volume London edition (*Log* 376).

Powell's second hasty book, *Living Authors of America,* which had no chapter on Melville, contained a number of quotations from poems by Emerson; Willis; Poe; Longfellow; Bryant; Halleck (with due attention to "Marco Bozzaris"); Richard Henry Dana (the elder, the "Idle Man," where Powell used space to quote from Crabbe, Goldsmith, and Wordsworth); and Frances Sargent Osgood. Powell stuck all of "The World is too much with us" into his Poe chapter, where he also buried his attack on Irving and Melville.

In his figurative or actual basket (Allan had saved articles for Gansevoort during 1844 in an actual bushel basket) Melville found the January 26, 1850, issue of the *Literary World* with Elizabeth Barrett Browning's "The Child's Grave at Florence" from the London *Athenæum.* The paper continued to promote her, even more than her husband. Cornelius Mathews, most likely, on September 14, 1850, denounced the two-volume *Poems* (New York: C. S. Francis) as "discreditable," notably in its dropping of two notes "complimentary to Mr. Mathews, her own chosen medium of communication with the American public." The reviewer took further swipes at the Francis edition in the February 1, 1851, second notice of it along with the

Chapman and Hall *Poems* (London, 1850). From the new poems in the London edition ("not to be found in the Francis edition") the reviewer quoted "Hiram Powers's Greek Slave" as Elizabeth Barrett Browning's tribute to "our country," the "West" whose grief was reflected in the face of the statue. The poem was a quarter century belated as an addition to the poems about Greek slavery; really, it was about the power of Art to effect political changes, to "break up ere long / The serfdom of this world!" (which would include American slavery as well as Italian domination by foreign tyrants). The reviewer reproached the poet for including "The Runaway Slave." She had failed to grasp that slavery was "purely a local institution": "The plan of the American Federation, which hereby proves itself essentially original, seems difficult of apprehension to the foreign mind; and statesmen and practical men have committed the confusion in which our respected poet is involved." In any case, the subject of a runaway slave was not "truly poetical." Mrs. Browning should not meddle with American institutions.

On June 21, 1851, the *Literary World* printed a review of the Francis and Company *"Casa Guidi Windows"* (as the heading read)— *Prometheus Bound, and other Poems; including Sonnets from the Portuguese, Casa Guidi Windows, etc.* The reviewer, a friend of Margaret Fuller, was presumably Mathews, whose poetic achievements she had praised in her essay on "American Literature," collected in the 1846 *Papers on Literature and Art.* As he read the part about the death of Garibaldi's wife and child, he remembered Fuller's fate off Fire Island and insisted that she deserved praise along with Mrs. Browning for "her devotion at Rome" and her (possibly factitious) "lost history of the time." America through Margaret Fuller had a claim on the Italian struggle for freedom. On July 5, 1851, the *Literary World* printed the second notice of "Mrs. Browning's Italian Poem," with ecstatic praise prefacing long quotations. On March 13, 1852, before Melville (angry since January) had succeeded in getting the Duyckincks to stop sending him their paper, the *Literary World* reviewed the new Francis edition of "Mrs. Browning's Poems," which more closely followed "the text of the author's copy," the London editions. There the reviewer concluded with a modern ranking: "The genius of Mrs. Browning, with the poems of her husband and Alfred Tennyson, and a few others, redeem the age succeeding that of Coleridge, Shelley, Wordsworth, and Keats, from the fear of abandonment by the Muses." Melville had the authority of the *Literary World* for thinking of the two Brownings and the new laureate as the greatest living poets.

In the sixteen months following the publication of *Mardi* in April 1849 Melville had his fill of seeing himself and his friends in the news, and particularly of dreading to see himself flecked with mud merely because he had been standing too close to reckless assailants in the petty New York literary feuds. In the early summer, his whaling book far along, he went off to the Berkshires for a vacation, and his buying a house in the Berkshires in September cannot have been wholly unrelated to his desire to escape from the cannibal island of Manhattan. He may have taken some contemporary poetry with him. The new poem of the early summer of 1850 was *In Memoriam;* the news in poetry was Tennyson's becoming poet laureate on Wordsworth's death. When *In Memoriam* appeared anonymously, at first some American reviewers did not know it was by Tennyson, though others did, right away. Melville borrowed it from Duyckinck somewhere about the time when Duyckinck gave a copy to Augusta. She wrote the donor on July 20: "Many thanks for 'The Vale of Cedars' [by Grace Aguilar] & Tennyson's new poem—I had been sighing for both of them. What a treat I shall have—the very titles breathe sadness!" (*New Log;* NYPL-D). Aguilar used poetic mottoes for her title page and all the chapters of her novel, some of them from a manuscript of her own, and the others from more or less conventional sources: Byron ("Hebrew Melodies" twice; *The Corsair,* "Well! Art thou happy," and *Parisina*); Mrs. Hemans eleven times; Shakespeare (*Richard II,* three times, *Othello, Measure for Measure* twice, *The Winter's Tale, The Merchant of Venice*); Sir Walter Scott (*The Lady of the Lake, Rokeby,* and the l'envoy from *Marmion*); Bulwer twice; Joanna Baillie twice; Charles Swain, James Grahame, and several from Grace Aguilar herself, identified as "MS." Chances are that Augusta and members of the household recognized quotations from Hemans almost as readily as quotations from Scott and Byron. Augusta, known as "the sad one," was a special lover of the sentimental and melancholy, and therefore of Tennyson. Melville, himself capable of writing a prose hymn to sadness, in chapter 188 of *Mardi* ("Sadness makes the silence throughout the realms of space"), particularly associated Tennyson with sadness. But just as Tennyson was never as interesting as his two early models, Keats and Shelley, he was never as important to Melville as the less likable Wordsworth. He was too much the melancholiac, too unable or unwilling to grapple for long with strenuous thoughts. In his longer works he was guilty of appalling aesthetic-intellectual lapses. On theological issues that mattered to

Melville, he was far too willing to collapse into blind faith and wishful thinking.

In 1850 and 1851 Melville had been skimming and plundering source-books for the whaling narrative and reading his new friend Hawthorne's books, reading poetry quoted in books and reviews rather than reading whole volumes of recent poetry such as Wordsworth's *Poetical Works.* That changed. He turned to Wordsworth, probably as early as the fall of 1851, as passages in *Pierre* show. He had not been able to look at *The Prelude* the summer before (when Duyckinck had Appleton proof sheets at Pittsfield), but he had scanned a number of reviews and posthumous reassessments in 1850, from one of which he probably took a hint for the way he used the cathedral of Cologne in *Moby-Dick.* Melville was always alert for coincidences between his circumstances and those of other great writers, so he would have paid special attention to one topic he repeatedly encountered in comments on Wordsworth. The *Literary World* in reviewing *The Excursion* (December 1, 1849) had quoted Wordsworth on retiring "to his native mountains, with the hope of being able to construct a literary work that might live." Although this review was published when Melville was abroad, he may well have skimmed the issues he missed, including this part of the first paragraph:

> It is a fine thing to think of a man, in a moral solitude, swung away into a quiet eddy beside the rushing current of the world's life, with mind full of imagery, and drinking in new draughts from its loving contact with this beautiful earth; full of profound and consoling thoughts upon human life and destiny, the harvest of a serene and blameless spirit; with heart blessed in its love of nature, and busy in active sympathies for the miseries of humankind; addressing himself to the labor of unfolding his inner mind, of sending forth his meditations, clad in the melody, and with all the adornments of noble verse, for the profit and comfort of mankind.

Melville was not a Berkshire "native," but his "first love" had been his uncle's Berkshire farm, and late in 1850 he "retired" (that is to say, withdrew) to his beloved American Lake District with the hope of being able to complete a literary work that might live. The Berkshires in topography constituted America's Lake District, the terrains so similar that lofty configurations were known as "Saddleback" in both regions.[6] In "Glimpses of Berkshire Scenery" (*Literary World,* September 27) Evert Duyckinck made the comparison explicit: "The mountains here are very closely grouped, descending rapidly in sharp outlines, and leaving narrow valley intervals, as the once beautiful valley of the Hoosac, which has the same elegance of a level floor, from which the hills rise at a well defined angle, which Wordsworth has noticed among the mountains of Westmoreland." He continued the comparison in regard to Stockbridge Bowl, below the Hawthorne cottage: "It has the cool freshness and life of some of our larger waters, with a more delicate sylvan beauty. The view partakes of the general breadth and expansiveness of American scenery, aided by the cold dry atmosphere, qualities which separate the landscape from the more limited, but softer lake country in England." Melville would quite naturally have associated his place as a writer in the Berkshires with Wordsworth's as a poet domiciled not in London but at Rydal Mount, as he had emphasized in chapter 11 of *White-Jacket*. In their 1855 *Cyclopedia* the Duyckincks declared that in the "comparative retirement" of Melville in the Berkshires was to be found "the secret of much of the speculative character engrafted upon his writings." Melville had been aware, all along, of similarities in his new "sequestered" situation and that of Wordsworth.

As Melville read Wordsworth he felt a growing diffidence toward the man along with admiration for much of the poetry. Many Americans had gained their sense of the poet as political reactionary from the Unitarian minister Orville Dewey's account of his visit to Wordsworth at Rydal Mount in 1833, as published in *Old World and the New* (New York: Harper & Brothers, 1836). Dewey, a Berkshire man, a native of Sheffield, Massachusetts, and a close friend of Lemuel Shaw, had by his own account lectured Wordsworth pompously but had enjoyed with him a memorable sunset at "Grassmere Lake." By contrast, John Wilson had made the Lake District a walkable guide to Wordsworth, endearing the man as he memorialized the landscape. Probably before he read Wilson, Melville had seen Wordsworth through the eyes of Lord Byron's *English Bards and Scotch Reviewers* and the introduction to *Don Juan,* as well as through Lord Jeffrey's skeptical essays in the *Edinburgh Review*—ironically, given Jeffrey's status as the chief of the "Scotch reviewers." Byron told him the man was a dullard author of a ridiculous theory and that his poetry was prosaic; and Jeffrey told him at start of his review of *The Excursion* that Wordsworth's "peculiar system" (his literary theory) was deplorable. "Theory" was an accusation in the air. O. W. Wight, the reviewer of *The Prelude* in the May 1851 *American Whig Review,* wrote that Wordsworth's name, "on account of his real merit," had begun to be associated with

Cowper and Goldsmith, despite "his theory." News of Wordsworth's death on April 23 arrived before the same reviewer recorded this in the July issue: "A theory, vicious in some respects, has led him, in many places, to use unpoetic language and imagery." Chances are that Melville fixed on the association of Wordsworth with theory from reading his friend Tuckerman's *Thoughts on the Poets*. Tuckerman declared that Crabbe had no "elevated theory of his own, like that of Wordsworth," and he treated Wordsworth as an important figure in "an intellectual history of our age," perhaps more important that way than as a poet. Melville may well have responded powerfully to Tuckerman's description of Wordsworth as choosing to "voluntarily remain secluded amid the mountains, the uncompromising advocate of a theory."[7] In Italy in 1857 on viewing Leonardo's Last Supper, damaged by his experimenting with paints, Melville thought of another great man, Wordsworth, and his theory—one with deleterious effects on the permanent value of at least some of his poetry. Furthermore, Melville came to resent Wordsworth's sense of superiority toward other writers.[8]

Advocating a theory was undesirable but there was much to be said, as far as Melville was concerned, for choosing to remain secluded amid mountains. By the first years of the 1850s Melville was absorbing some works now seldom read, notably *The Excursion*. *The Prelude* likely came at too awkward a time (the summer of 1850) for it to become important to him, except for portions that had been published before 1850, such as "Vaudracour and Julia" (a separate poem in his edition of Wordsworth, and just possibly an influence on *Pierre,* in the story of Isabel). *Pierre* begins with an evocation of Spenser's power to arouse a young reader sexually and aesthetically, but it progresses with passages that echo particular Wordsworth poems and show "active sympathies for the miseries of humankind" as well as for the unfolding of the inner mind in majestic natural settings. In *Pierre,* and in works written in the next years, Melville often described landscapes which derive a haunting part of their power from human associations with them—a familiar Wordsworthian situation. Furthermore, humble, resolute, suffering Wordsworthian cottagers appear in Melville's Berkshire writings, notably "Poor Man's Pudding and Rich Man's Crumbs" (1854). Wordsworth helped humanize the Berkshires for Melville, helped teach him "To look on nature, not as in the hour / Of thoughtless youth; but hearing oftentimes / The still, sad music of humanity" ("Lines Written a few Miles above Tintern Abbey").

Spenser, on Melville's mind as he wrote *Pierre,* was demonstrably off his shelf and in his hands by the end of 1853 or the beginning of 1854, when he used his father's copy of Spenser for mottoes in "The Encantadas" (first published serially in *Putnam's Monthly Magazine* beginning in March 1854).[9] Facing the title page he copied out: " 'Spencer to me (is dear) / whose deep conceit is such / As passing all conceit needs no defence' / Shakspeare." Now he recognized passages that later writers had echoed—Shakespeare (several times), Milton (several times), Pope (twice), Wordsworth, even Poe ("Ulalume"). Melville recognized a Milton borrowing in "The Ruins of Rome" (stanza 25: "To build with level of my lofty stile"), and annotated: "Build the lofty rhyme / Milton." Melville commented on a Wordsworth borrowing from "Vergil's Gnat," stanza 10, underlining "Now in the valleys wandring at their wills" and identifying a borrowing: " 'The river wanders at its own secret will' Wordsworth." He added, "How W. W. must have delighted in this stanza." Almost surely reading Spenser for the first time as a grown man, he saw the poet in the light of his own failing career as a writer. At 1.9.40 of *The Faerie Queene* he marked: "Sleepe after toyle, port after stormie seas, / Ease after warre, death after life, does greatly please." He marked the description of Scudamour (4.1.45) after Blandamour has denounced him: "He little answer'd, but in manly heart / His mightie indignation did forbeare." Then Melville turned the little volume around so the spine was facing him and wrote across the back flyleaf: "He little answered, but in manly heart / His mighty indignation did forbear." He had made no effort to influence or rebut any reviewer, or any treatment in the press, since he first defended the authenticity of *Typee.* At 4.6.1 he drew a line along the left margin and checked line 5: "What medicine can any leaches art" and annotated it: "Macbeth to the doctor." That passage dealt with a theme powerful in Melville's imagination, that of inward feeding:

> What equall torment to the griefe of mind,
> And pyning anguish hid in gentle hart,
> That inly feeds itself with thoughts unkind,
> And nourisheth her owne consuming smart?
> What medicine can any leaches art
> Yeeld such a sore.

Much later he recalled this passage in portraying a Spenserean character, Mortmain, who lies "with one arm wedged under cheek, / Mumbling by starts the other hand, / As the wolf-hound the bone" (*Clarel* 3.15.18–20). At 7.7.30 Melville did not bother to note "Autumne coming by" as a source for Keats's "To Autumn," but he marked lines 4–5: "And the dull drops that from his purpled bill / As from a limbeck did adown distill," and footnoted: "Keats—the monk in the chapel." In "Colin Clout's Come Home Again" Melville bracketed these lines: "Who life doth loath, and longs death to behold / Before he die, already dead with fear, / And yet would live with heart half stony cold, / Let him to sea, and he shall see it there." He annotated: "Absolute coincidence here between Spenser's conceit and another person's, in connection with a very singular thought." Melville knew his equals (he similarly noted a "singular coincidence" between his views on personal religion and Milton's). Melville took the Spenser volumes with him on his voyage on the *Meteor* in 1860 and, although he gave them to Augusta in August 1864, he retained a fresh memory of the poems all his life, as his annotations in other books show.

Melville's reading of Robert Browning is not well documented. Melville had seen some poems early, notably "My Last Duchess" in 1849, and some reviews. On December 8, 1849, while Melville was away but Allan or Lizzie was saving issues for him, the *Literary World* reviewed the new two-volume *Poems* by Robert Browning (Boston: Ticknor, Reed, & Fields). For "the poetic faculty" and poems "suggestive of thought" the reviewer ranked Browning second only to Tennyson among the poets of "the present generation," the next after the aged poet laureate. There was "too much of the metaphysical element" in Mr. Browning's poems, but he "everywhere shows that he possesses a mind of great originality, a strong and fervid imagination, a moderate fancy, a clear insight into character, and no ordinary skill in its delineation." The reviewer carefully explained that Browning's "poems are cast in a dramatic form, but they are dramatic poems rather than regular dramas. A few only can be considered as dramas, yet all have the dramatic element in a greater or less degree." Delineation of character, particularly feminine character, exhibited his creative powers to the best advantage. Perhaps most striking to Melville was the reviewer's quoting Landor's extraordinary praise (even while dissenting from it): "Since Chaucer was alive and hale / No man hath walkt along our roads with step / So active, so inquiring eye, or tongue / So varied in discourse."

By the mid-1850s Melville had grounds for taking Robert Browning seriously. He could not have missed high praise of Browning in the December 1855 issue of *Putnam's* along with the third installment of his "Benito Cereno." Then in the April 1856 *Putnam's* appeared an article on Browning which constituted an excellent guided tour of several poems (here using the titles given by the magazine): "Soliloquy of the Spanish Cloister," "In a Year," "Marching Along," "A Toccata of Galuppi's," part of "Master Hugues of Saxe-Gotha," bits of "Sordello" ("as hard reading as anything we know"), and a lurid section from "Pippa Passes." Toward the end the writer acknowledged that Browning "is called obscure, because he is not particularly easy reading; and immoral, because he recognizes every great fact of human development, but is never for a moment warped from the true vision of what is essentially true." For Melville the better defense had come earlier: "The fact of occasional obscurity is not to be denied. Upon the whole, Browning's poetry is harder to follow than that of any other great English poet. But the chief reason is, that he boldly aims to express what is, in its nature, so evanescent and shadowy—to put into words processes of thought and feeling, so delicately inwrought and fluctuating, that only sharp self-observers and students of human character can pursue them." What Melville had done in *Pierre* (where he pervasively used words like *evanescence, evanescent, shadowy, process, transient thought, feeling, feelings, fluctuate,* and *fluctuations*), Browning was credited with doing in poetry. Melville could not have missed this reminder of his own achievement in prose and the possibility of his pursuing his psychological investigations in poetry.

Two other contemporary poets, one a principal inspiration to the other, stand out as possible models, the Englishman Martin Farquhar Tupper, whose long pop-philosophic pseudo-biblical poems had been astonishingly successful during Melville's early career, and the American Walt Whitman. Melville carried Tupper's address with him to London, but did not call on him. (In the early 1850s Melville's mother idolized the Englishman as the Christian writer her son was not.) When he read *Clarel* Melville's brother-in-law John Hoadley identified one line as taken from "The Moon," a poem in a minor Tupper volume, *A Thousand Lines* (1848), not the book everyone knew, *Proverbial Philosophy* (published in Wiley & Putnam's Library of Choice Reading in 1846, the year *Typee* appeared in another Wiley & Putnam series, the Library of American Books). The New Yorker Walt Whitman (away in New Orleans during much of Melville's own early New York career) had taken strong hints for his poetic form, subject, and even his hope of wild popular success from Tupper, and Melville may have heard in 1855 or 1856 about the poet whose ambition to incorporate the country into his poetry was still more recklessly daring than Melville's own ambitions at the time of *Moby-Dick* and *Pierre*. A copy of the first edition of *Leaves of Grass* had been in Melville's brother-in-law Hoadley's library since soon after it was published in 1855, but apparently years passed before Melville sat down with *Leaves of Grass*. Late in his life, Whitman apparently meant much to Melville, judging by his responses to "Socrates in Camden," Robert Buchanan's tribute to Whitman with incidental exalted praise of Melville, and especially judging by Edmund Clarence Stedman's reference to his having said "so much" about Whitman that Stedman felt justified in sending him what he had written on the poet. In the early and mid-1850s, however, Melville did not take Tupper seriously and did not take any American poet seriously.

In the mid-1850s Melville continued to allude to poetry in his prose. Into the manuscript of *The Confidence-Man* in late 1855 or in 1856, for several instances, he made allusions to several of Shakespeare's plays (including a song from *The Winter's Tale*) as well as to William Makepeace Thackeray's parody of Goethe, "The Sorrows of Werther"; Wordsworth's "Immortality" ode and, later, "My Heart Leaps Up When I Behold"; John Ruskin's "Mount Blanc Revisited"; Dryden's translation of Virgil's *Aeneid;* Allan Cunningham (a line from *Songs of Scotland, Ancient and Modern*); Pope's "Elegy to the Memory of an Unfortunate Lady"; Hunt's "Bacchus in Tuscany"; Pope again (drawing the title of chap. 31 from the last two stanzas of "Sandys' Ghost; Or, A Proper New Ballad on the New Ovid's Metamorphosis: As it was Intended to be Translated by Persons of Quality"); and Burns's "Tam o'Shanter." Melville may have been reading much of Dryden besides the translation of the *Aeneid*. While he was at Arrowhead Melville owned the 1854 London edition (Sealts 191) of Dryden's *Poetical Works* published by George Routledge, who had pirated *Israel Potter*, although an 1854 Little, Brown edition was available in Boston. Melville may have picked his Dryden up in England in 1857. He did not mark the poems at the front, possibly because he already knew them. Toward the back he marked passages in *Tales from Chaucer*, "Palamon and Arcite," book 3. In Dryden's translations from Boccaccio he marked "Sigismonda and Guiscardo" and "Cymon and Iphigenia." Melville gave the book to Sarah Morewood, most likely in the late 1850s. In his customary way, he exhausted the book before giving it away.

In the 1850s, as throughout his life, Melville enjoyed many British poets even while harboring no illusions that they were great poets. This is clear in the passage from *Mardi* quoted early in this chapter, clear also in his 1862 marginalia on Hazlitt's dismissal (in *Lectures on the English Poets*) of Samuel Rogers as "a very lady-like poet," an "elegant, but feeble writer."[10] Melville offered a reasonable defense: "Rogers, tho' no genius, was a painstaking man of talent who has written some good things. 'Italy' is an interesting book to every person of taste." A poet of genius would be in the first rank, but "a painstaking man of talent" might well earn a place in the third or even second rank of poets. By contrast, in the same passage Melville read with apparent approval Hazlitt's indictment of Campbell's "Pleasures of Hope" for paying "a painful attention" when "there is little to express." When Hazlitt labeled *Gertrude of Wyoming* as "a kind of historical paraphrase of Mr. Wordsworth's poem of Ruth," showing "little power, or power enervated by extreme fastidiousness," Melville marked with a bow the continuation of the indictment, which included the accusation that Campbell is "so afraid of doing wrong, of making the smallest mistake, that he does little or nothing." Melville checked the line "The poet, as well as the woman, that deliberates, is undone." Melville marked Hazlitt's declaration that Thomas Moore lacks "intensity, strength, and grandeur," shows no "feeling of continued identity." "Lalla Rookh" was a mistake: "Fortitude of mind is the first requisite of a tragic or epic writer," Hazlitt declared, and Melville underlined the sentence and triple-checked it. Melville was an elitist, but not to the point of letting his sense of a poet's ultimate rank (as long it was in the top three) interfere with his enjoyment of "beautiful imaginings." He could learn something from minor British poets.

In the satirical "Young America in Literature" (bk. 17), which he recklessly interpolated into his completed manuscript of *Pierre* early in January 1852,[11] Melville all belatedly asserted that his hero "possessed every whit of the imaginative wealth which he so admired" in poetry when it was "by vast pains-takings, and all manner of unrecompensed agonies, systematized on the printed page." Melville was careful to say that Pierre had not really become a true poet himself: "Not that as yet his young and immature soul had been accosted by the Wonderful Mutes, and through the vast halls of Silent Truth, had been ushered into the full, secret, eternally inviolable Sanhedrim, where the Poetic Magi discuss, in glorious gibberish, the Alpha and Omega of the Universe. But among the beautiful imaginings of the second and third degree of poets, he freely and comprehendingly ranged." If Spenser, Milton, and Shakespeare were poets of the first degree of greatness, then Wordsworth, Coleridge, Byron, Shelley, and Keats might be ranked in the second degree, while a hoard of genuinely competent eighteenth-century poets and moderns like Cowper, Rogers, Crabbe, and Campbell might have helped populate the third degree, if not the lower reaches of the second. Tennyson, successor to Wordsworth as poet laureate, and younger poets like Elizabeth Barrett Browning and Robert Browning would already be recognized as newcomers, in the third rank but perhaps already earning their way into the second.

In the Berkshires Melville saw his career falter with *Moby-Dick*, his popularity all but lost with *Pierre* to the point that he could not publish his next book, *The Isle of the Cross*.[12] For three years he wrote short stories or serials—wrote almost unremittingly except during the worst of the illnesses that began to strike him. Being so ambitious ever since he had worked his way into *Mardi,* Melville would naturally have thought of what it might be like to emulate on their own grounds the greatest writers, the poets, with whom he knew he stood on equal footing, recognizing, more than once, singular coincidings between his thoughts and experiences and theirs. But there is no evidence that Melville in the mid-1850s was suffering any tension between having to continue to write prose while hoping to write poetry. Until after 1856, he was simply struggling against horrific odds to hang onto his career as a prose writer.

CHAPTER FIVE

The Status of Poetry and the
Temptation of Flunkeyism

UP FOR DEBATE ALL THROUGH THE NINETEENTH CENTURY HAD
been the question of whether there was a great modern poem and great
modern poet in English. Francis Jeffrey in the *Edinburgh Review* had
weighed candidate after candidate without discovering one. In May
1851, the month Melville left the manuscript of *The Whale* with the
stereotyper Craighead, the New York *International Magazine* featured
an excerpt from the London *Eclectic Review* focused not on poem but
poet: "Has There Been a Great Poet in the Nineteenth Century?" The
Eclectic Review listed twenty-three renowned British poets of the first
half of the century: "Bloomfield, Wordsworth, Coleridge, Southey,
Campbell, Moore, Byron, Shelley, Keats, Professor Wilson, Hogg,
Croly, Maturin, Hunt, Scott, James Montgomery, Pollok, Tennyson,
Aird, Mrs. Browning, Mrs. Hemans, Joanna Baillie, and the author of
'Festus'" (that is, Philip James Bailey). None of them, according to the
Eclectic, had "produced a work uniquely and incontestably, or even, save
in one or two instances, professedly GREAT." Then the *International
Magazine* grouched patriotically: "The critic appears never to have heard
of our Bryant, Dana [that is, the elder Dana, "the Idle Man"], Halleck,
Poe, Longfellow, or Maria Brooks, any one of whom is certainly superior to some of the poets mentioned in the above paragraph; and his
doctrine that a great poem must necessarily be a long one—that poetry,
like butter and cheese, is to be sold by the pound—does not altogether
commend itself to our most favorable judgment." The debate over who
might or might not be a great modern poet could rage year after year,
but everyone agreed that a great poet was needed and a great poem was
to be looked for. No serious critic said the day of poetry was over.

A misconception conspicuously promulgated in *The American Epic: Transforming a Genre, 1770–1860,* by John P. McWilliams, holds that by the time Melville wrote *Moby-Dick* he and his contemporaries would have seen the "prose epic" as the highest literary form for his time, not epic poetry. Analysis of hundreds of contemporary reviews of poetry (including dozens of reviews of particular poems such as *Evangeline* and *Hiawatha*) indicates that, to the contrary, most literary people in Great Britain and the United States looked upon poetry as the highest literary form and assumed that the great writers of a country would be its poets, not its prose writers. All during his early career in New York City Melville saw evidence that most critics who hoped for the emergence of great American literature were looking for it to come in the form of poetry, not prose. Late in 1847 and early in 1848, the months he was working his way deep into the manuscript of *Mardi,* Melville knew that some critics were hailing Longfellow's *Evangeline* as the great literary work they had been looking for. In the Washington *National Era* of November 25, 1847, had not Whittier cried out, "EUREKA!—Here, then, we have it at last! An American poem, with the lack of which British reviewers have so long reproached us"? However poetic his own prose was sometimes called in 1849 in reviews of *Mardi,* Melville could still see on every hand that the great American literary work was expected to come as a real poem, not as a poetic prose work.

The idea that impelled Whittier's enthusiasm for *Evangeline* flourished in the consciousness of many literary people: since a great national literature must come in the form of poetry, America, highly desirous of achieving literary independence from Great Britain, was on the lookout for a great national poem. The Washington *National Intelligencer* (November 23, 1855) opened the review of *Hiawatha* this way: "We have in this newest Poem of Mr. Longfellow perhaps the only American Epic. . . . What the greatest Poets have done for their lands Longfellow has done for his." Through the 1850s poems such as Longfellow's *The Golden Legend* and then *Hiawatha* (an adaptation of a Finnish epic) received far more extensive and admiring journalistic coverage than Melville's books (even allowing that much of the writing on *Hiawatha* dealt with charges that the metrics and subject were plagiarized). The bias toward poetry is clear in the fate of two works by Charles Kingsley. In the spring of 1855 his novel *Westward Ho!* tended to receive only slightly longer reviews in the United States than Melville's *Israel Potter.* The next year, while *The Piazza Tales* was receiving mainly short polite notices, Kingsley's *Poems* had five columns lavished on it in the New York *Tribune* of May 10, 1856.

To be sure, some critics complained that would-be epics were too long. As early as his review of Joel Barlow's *The Columbiad* in the *Edinburgh Review* (October 1809), Francis Jeffrey had acknowledged that "men certainly bore" (that is, endured) "long stories" (epic poems) "with more patience of old than they do now." (This review Melville owned in *Modern British Essayists*.) By the late 1850s ordinary British and American readers were seldom inclined to spend their evenings reading long poems by Spenser or Milton, and still less likely to read or reread lengthy poems by long-popular eighteenth-century writers like Thomson, whose *The Seasons* had been familiar to the Melvilles from the 1830s (so that as late as 1852 Augusta could casually apply a line from it to Melville's youthful school-teaching). Scott's beloved *The Lady of the Lake* and other long poems and even Byron's long narrative poems were read less frequently. Nevertheless, educated readers were still willing, and eager, to devote many hours to new poems. Melville's brother-in-law John Hoadley was far from the only man in the country who read Longfellow's *The Golden Legend* aloud to his assembled family nightly until he had finished it, and who expected to find in poetry a higher reward than in prose. All through the 1860s, the status of poetry remained higher than that of prose. The phrase "the great American novel" (famous now as the title of a January 1868 article by J. W. DeForest in the *Nation*) pre-dates by a decade or so the time when working critics stopped looking for great American literature to come in the form of an epic poem. Throughout the 1860s and even the early 1870s (when Melville was writing *Clarel*), the status of poetry, especially epic poetry, remained high. At some yet-to-be-established point toward the end of Melville's life, perhaps before the 1870s were over, a majority of influential literary critics ceased looking for great new literary works to come in the form of the long poem and began looking for such a great work to come as prose fiction.

That shift was too late to affect Melville. All his life he had heard the poets and critics say that the surest way to achieve ultimate immortality in literature was to write great poetry, and he believed them. If Apollo and the Muses inspired anything, it was poetry, not prose. When he read Milton's appeal to Urania at the start of book 7 of *Paradise Lost,* Melville noted, "Tasso's invocation," remembering the address to an explicitly Christian (not Hellenic) muse in *Jerusalem Delivered.* (He also marked heavily Wordsworth's obviously Miltonic

"Preface" to *The Excursion,* where Wordsworth also invokes Urania.) Therefore "Why poetry?" was not a question Melville would have thought to ask after his prose career floundered. If he wanted to keep writing, and ultimately to publish again, the supremely challenging alternative was poetry. Melville came to see, after 1857, that his own most prolonged mature wrestling with the "angel—Art" (a struggle memorialized in his short poem "Art," in *Timoleon*) would thereafter be in poetry, whether short poem or poetic epic. Without believing that Apollo or Urania had descended upon New York or Pittsfield and swept him to the top of Trinity Church or Greylock, Melville knew that he had the true "godlike gift" depicted by Collins in the "Ode on the Poetical Character," where God the Creator imagines the universe into existence, and, in Collins's daring analogy, the poet imagines a new literary world into existence. Becoming a great poet in the New World, however, was more problematical.

From the mid-1830s, at the latest, Melville had pondered Sydney Smith's infamous observations on what passed as poetry (and literature in general) in the United States. Even that early, from Simeon De Witt Bloodgood's lectures, if nowhere else, Melville caught reverberations from patriotic demands that America have its own national literature, and he knew from Bloodgood's comments on Joel Barlow that patriotism without poetic power would not win discerning and enduring praise. During his whaling years and his year in the navy, Melville missed some of the furor over the dubious merits of American poetry, notably the pyrotechnics of early 1844 when the *Foreign Quarterly Review* disdainfully reviewed the qualifications of most of the candidates Rufus Griswold had brought forth in his *Poets and Poetry of America.* The opening set the tone: "'AMERICAN Poetry' always reminds us of the advertisements in the newspapers, headed 'The best Substitute for Silver': if it be not the genuine thing, it 'looks just as handsome, and is miles out of sight cheaper.'" The reviewer was gentle with Peter Gansevoort's neighbor and friend, the Albany versifier Alfred B. Street, and considered a few to be competent poets—chiefly Bryant and Poe (although the latter was an imitator of Tennyson). The best American poet, Longfellow, could not really be considered "an indigenous specimen" of a poet because his mind had been "educated in Europe." Poe was sure Dickens was the writer of the article, and in fact Dickens may have had a hand in it, although John Forster, later his biographer, all but confessed to the chuffed Longfellow that he had written it himself (Moss 158).

American critics and some American versifiers of the young Republic had brought the scorn of the *Foreign Quarterly Review* on themselves. Rather than taking the risk of claiming high originality and power, these Americans had resorted to justifying and ennobling their poets by billing them as equivalents of established British poets, following the classical precedent whereby Romans exalted the creators of its fledging literature by comparing them to Greek masters. Just as Virgil had been called the Roman Homer and Plautus the Roman Aristophanes, now in the modern updating Washington Irving was the American Goldsmith, William C. Bryant the American Wordsworth, James Fenimore Cooper the American Scott, and Fitz-Greene Halleck the American Byron. Below these loftiest claimants was a range of other poets claiming equivalence or inviting favorable comparisons with British poets—including some British poets whose reputations did not long outlive those of their American imitators. In the *Foreign Quarterly Review* Forster was merciless, beginning with Lydia H. Sigourney, who was "usually advertised, as if it were something to boast of, as the American Hemans." Charles Sprague imitated Pope badly; Wilcox imitated Thomson badly (a compounded folly, since he should have imitated the Spenser of *The Faerie Queene* directly instead of imitating an imitator); Trumbull imitated Butler's *Hudibras;* Dwight imitated Pope; Robert Paine was "esteemed by his countrymen as a copier of Dryden's" (but he copied him "so badly" that Forster was "inclined to let him off as a worse original"); Pierpont imitated Burns; Poe was "a capital artist after the manner of Tennyson"; Hill toiled "hopelessly after the bounding lyrics of Barry Cornwall"; and Fairfield plagiarized Byron's *Don Juan* ("Ave Maria! 'tis the hour of prayer"). Charles Fenno Hoffman distanced "all plagiarists of ancient and modern times in the enormity and openness of his thefts," being merely Thomas Moore "hocused for the American market." There was no end to Hoffman's thievery: "The turns of the melody, the flooding of the images, the scintillating conceits—are all Moore. Sometimes he steals his very words." Hoffman's songs were "monkeyana," as in "monkey-see, monkey-do."

The next to last paragraph in the *Foreign Quarterly Review* was devastating:

> The result upon the whole examination may be thus briefly summed up: that American poetry is deficient in originality; that it is not even based upon the best examples; that it is wanting in

strength of thought, in grace and refinement; and errs largely on the side of false taste and frothy exuberance. The classical acquirements of the American poets are loudly insisted upon by their critics: but no such influence is visible in their works—Longfellow and three or four more excepted. It might rather be predicated that they are utterly ignorant of the principles of art, or that they hold all principles in contempt. The qualifications of the poet are lowered in them to the meanest and scantiest elements. They are on a level with the versifiers who fill up the corners of our provincial journals, into which all sorts of platitudes are admitted by the indiscriminate courtesy of the printer. . . . Numerous anecdotes are related, even by themselves, of their velocity in composition. We can readily believe them. But they will find out in the long run, that the go-ahead system is as fallacious in literature as they have already, to their cost, found it to be in more substantial affairs.

This issue of *Foreign Quarterly Review* was reprinted in the United States, as usual, probably in various cities, and the entire review was reprinted separately in Park Benjamin's *The New World* on January 27 and February 3, 1844, where it was cringingly read by everyone except Longfellow and his circle. Some of the other Cambridge-Boston poets were outraged at how Forster had dismissed the verse of the elder Richard Henry Dana. The only thing worse than being held up for worldwide contempt was being left out of Griswold's collection altogether, as young James Russell Lowell had been. A few months later, in July, the Boston *North American Review* printed a ferocious and at points downright Swiftian rebuttal exposing the social evils of contemporary England. Echoes of the barrage from the *Foreign Quarterly Review* and the retort from the *North American Review* were reverberating still in New York circles when Melville returned at the end of October 1844 and soon settled down to writing *Typee* in lower Manhattan. (There at the end of January 1845 he witnessed the hoopla over Poe's new American poem, "The Raven.")

From mid-1846 through 1851 Melville was on close terms with American literary nationalists associated with Evert Duyckinck, after 1847 joint editor of the *Literary World* (in a format blatantly copied from the London *Athenæum*). Rather than abandoning their self-glorifying comparisons to British writers after the contempt shown by the *Foreign Quarterly Review,* American critics and poets shamelessly persisted in applying these comparisons. Given the competitive climate, when Melville was hailed (mercifully, in London) as the modern

Crusoe or the new DeFoe, that seemed about as high a status as he could attain as a writer. Only after declaring his intellectual independence and lofty ambition in *Mardi* had Melville read Shakespeare and found him titanic but approachable. Indeed, the common assertion that Shakespeare was unapproachable was "Cant," according to Melville.[1] In his essay on Hawthorne (written at Pittsfield in early August 1850, with Duyckinck and Mathews at hand, and carried by Duyckinck back to New York to rush into the next two issues of the *Literary World*) Melville proclaimed that we needed no American Goldsmith, and, by implication, no American Dickens. As he wrote his way into this fervent essay, Melville adopted the persona of a hyperbolic Virginian summering in Vermont, an extravagant man who pleaded with America to "prize and cherish her writers." Melville as the Virginian says that even "were there no Hawthorne, no Emerson, no Whittier, no Irving, no Bryant, no Dana, no Cooper, no Willis (not the author of the 'Dashes', but the author of the 'Belfry Pigeon')— were there none of these, and others of like calibre among us, nevertheless, let America first praise mediocrity even, in her own children, before she praises . . . the best excellence in the children of any other land. Let her own authors, I say, have the priority of appreciation." The "I say," as always with Melville, was the sign that he was stemwinding his oratory. Since his Virginian was not sufficiently passionate, he invented an even more "hot-headed Carolina cousin" who on the fiery topic of American Literature once said, "If there were no other American to stand by, in Literature,—why, then, I would stand by Pop Emmons and his 'Fredoniad,' and till a better epic came along, swear it was not very far behind the Iliad." "Take away the words," says the Virginian, "and in spirit he was sound." In this manuscript version, before Duyckinck censored what he wrote, Melville was thinking of Emerson not as poet but as an essay writer; Dana was the younger Dana, the author of *Two Years Before the Mast,* not his poet father. Melville had praised only three poets, Whittier, Bryant, and Willis, but he had learned nothing he wanted to know from any American poets he had yet encountered, and none of these three meant much to him, once his rhetorical point had been made.

Once wound up in his argument, Melville went on with a personal criticism of Washington Irving (which somehow escaped Duyckinck's censorship but which outraged the old man and for many years rankled Pierre Irving, his nephew and biographer). That "graceful writer," he said, not needing to name Irving, "who perhaps of all Americans has received the most plaudits from his own country for his productions,—that very popular and amiable writer, however good, and self-reliant in many things, perhaps owes his chief reputation to the self-acknowledged imitation of a foreign model, and to the studied avoidance of all topics but smooth ones." Melville as the Virginian declared, "it is better to fail in originality, than to succeed in imitation." We "want no American Goldsmiths; nay, we want no American Miltons." Perhaps because Longfellow had received so much praise from British critics, Melville identified the Boston (or Boston-Cambridge) poets and critics as the most subservient: "Let us away with this Bostonian leaven of literary flunkeyism towards England. If either must play the flunkey in this thing, let England do it, not us."

"Hawthorne and His Mosses" caught the eye of literary people (Longfellow called it to Hawthorne's attention), but its fervent nationalism did nothing to stop the search for American equivalents of British poets. By the late 1850s E. C. Stedman, because he was a banker who wrote poetry, was called the American Rogers. Melville had been entertained by Rogers in London and had read much of Rogers's poetry, and Stedman was no Rogers. (Decades later, he became a decent, respectful admirer of Melville.) Richard Henry Stoddard, whom Hawthorne had thought of hiring to work at the consulate in Liverpool but instead went into the New York Custom House, brazenly set himself up as the American Keats. The Duyckincks in their *Cyclopedia* at the end of 1855 validated Stoddard's claims by printing in its entirety his ode called "Autumn": "Divinest Autumn! who may sketch thee best, / For ever changeful o'er the changeful globe? / Who guess thy certain crown, thy favorite crest, / The fashion of thy many-colored robe? / Sometimes we see thee stretched upon the ground, / In fading woods where acorns patter fast." Rowland Morewood signed his copy of Stoddard's *Songs of Summer* (Boston: Ticknor & Fields, 1857) "Broadhall / 1858," so over the hill from Arrowhead Melville could easily have sampled some of the poems by Stoddard in his later Browningesque phase.

Sam Shaw visited Arrowhead in the summer of 1859 bringing Melville a copy of a recent printing of Emerson's *Poems* (Boston: Phillips, Sampson, 1858; Sealts 206), which Melville may not have read before, although chances are that he had sampled some Emerson poems in his promiscuous reading of his countrymen's and countrywomen's poetry. Emerson, by contrast with the others, was a poet to be taken seriously in the late 1850s, the way Melville took Robert

Herrick, a copy of whose poetry he acquired late that summer of 1859 (*Hesperides: or The Works Both Humane and Divine* [Boston: Little, Brown, 1856; Sealts 271])—all the more so because Melville had begun writing short poems as a way of learning the craft, and Emerson had never been visited by the epic muse. In Emerson's "Merlin" Melville scored the injunction that a poet should not try to write poetry in "weak, unhappy times" but should wait "his returning strength" (after which his rhymes might again be "efficacious") and the injunction not to force poetry into existence through the use of mere "meddling wit" but, again, to wait until the mind is "propitious," for the mind of the poet will publish, produce, only when it is inclined to do so. It might have been better for Melville to read advice less in accord with his own early vaunting of the certain something unmanageable in a writer, but at least he got from Emerson's poem confirmation that elsewhere in the United States, and in fact in his own Massachusetts, someone had been grappling with some of his own "poet-problems" (the term he used in a verse-epistle to Daniel Shepherd, dated July 6, 1859).

Melville may have recognized as a poet-problem the difficulty of connecting his admiration of the classical past with genres he might imitate in his own poetry, but he had little guidance. He had read the vague address to the "Genius of Ancient Greece!" by Akenside, which ends with the poet's pointing the high example of the Greek poets to his "compatriot youth" and urging that the British lyre be tuned to Attic themes: could he derive anything suggestive for tuning his American lyre to Attic themes? Whether he was defining himself in relation to his contemporaries or in opposition to them, as a writer of some poetic prose he had ample reason for thinking that he might make a new career as a poet. The Melville who made confident judgments as to the first, second, and third degree of poets would never have started to write poetry with the thought that he would be one more American mediocrity. Having experienced what being called the American DeFoe amounted to, Melville felt no urge as a poet to become the American Alfred Tennyson or the American Robert Browning. He would not have become a poet at all unless he thought he could become as good a poet as they were. After all, even Shakespeare was approachable.

CHAPTER SIX

A Nonpartisan Becoming a Poet
During the Risorgimento

FROM HIS YOUTH MELVILLE KNEW POETRY THAT DEALT WITH IMME-
diate political issues and more ambitious poetry that dealt with the
destiny of nations. In their ways the American *The Columbiad* and *The
Fredoniad* (and even the less sweeping *M'Fingal*) had been, like Virgil's
Aeneid, attempts to celebrate the founding of a nation. Melville may
not have known that Spenser had been an ultra-partisan in *The Present
State of Ireland.* His annotations in *The Faerie Queene* do not suggest
that he knew that Duessa was sometimes thought to be a portrait of
the beheaded Mary Queen of Scots, yet in "Prothalamion" he queried
"Essex?" as the man alluded to as the "noble peer" (one "Whose dread-
full name late thro' all Spain did thunder"). The editors of *The Life and
Death of King Richard the Second* in Melville's Hilliard, Gray Shakespeare had taught him that the name of Essex was politically explosive
in the mid-1590s. From *Richard II,* Melville also knew the "this England" passage, perhaps the greatest patriotic tribute to the isle (never
mind that the island did not consist only of England). He knew, and
probably did not admire without reservations, Milton's "To the Lord
General Fairfax" and "To the Lord General Cromwell." Milton's sonnet "On the late Massacher in Piemont" (1655) would have appeared,
by Melville's time, to be the first great English denunciation of
Catholic Italy, the "triple tyrant" accused of the murder of the
Waldenseans being the pope, from the bejeweled three-tiered papal
tiara. Melville knew Samuel Butler's *Hudibras* (London: Baker, 1710;
Sealts 104), in which part 3, canto 2 (1678) is a partisan political his-
tory of the period between the death of Oliver Cromwell and the
Restoration, scathing toward both Presbyterians and Jesuits, and

singling out for contempt the slippery side-switching Earl of Shaftesbury. (He knew that Butler, for his own epic adventures of knight and squire, had revived Spenser's Hudibras, a minor character in *The Faerie Queene.*) Melville almost surely knew Dryden's "Absalom and Achitophel" (1681), in which Achitophel was a portrait of Anthony Ashley Cooper, the Earl of Shaftesbury, whose most recent schemings were to exclude any Catholic from succession to the throne, particularly the king's brother James. Melville had seen Thomson's five-part *Liberty,* the first part a comparison of ancient and modern Italy and the fourth a consideration of the advantages of modern Britain, and he would have known Thomson's inescapable lyrics to "Rule Britannia" ("Rule Britannia, rule the waves; / Britons never will be slaves").

One of the standard poems of Melville's childhood, Campbell's "The Pleasures of Hope" (1799), had a section on the evils of Negro slavery (written before Britain's abolition of the slave trade) and a section on the sufferings of the Polish people after the first and second partitions. Tadeusz Kosciuszko, the Colonel of Engineers in the Continental Army, who led a revolt against the Russian army in 1794, after his capture and release from prison, had spent a year in Philadelphia, 1797–98, time enough to confer with many of his old friends like Thomas Jefferson and confirm his position as a hero of the world, not merely of the former colonies. His residence in the United States helped to make the sufferings of Poland real for many Americans. The Partitions of Poland constituted an early international cause about which the young American Republic could express the sort of polite sympathy that made them feel better about themselves as an altruistic people but cost them little or nothing and did no practical good for the Poles. Melville reflected this general knowledge in *Moby-Dick* when he referred offhand to the three pirate powers, Russia, Prussia, and Austria, who had dismembered Poland while England and France had stood by without helping the Poles.

Melville's first ideas about the French Revolution came from appalled comments he heard from his Melvill grandfather and other elderly relatives. The issues all his life were embodied by two mighty opposites, Edmund Burke and Thomas Paine. In his maturity the image that stuck in his mind was derived from Carlyle's history of the revolution, Anacharsis Cloots addressing the first French Assembly as a representative of all mankind. Apparently none of his main ideas about the French Revolution came from poetry. Wordsworth's "Vaudracour and Julia" in Melville's edition was extracted from its context in *The Prelude* in such a way that it was not obviously a poem about the French Revolution. Melville did know some poetry of the Napoleonic era, and respected Napoleon profoundly all his life despite the hostile tenor of some of that poetry. Melville probably knew from early life Campbell's tribute to Horatio Nelson's victory, "The Battle of the Baltic" (1801), though his surviving reference to it is in the late *Billy Budd, Sailor* manuscript.[1] (Later he knew Tennyson's 1852 tribute to Nelson in the poem on the death of the Duke of Wellington, and recalled it in *Billy Budd,* also.) Melville probably read but did not mark Wordsworth's "Sonnets Dedicated to Liberty" or the following 1816 "Thanksgiving Ode." From his comment in Hazlitt's *Lectures* we know that he was offended by Wordsworth's repeated criticisms of Napoleon, such as Wordsworth's hostile interpretation of R. B. Haydon's painting of Napoleon on St. Helena (a sonnet which Melville did not mark).

Felicia Hemans in "Modern Greece" (1817) was sure that modern Greeks were so slavishly docile to their Muslim rulers that they did not deserve to look at the great marbles on the Parthenon. Some of those marbles, thanks to Lord Elgin, now served a higher purpose in London, she thought, where they could inspire new generations of British artists to great achievements. (Others in the family possessed Hemans's poetry, but Melville's own copy of *The Poetical Works* [Boston: Phillips, 1859; Sealts 269] was purchased late, 1859.) Given the classical training some women and all educated men still received, it was natural that other British poets soon found in the efforts of the Greeks to free themselves from Turkish oppression a political cause more appealing than the plight of Poland, whatever their varying views on the Elgin marbles. Most of the poets of the time, British and American, championed the cause of Greek liberty. Lord Byron, Melville knew, had joined Greek fighters for independence and died on the field, albeit from medical mistreatment rather than wounds. Melville knew Byron's poems celebrating the Greek struggle for independence, a theme in *The Giaour,* from the opening invocation to the tomb supposed to be that of the Greek hero Themistocles. Judging from his allusion in 1846 to Byron's waking one morning to find himself famous, Melville knew Thomas Moore's *Life of Lord Byron* (which details the importance of Greece to Byron) long before he bought the surviving set (Boston: Little, Brown, 1853[?]; Sealts 369), probably in 1862. Shelley celebrated the Greek spirit in *Hellas* (1822), which he hoped would sway British public opinion in favor of the Greek revolt against the Turks. In the United States, William Cullen Bryant by speeches and poems in the early 1820s and Fitz-Greene Halleck by the great popularity of "Marco Bozzaris" (a celebration of a great hero of the war) stirred high feelings for the Greek cause. Melville, of course, knew from childhood that "Marco Bozzaris" had affected a national mood, if not national policy. As it turned out, this great European political cause of the 1820s ended with Greek freedom from the Turks, whether or not British and American good will facilitated that result at all. Allowing for a few exceptions (Shelley, Whittier), the political poetry Melville encountered tended to focus attention on foreign injustices while disguising or glossing over the fissures in the society at home, whether that was Great Britain or the United States.

Avidly following news reports of the European revolutions of 1848, Melville had eagerly engorged the manuscript of *Mardi* with international and national political allegory. His own response, like that of most Americans, was intense but brief. The uprisings in Europe were widespread and quickly suppressed, so that Americans turned their attention back to the consequences of their own just-ended war against Mexico, the discovery of gold in California, and the perturbing new focus on slavery in the national political campaign, especially in upstate New York. Melville's impulse to make himself a national and international political commentator, to record "the peculiar thoughts & fancies of a Yankee upon politics & other matters" (as he called it on June 5, 1849), was further dashed by the reception of *Mardi*. Any residual impulse to meddle with local political controversies died in the days after May 8, 1849, when he incautiously put his name to the petition urging the English actor Macready to play Macbeth at the Astor Place Opera House despite the intimidation of Bowery ruffians, champions of the Macbeth of the American actor Forrest. By encouraging Macready without protecting him, he had played a small part in bringing on the Astor Place riots, and he never again let anyone else vote his proxy. The evidence is that he did not vote at all during his years at Pittsfield, and perhaps never.

Late in 1851, when all good Whigs and Democrats were still telling themselves they had set the slavery issue to rest for their generation by the Compromise of 1850, which included the Fugitive Slave Law, Americans gave Lajos Kossuth a triumphal tour of the country on behalf of the liberation of Hungary from Austria. Pretty clearly, in this national obsession with Hungary at a time when the

United States should have been confronting its own political crisis, there was an element of hysterical displacement, a feel-good ineffectual celebration which required no national outlay of money and no commitment of American troops. Melville would have read in the *Literary World* of December 6, 1851, the "Lines Addressed by Walter Savage Landor to Kossuth on his departure for America," an appeal to the north wind Boreas to spare him so that the United States might arm him for a return to his home: "Hungary! no more / Thy saddest loss [Kossuth] deplore; / Look to the star-crowned Genius of the West, / Sole guardian of the opprest. / Oh! that one only nation dared to save / Kossuth the true and brave!" Melville heard firsthand reports of Kossuth's triumphant address in New York City. His attitude, expressed in a grim pun as he was completing the short version of *Pierre,* was that if he left home to look after Hungary (that is, to join in the feting of Kossuth) the cause of supporting his family "in hunger would suffer" (Parker 2:49). After Kossuth's departure, Americans, already manifesting a short national memory, turned their attention elsewhere, although for a while people remembered Kossuth whenever they saw an ostrich plume on a man's hat. The fad he created outlived his cause.

After the preoccupation with the liberation of Greece in the late 1810s and 1820s it was the dream of Italian liberty and unity, not the freedom of Hungary or any other country, that enlisted the passionate attention of English poets of Melville's time. Through his friend Henry T. Tuckerman's *Thoughts on the Poets* (New York: C. S. Francis & Co., 1846) Melville may have known that Felicia Hemans, having celebrated the presence of the Elgin marbles in London, had shifted her ground on national thievery of another nation's art. In "The Restoration of the Works of Art to Italy" (1816) she exposed the French under Napoleon as looters and spoilers and celebrated the return of treasures to Italy. Melville may have known her "Sonnet—To Italy," where she celebrates Italy as luxuriant, genial, fragrant, and lightly concludes with one caveat: "Yet far from thee inspiring freedom flies, / To Albion's coast and ever-varying skies." By 1862, and probably long before that, Melville knew at least one version of Samuel Rogers's *Italy,* in which his host of 1849 contrasted the beauty of the country with its present status, foreseeing a time when it would be both liberated and unified. In Melville's copy of Wordsworth was "On the Extinction of the Venetian Republic" as well as "On the Departure of Sir Walter Scott from Abbotsford, for Naples," where Wordsworth wished the brave, sick Scotsman safe passage to "soft Parthenope" (Naples). (That was, Melville knew, a precedent for the Landor poem on Kossuth.) Melville knew how important Italy had been to the poets of his childhood—Byron, who had lived there, and Shelley and Keats, who had perished there. Byron and Shelley had been scornful of the Congress of Vienna's sorting out the governing of northern Italy so high-handedly that the Austrians were still in charge in 1857, during Melville's visit there. He knew Shelley's "Lines Written Among the Euganean Hills," where the "Sun-girt City," Venice, now with her "conquest-branded brow," stooped "to the slave of slaves." Before visiting the ruins of the Baths of Caracalla in 1857, Melville knew that Shelley had written part of *Prometheus Bound* there. When he said that from the Baths he was led by a natural process down to the Protestant Cemetery, he did not have to specify that he was following poetical associations, thinking of Shelley, then of the cemetery. He was so steeped in the poetry and the biographical accounts of the poets of his youth that his going from locale to locale in a foreign city was altogether natural, even though the previously unknown way down to the cemetery turned out to be torturous. Byron and Shelley were not remote figures. At least one member of Dr. Francis's circle in Bond Street, the painter William E. West, had known them and had painted Byron (and Felicia Hemans) and had met Shelley. A gondolier in Venice had regaled Melville with personal tales of witnessing Byron en route to sexual adventures.[2] These poets had been approachable men, and in making his notes in the 1857 journal, in Venice, say, Melville would naturally have been thinking of what Byron or Shelley might have done had they been with him on an excursion or experienced such an event as he had just experienced. They were, after all, no older than many living men he knew, and both in his mind were as much associated with Italy as England. How could he think of the Coliseum without thinking of Byron or the Baths of Caracalla without thinking of Shelley? Or the Baths of Caracalla without thinking of the Protestant Cemetery and not only Shelley but Keats and his heartbreaking tombstone?

Yet Melville had been no faster than most Americans to interest himself in the liberation and unification of Italy. In *Mardi,* chapter 145, written in 1848 well after the European revolts early in the year, Melville glided over any problems in Italy. There were "many chiefs of sunny Latianna; minstrel monarchs, full of song and sentiment; fiercer in love than war; glorious bards of freedom: but rendering tribute while they sang;—the priest-king of Vatikanna; his chest marked over with antique tatooings; his crown, a cowl; his rusted scepter swaying over falling towers, and crumbling mounds; full of the superstitious past." The ruler-bards might sing gloriously even while paying tribute to Austria, the pope, or the Bourbons imposed upon the two Sicilies (Sicily and Naples), recently or long ago, by outside powers. Melville may have learned a different attitude in Robert Browning's "Italian in England" after he returned from England, for that Hamletlike dithering of a patriot in exile was in the late 1849 *Poems* (Boston: Ticknor, Reed, & Fields, dated 1850). Browning had made the subject of Italian resistance to Austrian rule a fit subject for poetry long before Melville looked askance at the Austrian soldiers in northern Italy in 1857. The year before, in April 1856, Melville had surely seen in *Putnam's Monthly* (where he had published the month before and the month after) an essay on five books by Robert Browning—the Ticknor and Fields (so it said) *Poems* (1848) and *Men and Women* (1856) and the London *Sordello* (1840), *Christmas Eve, and Easter Day* (1850) and *Strafford, an Historical Tragedy* (1837). This ten-page article, which celebrated Browning as "the most purely dramatic genius in English literature since the great dramatic days," identified him with Italy: "The secret sympathy of Browning's genius with everything Italian, is one of the most remarkable peculiarities of his poetry. It is the key, also, to the character of his genius. Many of the recent English poets have had the same fondness for Italy. Byron was never so much Byron as in Italy; Shelley lived there; Keats died there [as of course did Shelley]. But none of them has so completely and dramatically reproduced the romance and tragedy of the Italian nature as Browning."

Melville's friend Tuckerman owned a great run of American editions of both Brownings and had included a chapter on "Miss Barrett" in his *Thoughts on the Poets.* Elizabeth Barrett Browning was an even stronger partisan for Italian freedom and unity than her husband, and her "Casa Guidi Windows" had been available in the United States since 1851 in the C. W. Francis edition, where Melville would have learned of it from the June 21 *Literary World* article headed "Casa Guidi Windows," a review of *Prometheus Bound, and other Poems; including Sonnets from the Portuguese, Casa Guidi Windows, etc.,* published by Francis and Company. It consisted mainly of long quotations: "Freedom's Hopeful Day," "The Return of the Grand Duke," passages on Michelangelo, on Cimabue, on the wife of Garibaldi (martyred in the lost cause of Italian independence), and a sequel on "Charles Albert," the king of Piedmont-Sardinia. The second part of the review (July 5,

1851) celebrated the poet's "great thought threading the history of a great people. Liberty and Rome!" The section "What's Italy?" took the poet's own question, which she answered by naming great men of the remote past through the Renaissance but expressed her hope that "one quick breath would draw an avalanche / Of living sons around her, to succeed / The vanished generations" in creating a new heroic Italy. The reviewer devoted almost all his space to other quotations under the section titles "Vallombrosa" and "Our Italy." Unable to let go, the *Literary World* printed almost another column on September 6, 1851, titled "A Poet's Sight of the Exhibition" (the new Crystal Palace in London). Altogether the *Literary World* gave more than four full three-column pages to the poem. Since the first installment arrived in Pittsfield when Melville was about to become a "disengaged" man,[3] he gained from it and the following pieces a good working knowledge of what the reviewer called "the fair and active morning of 1848 sinking into the heavy lethargic noon of 1851." On March 13, 1852 (during the time Melville was trying to get the Duyckinck brothers to stop mailing the paper to him), the *Literary World* printed a favorable review of the new edition of "Mrs. Browning's Poems" by Francis and Company, who made amends for textual errors in its earlier edition.

Melville knew that in "Casa Guidi Windows" Elizabeth Barrett Browning had identified the first part as written during the initial success of the Risorgimento, in 1848, and the second part in 1851. Beginning with "Italy enchained," she traced the course of hopes as she witnessed the lighting of the "first torch of Italian freedom," and then wrote resolutely: "Will, therefore, to be strong, thou Italy! / Will to be noble! Austrian Metternich / Can fix no yoke unless the neck agree." Yet despite Mazzini and Garibaldi there was not a hero strong enough, so that she resorted to hoping indefinitely for "Whatever hand shall grasp this oriflamme" and "insphere / These wills into a unity of will, / And make of Italy a nation." Then as the revolution collapsed she cried: "Help, lands of Europe!" Part 2 began with the betrayal of Florence by the Grand Duke, who returned supported by Austrian troops, so that she beheld "the armament of Austria flow / Into the drowning heart of Tuscany." In 1851 she called on Giuseppe Mazzini to persevere and record the fate of Giuseppe Garibaldi's wife (dead in 1849 while following his troops, she and the baby were so hastily buried that dogs dug up their bodies). Mazzini and other revolutionists had proclaimed Rome a Republic late in 1848 but the pope called in French troops to restore him to power, and in early July the troops took Rome and the Republic was dead. Some of Elizabeth Barrett Browning's most scathing passages dealt with the Catholic hierarchy and in particular the pope. She praised King Charles Albert of Piedmont-Sardinia, who supported the revolt in Milan and struggled to repel the Austrians until in 1849 he abdicated in favor of his son and went into exile and speedy death. She evoked Romans of classical times and Renaissance writers and artists to shame modern Italians, those "oil-eaters," their mouths "Agape for maccaroni," who shouted for freedom then submitted to tyranny. Looking a little back in the history of resistance to tyranny, she mentioned "Pellico's Venetian dungeon" and the Neopolitan Masaniello, who dried his nets in haste when the sky was blue—two heroes recalled also by Melville in his poem on Naples (Pellico in a passage removed from the poem as "Pausilippo"). Insofar as Melville was moved by contemporary political writings, it was probably the poetry of English poets who had been protesting the oppression of parts of Italy under the Austrians in the north and the Bourbon Ferdinand II in the Kingdom of the Two Sicilies.

Melville's travels in the Mediterranean in 1856 and 1857 made him more sensitive than ever to the tradition of the English poem written in or about a famous location in Italy. Some of this poetry he probably knew before he visited Italy; he read and reread this poetry with quickened interest after being on the scene, especially since Italy was little short of an obsession of his friend Tuckerman. A year or two after Melville met him, Tuckerman heard the exiled Garibaldi at a meeting called to deal with the funds raised in the Italian cause in 1850, the cause familiar to New Yorkers from Margaret Fuller's letters to Greeley's *Tribune.* Tuckerman then, in 1850, at the time of his early acquaintance with Melville, a sailor like Garibaldi, had been reminded "of some masterly portraits of mediaeval celebrities which haunted our memory, almost alive with courage, adventure, and loyalty,—whose effigies hint a stern romance and a chivalric history."[4] Tuckerman idolized Garibaldi as "one of Nature's noblemen," his complexion "bronzed by exposure to the elements; his gait rather that of a sailor than of a soldier; but through, within, and above all these traits was distinctly visible the hero." Tuckerman's intimacy with Melville was still flourishing in the mid-1850s. During the war, when he was working on an introduction to a reissue of Dr. Francis's *Old New York,* Tuckerman misdated to 1850 an important document of his friendship with Melville, but he had in his hands, in the 1860s, both an article he had saved from the New Orleans *Commercial Bulletin* in November 1854 and its reprinting in the New York *Times* in January 1855, for he drew on both of them (and perhaps the originals, for he was probably the author). This was the tribute to Dr. Francis which identified four men as habitual intimate guests at the Bond Street house of the great old man—Tuckerman, Griswold, Duyckinck, and Melville (on his visits to town from Pittsfield).

Melville could have found a powerful theme in the Crimean War, which during 1854–56 had astonished Americans with the magnitude of the arrayed forces, like nothing since the Napoleonic era—Russia poised to take Constantinople from Turkey, Great Britain and France sending forth a great combined fleet to fight the Russians. In the late 1850s, having passed through waters which warships had sailed just about the time he was deciding to become a poet, Melville might understandably have chosen a topic from that war for a theme. Other international topics were available, not least the Great Revolt in India in 1857. Alternatively, he might have found robust current subjects from the American Northern Hemisphere in the filibustering in Nicaragua, where William Walker had captured Granada in 1855 and made himself president, only to be driven out by the British in mid-1857, after Melville's return home from Europe. During the years Melville became a poet, Walker remained in the news, repeatedly trying to control a route across the isthmus until the British captured him in Honduras and turned him over to local forces who executed him by a firing squad in 1860. Through family news of Samuel Savage, a cousin of his wife's half brothers, Melville had intermittent news from Central America. In 1855 he bought Ephraim George Squier's *Waikna: or, Adventures on the Mosquito Shore* (New York: Harper, 1855; Sealts 485). Squier, Melville probably knew, had also written *Nicaragua: Its People, Scenery, Monuments, and the Proposed Interoceanic Canal* (New York: D. Appleton, 1852), a two-volume work with evocative fold-out maps. He knew accounts of the horrendous sufferings of the Strain expedition (Parker 2:375). His awareness of Walker's filibustering and the construction of the railroad across Panama are topics in his second lecture, "The South Seas." Melville could have written with some confidence about the epic construction of the Panama Railroad with its uncountable sacrifice of human life, since he could have relied on his copy of the chronicle of that achievement written by his old friend Robert Tomes and published by the Harpers, *Panama in 1855: An Account of the Panama Railroad, of the*

Cities of Panama and Aspinwall, with Sketches of Life and Character on the Isthmus (New York: Harper, 1855; Sealts 528).

After finishing his book on Panama, Tomes had become the recording author on the great expedition led by Matthew Perry that opened Japan to Western commerce. No one in the Melville family could have forgotten the report of Gansevoort Melville's impromptu speech in Cambridge, England, in March 1846, as reported in American papers after his death, a description of Gansevoort's "walking up to an immense terrestrial globe suspended in the centre of one of the rooms, and placing his hand upon it," then declaring:

> "Look here, gentlemen, and see if any American can carefully examine the map of our globe, and not feel a gratitude and just pride at seeing the geographical position our country holds upon its face. Here lies Asia and the whole East, with its immense wealth. There is the mouth of the Columbia River, almost as near Canton as London is to New York. Now here is a little speck called Europe, upon the Eastern shores of the Atlantic, and a smaller speck on its Western shore called New England, including New York city, which have ever held the trade of this immense region, at the expense of passing Cape Horn, or the Cape of Good Hope, the South Atlantic, Indian Ocean, &c. &c. . . . Look here," said he, "and tell me if any American can give up, or barter away the valley of the Columbia, and not, Esau like, sell his birth-right?" (Parker 1966, 51)

Knowing as he did that Camoëns's *Lusiad* celebrated the Portuguese establishing of trade with India and the Far East, Melville would have seen a theme for a modern epic in the ongoing conflict between the British, French, and Americans for military and commercial control of the Pacific (a conflict to which he had been an eyewitness). His second lecture, "The South Seas" (1858–59), sufficiently confirms his well-informed interest in current Pacific affairs, but judging by what survives, he rejected Central America and the Pacific as a theme for poetry, although, as we will see later, he tried for a time to work up, presumably into poetry, a Hawaiian legend.

At home the slavery issue, supposedly laid to rest in 1850, had erupted the next year, when his father-in-law had been party to one of the most dramatic scenes involving the enforcement of the Fugitive Slave Law (see Parker 1:831). In the mid-1850s, when slavery was dividing Democrats from the dying Whig Party and the emerging Republicans, Melville could have made high tragic use of stories fully reported from Kansas, or only briefly publicized and then suppressed

for years, like news from Pottawattamie. But rather than brooding
over the slavery crisis or over the broader topic of what had happened
to the American national character (as he had done in *The Confidence-
Man* in 1856) Melville seems to have started with Italy, following, in
his way, the Brownings. At least, Melville's first known poem of the
late 1850s, "To Daniel Shepherd" (July 6, 1859),[5] begins with an allusion to the current military and political situation in Italy. This
verse-epistle to his and his brother Allan's friend Daniel Shepherd is
far from amateurish, especially when one considers that it served a
mundane purpose, to invite the friend to Arrowhead. In the nature of
things Melville would not have spent much time on it—an hour or
two? Therefore it testifies to Melville's facility as well as his competence in writing verse. Characteristically, Melville plays on the name
of his friend and that of the Hebrew prophet, making Shepherd the fit
expounder of his dream:

> Come, Daniel, come and visit me:
> I'm lost in many a quandary:
> I've dreamed, like Bab'lon's Majesty:
> Prophet, come expound for me.
> —I dreamed I saw a laurel grove,
> Claimed for his by the bird of Jove,
> Who, elate with such dominion,
> Oft cuffed the boughs with haughty pinion.
> Indignantly the trees complain,
> Accusing his afflictive reign.
> Their plaints the chivalry excite
> Of chanticleers, a plucky host:
> They battle with the bird of light.
> Beaten, he wings his Northward flight,
> No more his laurel realm to boast,
> Where now, to crow, the cocks alight,
> And—break down all the branches quite!
> Such a weight of friendship pure
> The grateful trees could not endure.
> This dream, it still disturbeth me;
> Seer, foreshows it Italy?

The Austrian eagle had been "afflictive" but the plucky troop of roost-
ers who drove it back home may do more destruction than the eagle:
disintegration of the whole Italian fabric might follow such success,
particularly if the "friendship pure" (presumably of France) might

prove an ironic illusion. He had long ago acknowledged the danger of trying to promulgate his political opinions, but it was hard not to be drawn into commentary on bloody battles in the Holy Land of Art.

As *The Confidence-Man* had demonstrated, Melville had even recently been willing to venture into national criticism, but after writing *Mardi* he never again assumed the role of partisan. Partisanship, he decided, was always inappropriate for poetry, commenting on lines 115–31 in Milton's "Lycidas": "Mark the deforming effect of the intrusion of partizan topics & feelings of the day, however serious in import, into a poem otherwise of the first order of merit." Aware of and influenced by the English poetry of the Risorgimento, Melville kept to his own preoccupations rather than merely echoing the political stances of other poets or his acquaintances, even those of his friend Tuckerman. Without becoming a partisan, Melville might, in the spirit of Akenside, see what of value he might derive by tuning his new American lyre to Attic themes, or Roman themes, drawing on his recent experiences and observations in the Mediterranean.

CHAPTER SEVEN

Melville's Progress as Poet,
1857(?) to May 1860

IN LATE MAY 1857 IN BOSTON UPON HIS RETURN FROM HIS TRIP TO
the Mediterranean Melville reportedly said that he was not going to
write any more at present (*Log* 580). This was good news to the man
who told the story, Elizabeth Melville's half brother Lemuel Shaw Jr.,
who had been convinced ever since *Mardi* that Melville had written
too many books. Whatever Melville actually said, he probably meant
he was not going to write any more fiction right away, for he may have
decided already to write a lecture during the summer. As it turned
out, he wrote the lecture "Statues in Rome" and delivered it from November 23, 1857, to February 23, 1858; he wrote "The South Seas"
and delivered it from December 6, 1858, to March 16, 1859; and
wrote "Travel" and delivered it between November 7, 1859, and February 21, 1860. Howard Horsford, the editor of Melville's *Journals,*
calls attention to memoranda Melville added on the pages following
the last dated entry for his 1856–57 travel journal. Whether these
were made on his voyage home or later is not certain, but they include
titles: "Frescoes of Travel" and "Subjects for Roman Frescoes." These
may have been titles for a lecture, but they may have been titles for
poetry (or even fiction, despite Melville's demurral). The full entry on
the first title consists of "Frescoes of Travel / by / Three Brothers / Poet,
Painter, and Scholar" (later he changed "Scholar" to "Idler"). Adjacent
to these lines were four names of men followed by an open bracket and
four more names, three of cities and one of a man: Rosseau [*sic*], Cicero, Byron, and Haydon in one column facing Venice, Olympus,
Parthenon, and Leonardo on the other side of the bracket. These eight
words have not been satisfactorily accounted for, not even to the point

that we can say whether Rousseau was meant to be associated with
Venice, Cicero with Olympus, Byron with the Parthenon, and Haydon with Leonardo.

Horsford makes clear that Melville did plunder his recent journal
for his first lecture, as his marks on the pages show and as the lecture itself reveals. Horsford cautiously comments on the possibility that
Melville also consulted his journal as he wrote some of his early poetry:

> Melville began writing poetry seriously in those years [starting in
> 1857], seriously enough and extensively enough that he had a book
> of poems ready in 1860 for publication, though it found no pub-
> lisher; and he continued writing poems for the rest of his life. Most
> of them are difficult or impossible to date very precisely. But when-
> ever written, many of them make direct and repeated levy on the
> experiences recorded in the journal. Still, as with the lectures, there
> is very little in the way of supplementary marking of the journal re-
> lated to them. Quite possibly in reading it over for other purposes
> Melville was prompted, incidentally as it were, to render his imagi-
> native impressions in poetic form. But even the passages on the
> Egyptian desert and the heavily reworked ones on the Pyramids . . .
> only indirectly foreshadow his two published poems on these sub-
> jects, "In the Desert" and "The Great Pyramid." Both were among
> eighteen poems in a section titled "Fruit of Travel Long Ago" in
> *Timoleon* (1891), all of which relate to experiences recorded in the
> journal in passages without later markings suggesting such use;
> their dates of composition are conjectural. (191–93)

As Horsford indicates, if Melville did consult his journal as he wrote
these short poems, he did not work directly from it, in contrast to the
way he worked on the poem "Morning in Naples" and parts of *Clarel.*

Already in May 1857 Melville may have been planning to write
poetry as well as a lecture. In the next months after his return from his
travels, within a year or so at the latest, perhaps even while he was
traveling with his first lecture in 1857 and 1858, Melville set about
making himself a poet. We know that he had a volume of poetry ready
for publication in May 1860. Two years or so for the composition of
Poems fits with Melville's letting George Duyckinck know in July
1858 that he was "busy on" what George understood to be "a new
book."[1] In his report George seems to have taken for granted that
Melville was writing prose, but this may be the first known reference
to the book of poetry Melville completed early in 1860. The second
possible reference is a letter apparently to the Harpers on May 18,

1859: "Here are two Pieces, which, if you find them suited to your Magazine I should be happy to see them appear there.—In case of publication, you may, if you please, send me what you think they are worth." Since he knew what the Harpers were likely to pay for prose pieces, the likelihood is that these were unlike what he had sold to *Harper's Monthly* in the mid-1850s. The use of the term "piece" may or may not be significant. In Melville's known letters about the stories he published in *Harper's* and in *Putnam's New Monthly Magazine* from 1853 to 1856, he calls them "pages" or a "parcel" or an "article" (lowercase or capital) and only once refers to a short prose work as a "piece"—when he identifies "The Piazza" as the "accompanying piece." In his instructions to his brother Allan about the publication of his book of poems, printed below, he uses a form of the word "piece" three times to mean "poem." These pieces were not published in *Harper's New Monthly Magazine,* and their rejection may be one reason Melville ruled out offering the Harpers his full book of poems when it was ready the next year: there was no point trying them for the whole book when they had rejected two poems already. *Putnam's Monthly* folded with the September 1857 issue, but on August 19 of that year, in response to an invitation from the publishers, Melville expressed willingness to write for the new *Atlantic Monthly.* A reason for not sending the two rejected pieces to the *Atlantic* or another magazine may have been that by mid-1859, after the rejection by the Harpers, he thought himself far enough along that he could wait for exposure and criticism until he could publish his book of poetry.

Whenever Melville began writing poetry, it was in the profoundest secrecy possible in the Melville-Shaw family, which on scandalous matters could be cautiously reticent but normally was briskly communicative. You "know how such things spread," Elizabeth Melville wrote to her stepmother in 1875 (*Log* 741), in the act of violating Herman's wish that she keep it secret that he had been writing poetry again, as he had asked her to keep it secret in the late 1850s. On June 23, 1860, when she was trying to think of a likely publisher for the volume of poems, Lizzie commented to Evert Duyckinck that Melville's writing poetry had "been such a profound secret" between the two of them "for so long" that she was glad now to talk openly about it, and to solicit an objective opinion about it (*Log* 620). "For so long" is indefinite—probably more than a year, possibly two years or more, up until around May of 1860, when two of the sisters were told: Helen, who was with Elizabeth the second time she wrote Evert A.

Duyckinck about Melville's volume of poems, and probably Fanny, who had been released as caretaker of Allan's motherless children upon his remarriage and who had probably stopped at Arrowhead before going to Boston, where she saw Herman and Tom off on the *Meteor* on the voyage around Cape Horn.

After the letter to the Harpers on May 18, 1859, the next evidence about Melville's poetry is from July of that year, when he wrote the verse-epistle directed to Daniel Shepherd, whom Allan had known since 1850 at the latest. It survives as a draft, found in Allan's papers, but it was a letter to be copied out and mailed, not a poem to go into a growing stack of poems that would become a book. Judging from its competence as an impromptu composition, it was far from his first poem (whether or not the two "pieces" mentioned in May were poems). No other poem of Melville's (not counting effusions such as those in *Mardi*) can be assigned an earlier date. The first known reference to the poems as a collection to be published is Melville's letter to Duyckinck, May 21, 1860, although this letter does not itself specify that the subject is poetry, not prose. There Melville begins with a reference to his brother Allan, who had taken his second wife only the month before: "If you have met Allan lately he has perhaps informed you that in a few days I go with my brother Tom a voyage round Cape Horn. It was only determined upon a short time since; and I am at present busy, as you may imagine in getting ready for a somewhat long absence, and likewise in prepareing for type certain M.S.S." Then followed a request for Duyckinck's editorial services in Melville's absence: "Now may I with propriety ask of you, conditionally, a favor? Will you, upon the arrival of the M.S.S. in New York—that is, in the course of two weeks, or less—look over them and if they seem of a sort that you care to be any way concerned with, advice [advise] with Allan as to a publisher, and form of volume, &c. . . . In short, may I, seeming too confident, ask you, as a veteran & expert in these matters, and as an old acquaintance, to lend something of an overseeing eye to the launching of this craft—the committing of it to the elements?" Evert's response, which Melville on May 28 referred to as "a very welcome one—quite a wind from the feilds of old times," included an agreement to help see the volume into print.

On May 22, the next day after he wrote Duyckinck, Melville "jotted down" for his wife's copying a set of "Memoranda for Allan concerning the publication of my verses." These "Memoranda for Allan" (known in his wife's transcription) constitute the fullest instructions he had ever given for the publication of one of his works, as far as we know:

Memoranda for Allan
concerning the publication of my verses.

1—Don't stand on terms much with the publisher—half-profits after expenses are paid will content me——not that I expect much "profits"—but that will be a fair nominal arrangement—They should also give me 1 doz. copies of the book—

2—Don't have the Harpers.—I should like the Appletons or Scribner—But Duyckinck's advice will be good here.

3—The sooner the thing is printed and published, the better—The "season" will make little or no difference, I fancy, in this case.

4—After printing, dont let the book hang back—but publish & have done.

5—For God's sake don't have *By the author of "Typee" "Piddledee" &c* on the title-page.

6—Let the title-page be simply,

Poems
by
Herman Melville.

7—Dont have any clap-trap announcements and "sensation" puffs—nor any extracts published previous to publication of book—Have a decent publisher, in short.

8—Don't take any measures, or make inquiries as to expediency of an English edition simultaneous with the American—as in case of "Confidence-Man".

9—In the M.S.S. each piece is on a page by itself, however small the piece. This was done merely for convenience in the final classification; and should be no guide for the printer—Of course in printing two or more pieces will sometimes appear on the same page—according to length of pieces &c. You understand—

10—The poems are divided into books as you will see; but the divisions are not *called* books—they are only numbered—Thus it is in the M.S.S., and should be the same in print. There should be a page with the number between every division.

11—Anything not perfectly plain in the M.S.S. can be referred to Lizzie—also have the M.S.S. returned to her after printing.

12—Lizzie should by all means see the printed sheets *before* being bound, in order to detect any gross errors consequent upon misconstruing the M.S.S.—

These are the thoughts which hurriedly occur to me at this moment. Pardon the abruptness of their expression, but time is precious.—

—Of all human events, perhaps, the publication of a first volume of verses is the most insignificant; but though a matter of no moment to the world, it is still of some concern to the author,—as these *Mem.* show—Pray therefore, don't laugh at my *Mem.* but give heed to them, and so oblige

Your brother

Herman—

Aware of the insignificance of a volume of American poetry in a glutted market ("Of all human events, perhaps, the publication of a first volume of verses is the most insignificant"), Melville nevertheless admitted that it was "still of some concern to the author,—as these *Mem.* show," and left Lizzie, Allan, and Evert Duyckinck all aware of their responsibilities toward him and his poems. The twelve points reveal the seriousness with which Melville took the poetry he had been writing during the past two years or more. No one preserved a table of contents, however, so we are left to what deductions we can make about such matters as the numbered sections—not "called" books, the way the sections of, say, *Paradise Lost* are called books, but nevertheless constituting books in the sense of separate and presumably unrelated sections.

The twelve points are almost all self-explanatory. Melville gave no reason for not having the Harpers, natural enough if what they rejected in 1859 had been two poems. The one problematic point, the ninth, seems to say flatly that every poem was so short that it was contained on a single page. However, Melville is saying he knows that the printer will need to put two or possibly more short poems on a single page, even though in the manuscript short poems are not put on the same page. We know from Mrs. Melville (see p. 132) that the manuscript ran to 111 pages, at the least, and presumably beyond that. Taking the ninth memorandum literally would mean that *Poems* consisted of a great many very short poems, perhaps many more than a hundred, even allowing for pages left blank except for section numbers. Melville's haste in jotting down the notes (or Lizzie's difficulty in making a perfect copy of them) may account for the imprecision, for Melville most likely meant to say that in the manuscript every poem *started* on a separate page. Points 11 and 12 constitute the earliest evidence that Lizzie was so intimately familiar with the poems that she could explain anything that was confusing and would have to be the one to exercise final judgment over the proofs.

In the letter Melville wrote to Evert Duyckinck on board the *Meteor* in Boston Harbor on May 28, he explained that his wife would send "the parcel" of poems "in the course of a week or so—there remaining something to be finished in copying the M.S.S." His wife, he explained, had "interested herself a good deal in this matter," to the point that she seemed "to know more about it" than he did, "at least about the *merits* of the performance." George Duyckinck, he hoped, would also look over his "scribblings"—this he added before breaking off his "egotistic" requests. Constitutionally Melville loathed asking favors of anyone, as his mother had observed long before, so his "egotistic" placing of his poetry in the capable editorial hands of the Duyckincks reveals how momentous to him the publication of his *Poems* was.

The memorandum to Allan left out any consideration of physical aspects of the book such as binding and typeface, although it mentioned some internal features such as the numbered page Melville wanted before each section. Melville may have been taking for granted that his book would be in black or brown cloth, in octavo or twelvemo. Once in Boston, Melville must have looked sharply at the appearance of poetry books he came across in the publishers' houses and bookstores. Ticknor and Fields may have been displaying *Lucile* by "Owen Meredith" (the novelist Bulwer-Lytton's son), officially published on May 24, 1860, although advertisements have not been found. *Lucile* was in Ticknor and Fields' "blue and gold" poetry series—blue cloth, stamped blind, gold title and cartouche on spine, gilt edges, brown glazed endpapers. There in Boston Melville seems to have reacted strongly to this or another "blue and gold" book. Overgilt would be bad enough, but the fussy preciousness of Ticknor and Fields' "blue and gold" was egregious and not to be endured. Realizing that he had to head off Duyckinck from putting his own volume in blue and gold, he took the trouble to write Lizzie immediately to ask her to add another item to his dozen points in the memorandum to Allan.

Accordingly, on June 1, Elizabeth Melville wrote to Evert Duyckinck:

On Monday or Tuesday of next week I shall forward to you by Express, the manuscript of which Herman wrote you—and with this I

enclose a copy of the memoranda which he jotted down for Allan,—
according to his request—

To this also should have been added an item which Herman
omitted in his haste—and that is, that the book should be plainly
bound, that is, not over-gilt—and to "blue and gold" I know he has
a decided aversion—He may have mentioned it in his letter to you,
from Boston—[2]

On June 4, Elizabeth Melville sent Evert Duyckinck the manuscript
of the whole volume, accompanied by a letter:

I send you the manuscript and hope the printers will find no difficulty
in reading it—though it has been (the greater part of it) necessarily
copied in great haste—If anything in it should be obscure, please enclose the page to me and I will compare it with the original draught—

In making up the table of "contents," I am not sure I have always used capitals in the right place—will you have the kindness to
overlook it, and right it, if wrong—In the printed book, the titles
of the verses are all in capitals, I believe—so of course the printer
will arrange that—and I see that in the manuscript they are sometimes underscored which is accidental—

One question more occurs to me about titles—which is this—
When the first line is quoted at the heading (as on page 111) what
punctuation should be used about it? quotation marks and *period,* or
with whatever punctuation immediately follows in the verse?—
With this the contents should also correspond—

I am sorry to trouble you about these little matters, Mr
Duycinck, but Herman was obliged to leave much in an unfinished
state, and I should feel much easier, as I know he would, if you
would overlook the sheets for these little inaccuracies—

When you have read the manuscript, I should be very glad to
have your opinion of it, as a whole, and you need not be afraid to say
exactly what you think,—I am the more desirous of this, because as
yet, no one has seen the sheets, excepting two of Herman's sisters,
who are now with me—and I want to know how they would strike
an unprejudiced person—If your brother also would add his impressions, so much the better—[3]

The reference to "unfinished state" meant that the poems were not
fully arranged in final order with proper divisions, not that poems
themselves were not completed.

Melville had suggested Scribner as a "decent" publisher. Long afterward, Richard Henry Stoddard wrote a chapter on Edmund Clarence
Stedman in *Poets' Homes: Pen and Pencil Sketches of American Poets and Their*

Homes, by "R. H. Stoddard and Others" (Boston: D. Lothrop & Co., 1877). Before June 19, 1860, Charles Scribner had obliged Stoddard:

> My good friend Bayard Taylor and I were living together in the same house when these poems [by E. C. Stedman] appeared [in the *Tribune*], and I remember his coming home one afternoon and telling me that he had that day, or the day before, met their author in the editorial rooms of the *Tribune,* and had had a talk with him, and that he liked him very much. A few evenings afterwards this likable young poet came to see me, and I was charmed with him. . . . I asked him to show me his poems printed and unprinted, for he told me that he had enough to make a small volume, and he did so. I read them with great care; I corrected them where I thought they needed it, and I tried to get a publisher for him. I think that my opinion was not without weight with the gentleman who became his publisher—the late Mr. Charles Scribner.—(255)

The weight of that opinion is clear. Scribner returned Melville's manuscript to Duyckinck, writing him on June 19: "I have looked over Melville's Poems. I have no doubt they are excellent, they seem so to me, and I have confidence in your judgement—But I have not got the heart to publish them—I doubt whether they would more than pay expenses, and as I have issued two vols of Poems [by E. C. Stedman and G. P. Morris] this season and the prospect is that neither of them will pay I don't feel like making another venture in that line" (*Log* 619–20). Upon the refusal from Scribner, Duyckinck sent the manuscript to Rudd and Carleton, and wrote to Elizabeth Melville. Her reply is dated June 23:

> I received yours of the 19th yesterday, and hasten to thank you for your kind endeavors about the manuscript, regretting that its course does not run smoothly, thus far—For myself, I am willing to wait patiently for the result, so that the publication is eventually accomplished—and do not consider its rejection by the publishers as any test of its merit in a literary point of view—well-knowing, as Herman does also, that *poetry* is a comparatively uncalled-for article in the publishing market—I suppose that if John Milton were to offer "Paradise Lost" to the Harpers tomorrow, it would be promptly rejected as "unsuitable" not to say, denounced as dull—
>
> I think infinitely more of yours and your brother's opinion of it, and feel more confidence in its worth, since it has been looked at by persons of judgment and taste, than ever before—it has been such a profound secret between Herman and myself for so long, that I rejoice to have my own prejudice in its favor confirmed by some one

in whose appreciation we can feel confidence—for I do not believe you would speak favorably of it, unless you could do so sincerely—so for that, your letter gives me great satisfaction—

The name of one publishing firm in New York occurs to me who might possibly take a personal interest in the matter—that of "Derby and Jackson" the first named being a brother-in-law of "Toby" of Typee memory—if he is the same that I think he is—"C.L. Derby"—former "Actuary of Cosmopolitan Art Association"—I do not know of what standing the firm may be, but I merely offer the hint, in case "Rudd and Carleton" should decline to publish—

I feel that you and Allan will do everything that is suitable and proper about it and am deeply sensible of your kindly efforts to fur-ther its success—indeed I feel that it is in better hands than even with Herman's own management for he might be disheartened at the outset, by its rejection, and perhaps withhold it altogether, which would be a great disappointment to me—

I am prepared to be very patient in any delay that may ensue, even when the book shall have been accepted for publication—bearing in mind the "midsummer" "stagnation in trade"—"season"—and all that—though I shall count on your promised report of progress in good time.[4]

What Lizzie says about Milton offering *Paradise Lost* to the Harpers tomorrow is a secularized version of Melville's comment to Hawthorne about what would happen if he wrote the Gospels in his century. She may have been echoing him, if he had said much the same thing to her as he had written to Hawthorne.

Rudd and Carleton must have declined the volume, leaving Duyc-kinck with only Lizzie's somewhat imprecise suggestion about Derby and Jackson. Of the four Derby brothers—James, George, Henry, and Chauncey—active in publishing and bookselling, the one who had a link to Toby, Thomas F. Heffernan explains,[5] was Chauncey, whose marriage to Charlotte Flower, sister of the widowed Mary Jane Flower Stone (Toby's wife), made him and Toby brothers-in-law, by common American usage. The Derby who was a partner in Derby and Jackson was James Derby, not Toby's brother-in-law Chauncey. As far as we know, Duyckinck did not follow up on this hint, and the Rudd and Carleton rejection marked the end of anyone's efforts to publish *Poems* by Herman Melville in 1860. Naturally Melville expected to find a copy of his *Poems* waiting for him in San Francisco, sent by way of the celebrated new Panama Railroad. Instead of the book he found one or more letters from his wife telling him the fate of his verses.

CHAPTER EIGHT

Possible Contents of *Poems* (1860)

WHAT WE KNOW ABOUT THE DATING OF MELVILLE'S POEMS IS RUDImentary and may remain so unless new documentary evidence is discovered. We know, to display the level of current ignorance, that the poems in *Battle-Pieces* (1866) were written during and just after the Civil War and that certain ones could not have been written before battles and other datable events took place. It is now almost certain that Melville wrote *Clarel* (1876) between early 1870 and the first half of 1875. Of the poems in *John Marr* we know only that they were written before the publication of that little book in 1888, just as we know only that the poems in *Timoleon* were written before the publication of that little book in 1891. We strongly suspect, but cannot now prove, that many of the poems in *Timoleon* antedate some if not most of the poems in *John Marr.* Of the many poems that Melville left unpublished (some in provisionally titled collections), few have been dated at all closely. Only one poem by Melville seems absolutely certain to date from the late 1850s, the July 1859 verse-epistle, "To Daniel Shepherd." Not a single poem of Melville's can be identified as one indisputably included in the 1860 collection Melville called *Poems.* It is possible, although not likely, that not one poem survives from all those that were in *Poems.* Yet despite all this uncertainty we need to try to speculate reasonably about the possible contents of *Poems* and about the possibility that some poems Melville published late in life or left unpublished might (perhaps in an earlier form) have stood in the 1860 collection.

Our imperfect knowledge about Melville's poetry got off to a grotesque start in 1921 when Raymond Weaver (360) put the date

1859 on a confidential letter from Melville's wife to her stepmother about his writing poetry (a letter written in 1875), then said nothing more of Melville's writing poetry in the late 1850s and did not mention *Poems*. Meade Minnigerode in 1922 became the first modern researcher to know that Melville had written a volume he called *Poems*. The name "Duyckinck" is not in Weaver's index, but Minnigerode located many Melville items in the Duyckinck Collection of the New York Public Library, among them the letters written in 1860 by Melville and his wife to Evert Duyckinck about the volume of poems and Melville's memorandum of instructions to his brother Allan. Rushing the information into his bibliography, Minnigerode guessed that this 1860 poetry might be *Clarel* (77). By reading more carefully the memorandum to Allan which Minnigerode printed, Lewis Mumford (1929) realized that *Poems* must have consisted of shorter poems, not *Clarel*. In 1938 Willard Thorp ventured to speculate about the contents of *Poems*: "There is reason to suppose the book contained some if not all of that little group of poems which were printed in *Timoleon* (1891) under the caption 'Fruit of Travel Long Ago.' The themes treated in these poems can all be traced to impressions of the 1856–1857 journey and many of them are foreshadowed in the diary which he kept at that time" (lxxxv). Here Thorp was more cautious ("some if not all") than some later commentators have been.

Demonstrably, Melville worked up portions from his early 1857 journal as he wrote his first lecture, "Statues in Rome," for the 1857–58 season, the topic being ancient statues, not Renaissance or modern statues. Therefore Thorp reasonably assumed that in the two or three years after his return from the Mediterranean, when he seems to have begun his career as a poet, Melville had also made much use of his recent impressions and had refreshed his memory by looking over pages of his journal. For all we know, some poems in the 1860 volume could have been grouped under the title (or at least the idea) listed in his journal, "Frescoes of Travel / by / Three Brothers / Poet, Painter, and Idler" ("Idler" replacing what he first wrote, "Scholar"). When a number of poems associated with long-ago travel are published late in life, some of them in a section called "Fruit of Travel Long Ago," as part of a grand erratic campaign aimed at cleaning accumulations out of a writing desk and getting poems into print one little self-subsidized volume at a time, the sensible thing is to assume, as Thorp did, that some of the pieces may have languished in the desk for a very long time. The foliation of surviving pages of Melville's poetry does not suggest that any pages survive from *Poems,* but some of the poems in *Poems* may survive after having been recopied (and presumably revised) during the years or even decades after 1860. The eighteen poems of "Fruit of Travel Long Ago" (Weaver counted twenty-one), all set in the Mediterranean regions Melville had visited from December 1856 through early April 1857, are "Venice," "In a Bye-Canal," "Pisa's Leaning Tower," "In a Church of Padua," "Milan Cathedral," "Pausilippo" (written as part of the much longer "Naples in the Time of Bomba," which Melville did not live to publish), "The Attic Landscape," "The Same," "The Parthenon," "Greek Masonry," "Greek Architecture," "Off Cape Colonna," "The Archipelago," "Syra," "Disinterment of the Hermes," "The Apparition," "In the Desert," and "The Great Pyramid." At least one of them, "Disinterment of the Hermes," was occasioned by a widely reported discovery in 1877, but as Melville arranged poems for *Timoleon* he could have thought of it as fairly recent fruit of travel long ago, since in Rome he had been powerfully moved by what he learned of the excavation of colossal horses from the ruins of the Baths of Caracalla ("like finding the bones of the mastadon," he noted in his journal on February 28, 1857). The other seventeen may have been poems written long ago, soon after the long-past travels. No one has suggested any other plausible reason for Melville's segregating these poems (even allowing for his putting at least one late poem into the group). "Fruit of Travel Long Ago," without the "Hermes" poem, could not have constituted the entire *Poems* (1860); many more pages of poetry were included in that lost manuscript.

Disgusted with the late 1850s' worship of technology, Melville for many months after the summer of 1857 found an intellectual home in ancient Greece and Rome. In the 1857–58 lecture Melville announced his preference for classical values in a passage contrasting the Vatican as the index of the ancient world with the Washington Patent Office as the index of the modern, then contrasting the Apollo Belvedere with a locomotive and the Coliseum with the Crystal Palace. He concluded with a quotation from Byron's *Childe Harold's Pilgrimage* that everyone knew: "While stands the Coliseum, Rome shall stand; / When falls the Coliseum, Rome shall fall; / And when Rome falls, the world." The statuary and architecture of Rome would outlast the institutions, inventions, and buildings of the progressive modern world. Two lads from Williams College, Titus Munson Coan and John Thomas Gulick, who made a literary pilgrimage to

Arrowhead in late April 1859, testified that Melville harangued them on the superiority of classical times to the present, just the position he had taken in his first lecture a year and a half earlier.[1] Influenced by Edward Gibbon's *Decline and Fall of the Roman Empire,* he idealized the reigns of Antoninus Pius, Marcus Aurelius, and Lucius Verus (A.D. 138–69). A family report suggests that Melville left a set of Gibbon behind at Arrowhead when he left at the end of 1863 (see Sealts 223b), so the poem praising that golden era, "The Age of the Antonines," may have dated to his first years as a poet although it was not printed until *Timoleon* (1891). Retreating into an idealized Golden Age of politics and literature could not, of course, be complete, however much Melville wanted to avert his eyes from the political realities of the late 1850s. Having already written an exhaustive anatomy of American overconfidence in 1855 and 1856, it was understandable that now (like many other Americans) he would turn to contemporary Mediterranean politics rather than the crisis in the United States. His verse-epistle "To Daniel Shepherd" (July 1859) begins with an allusion to the current military and political situation in Italy. Surely not his first poem, it probably followed other poems set in Italy and elsewhere in the Mediterranean. In the late 1850s, when memories of his travels were sharpest and when Italy was more and more in the news, Melville very likely wrote some, most, or perhaps even all of his poems that drew on his journals and his memories of the Mediterranean. Besides such poems as those on the Parthenon and the Great Pyramid in "Fruit of Travel Long Ago," Melville might also have tried his hand at poems based on classical history, such as the story of Timoleon and his brother.

Melville could have written "In a Bye-Canal" without reading Browning's lurid "In a Gondola," but it seems unlikely that he would not have known that poem. Before he wrote "After the Pleasure Party" Melville almost surely knew some of the striking examples of dramatic monologues or soliloquies in Browning's *Poems* (Boston: Ticknor, Reed, & Fields, 1850) and Browning's *Men and Women* (Boston: Ticknor & Fields, 1856). "After the Pleasure Party" may show the influence of Tennyson. Melville kept up with Tennyson's poetry, and continued to do so for decades, reading new poems probably as late as the 1882 tribute on the nineteen-hundredth anniversary of Virgil's death. Very late in life, in the manuscript of *Billy Budd, Sailor,* Melville had, as previously noted, recalled the tribute to Lord Nelson from the 1852 "Ode on the Death of the Duke of Wellington": "Alfred in his funeral ode on the victor of Waterloo ventures not to call him the greatest soldier of all time, though in the same ode he invokes Nelson as 'the greatest sailor since our world began' " (chap. 4). Already by the late 1850s Melville had gone far beyond his "Will Waterproof" phase of reading Tennyson. At some point Melville bought Ticknor and Fields' 1855 *Maud, and Other Poems.* In "The Piazza," written early in 1856, he probably echoed Tennyson's weary "Mariana" as well as *Measure for Measure;* he had known it a long time. In August 1861 Melville bought *The Poetical Works of Alfred Tennyson* (Boston: Ticknor & Fields, 1861; Sealts 508), in two volumes. Later, pasting in a newspaper clipping which disparaged "The Charge of the Light Brigade," Melville defended the poet, labeling the criticism "stuff by a small man" ("small man" being a phrase from Carlyle employed by Melville in "Hawthorne and His Mosses" and in *The Confidence-Man,* chap. 22).[2]

On the grounds that one is usually more likely to write about something when it is fresh in mind, and on the basis of echoes of words and themes from Tennyson's *The Princess,* one could suspect that the 1860 volume may have included the second poem in *Timoleon,* "After the Pleasure Party." Much of that poem consists of a strong, self-revealing dramatic monologue by a female astronomer presumably suggested by Maria Mitchell, who had impressed Melville in 1852 during the evening he and his father-in-law spent "with Mr. Mitchell the astronomer, & his celebrated daughter, the discoverer of comets" (see *Log* 452). Although using an Italian setting for the poem, Melville may have adapted some details from Tennyson's *The Princess,* which is set in England. Melville knew about it, at least, from Powell's description of it, and probably from the 1848 William D. Ticknor edition or the 1855 Ticknor and Fields "New Edition" (lacking some lines criticized by the first reviewers). Here Tennyson, poet laureate since 1850, explored the topic of female education, specifically the challenge that "with equal husbandry / The woman were an equal to the man" (1.129–30), and the proposition that men hate "learned women" (1.442). Some of the names and images in *The Princess* and "After the Pleasure Party" are suggestive even though they do not prove that Melville drew them from Tennyson. The words "terrace" and "balm," not extremely common words, occur six lines apart in Tennyson and five lines apart in "After the Pleasure Party." Tennyson has Cupid and Uranian Venus: "The seal was Cupid bent above a scroll, / And o'er his head Uranian Venus hung" (1.238–39). Melville's poem begins with "Lines Traced Under an Image of Amor Threatening," Cupid warning virgins not to slight him. In Melville the name of the female astronomer is "Urania," but she is not Milton's or Wordsworth's muse. She is a woman tormented by Amor, who "boy-like" (line 112) wreaks his boyish spite on her. Melville's Urania prays to an "arm'd Virgin," the "Helmeted woman" Athena (lines 132, 134), and there is a bust of Pallas (Athena) in Tennyson's poem (1.219). (In *The Princess* 1.131 is a woman "that arm'd / Her own fair head.") This is *The Princess* 3.283–85: "either sex alone / Is half itself, and in true marriage lies / Nor equal, nor unequal." This is Melville: "For, Nature, in no shallow surge / Against thee either sex may urge, / Why hast thou made us but in halves— / Co-relatives?" (lines 84–87). Finally, *The Princess* deals with the topic of "After the Pleasure Party"—the repressed sexuality of educated women, particularly the idea that "one's sex asserts itself."

Two others of Melville's surviving longer poems set in the Mediterranean (or at least involving old Italian artists and, in some stages of composition, recent Italian history) may well have been written in the late 1850s and may have been in *Poems*. One at an early stage was entitled "A Morning in Naples" and later retitled in various ways, including "An Afternoon in Naples" and "Naples in the Time of Bomba" ("Bomba" being the contemptuous name Ferdinando II earned by bombarding Messina into submission in 1848 and Palermo in 1849). The other is "At the Hostelry." Fairly soon after *Clarel* was published, Melville took one or both of these two poems out of his desk and attempted to salvage them by prefacing them with newly composed prose headnotes and supplementary sketches which introduced dramatic characters to speak the poems as well as (later) an editor who transcribes and prepares them for publication. Melville worked on the headnotes intermittently even during the later years when he was also engaged in writing or salvaging other poems and when he was, also intermittently, engaged in elaborating a burgeoning time-and-energy-consuming prose headnote to a poem, the manuscript, left nearly finished at his death, about a sailor named Billy Budd. There is as of now no way of saying which of the two poems was written first, but the lines about Garibaldi in "At the Hostelry" seem to have begun as an (early 1860s?) updating or continuation of the Naples poem and then been moved over into the poem about a symposium of artists (Italian and Dutch) discussing the idea of the picturesque. The topic of discussion in "At the Hostelry," the picturesque, is a theme that Melville recurred to several times in the 1850s. It is also present in poetry that may have been composed much later, particularly in the prose headnote to the poem about Rip Van Winkle, but, as Dennis Berthold has shown, it constitutes a significant motif in *Pierre* and some stories of the mid-1850s. The chapters on literary theory in *The Confidence-Man* are not aesthetically complicated, and Melville in his first lecture, on "Statues in Rome," reveals himself as still lacking a vocabulary of aesthetic terminology and as not having worked through some basic aesthetic problems. In "At the Hostelry" Melville amuses himself by vividly describing some low Dutch scenes but he does not grapple with aesthetic issues there beyond what he had done in *The Confidence-Man*.

On the admittedly weak grounds of Melville's rather unsophisticated treatment of the topic, the picturesque, it is tempting to argue that the initial composition of "At the Hostelry" belongs in the late 1850s. (Revisions made later include references to more recent Italian events, the substitution of a ship name famous in the Civil War for an earlier name, and possibly a reference to an engraving of Dürer that Melville may not have seen before it appeared in *Harper's Magazine* in 1870.) Melville's interest in art antedates the 1850s, but his known study of art and artists dates from 1859, when he borrowed from Evert Duyckinck four volumes of a five-volume set of Giorgio Vasari's *Lives of the Most Eminent Painters, Sculptors, and Architects* (London: Bohn, 1850–52; Sealts 534a) and a three-volume set of Luigi Lanzi's *The History of Painting in Italy* (London: Bohn, 1847; Sealts 320). When he wrote *Poems*, Melville surely had at hand not only poems by both Brownings about political turmoil in Italy but also poems by Robert Browning about Renaissance artists in Italy. (He would have devoured a poem like Browning's "Fra Lippo Lippi" in the 1856 Boston edition.)

Much of "A Morning in Naples" is directly based on Melville's own experiences. On February 19, 1857, Melville had pushed into the vast crowded Neapolitan streets that reminded him of Broadway, at least until there was a most un-American show of armed force: "Palace—soldiers—music—clang of arms all over city. Burst of troops from archway. Cannon posted inwards." Two days later he himself experienced the small adventure he recorded in his journal. The long poem he wrote based on his own drive through Naples examines the speaker's desire to avert his eyes from a political reality that intermittently imposes itself on him, however unwilling he is to face it. This continues Melville's moral scrutiny of the picturesque, for in *Pierre* and afterward he had been distrustful of aesthetic appreciation of the picturesque that came at the cost of ignoring economic injustices. The speaker of the poem, Melville, or a tourist seeking guilt-free enjoyment of the picturesque, is pulled in two directions—toward a denunciation of the displays of military power and an amelioristic acceptance that vineyards glow even if bayonets flash, that Nature's beauty makes living in Naples possible and even agreeable, even under an oppressive dictatorship. The speaker broods over Virgil, "here inurned / On Pausilippo, legend tells—/ Here on the slope that pledges ease to pain" (Pausilippo meaning freedom from pain). This leads into a passage on the world as two poet laureates knew it, Virgil and now Tennyson, a "Melancholy sphere" set in motion by some Deistic force ("Ruled by the primary impulse given—/ Forever revolving on"). In this sphere "Opinion and vogue" are "recurring still," although some things wait long before recurring: "life's too brief to note some long returns." In this melancholy sphere wise unconsciousness is lord, and "reason, that gladdens not the wise," alarms the fool. (That seems to be the sense, but so far the passage is imperfectly transcribed.[3]) In this world there is more to fear from life than there is from death; and in this world "truth takes falsehood graft, and hence / Equivocal fruit—." Beginning with a meditation on Virgil and Tennyson's both having "known" the world as a "melancholy sphere," the speaker has worked himself into a state of depressed brooding which is broken not by anything within but by a cheery distraction from without, the sight and fancied speech of the flower in his lapel.[4]

The narrator of the Naples poem is unable to suppress his historical memory any more than he can suppress awareness of present military displays. A "flash of thought" carries him back to Queen Joanna, the cool murderer of her husband, then that scene is replaced by an older one, Agrippina, the granddaughter of Augustus, who starved herself to death when "In cruel craft exiled from Rome / To gaze on Naples' sunny bay." Pulled as he is by the rose, the symbol of present beauty of life, the speaker is haunted by fearful images from history, "Spectres of Naples under Spain"; an "incensed Revolt" in the seventeenth century, led by Tomaso Aniello (Masaniello); and the Terror imported from France, so that beautiful and bountiful Naples became "Hell's cornucopia crammed with crime!" As Melville wrote this part, he included the lines on Silvio Pellico (1789–1854), seized from his house, at night, never tried, imprisoned for many years and kept at hard labor, all because he wrote a "patriot ode / Construed as treason." He was internationally famous as a political prisoner, as shown by Felicia Hemans's honoring him with "To Silvio Pellico, on Reading his 'Prigione.'" This section, however revised, was published as "Pausilippo (In the Time of Bomba)," sixth in the "Fruit of Travel Long Ago." The whole of the "Naples" poem in an early version, one including this section on Silvio but lacking a reference to Garibaldi, may well have been part of the 1860 *Poems*. The surviving manuscript of the longer version, which Melville never published, shows that the ascription of the poem to the character Jack Gentian was an addition of the mid-1870s, and nothing prevents one's taking the speaker as "Melville" or an invented character reenacting Melville's own adventures and elaborating his own thought processes as he went about Naples, looking from superb palaces to smoking Vesuvius, visible from the main square. Very possibly Melville completed "Naples in the Time of Bomba" in the late 1850s and later added a few lines on the conquest of Bomba's son by Garibaldi's Red Shirts. The poem does not exist in an early, complete form but only as revised for inclusion in a volume which was also to contain prose introductory sketches and prefaces, and another long poem, "At the Hostelry"—perhaps written after it but placed before it.

Robert Milder has objected that "a fledgling poet seems unlikely to write a poem so thematically and technically accomplished" as "After the Pleasure Party" (2005, 57n. 43). But Melville was a fast learner. He went from *Typee* to *Moby-Dick* in five or six years and had been a great prose writer for several years by 1857 or 1858, when he began writing serious poetry. For the best part of a decade, he had also been an extraordinarily sensitive reader of poetry, including some of the greatest poetry in the language. It is almost certain that Melville offered poems for publication early in 1859 and there is hard evidence of his facility as a poet in July 1859. *Poems* (1860) was Melville's first book of poetry, but it did not consist of the amateurish verse of a "fledgling poet."

CHAPTER NINE

On the *Meteor:* Melville When He Thought
He Was a Published Poet

WHEN HE DEPARTED ON THE *GLASGOW* FOR EUROPE IN 1856 Melville had left his brother Allan to see that *The Confidence-Man* would be published in New York and London. When he sailed on the *Meteor* in 1860 Melville was equally sure that his *Poems* would be published, guided not only by Allan but also by Evert Duyckinck, while Lizzie, after relaying his last-minute instructions, would make herself available to answer any questions that might arise about his intentions. With his secret apprenticeship and early mastery of poetry behind him, soon to be enshrined within covers, Melville was free to think about taking the next ambitious step. He had heard of Krakens, he said (perhaps from a recent reading of Tennyson), just after *Moby-Dick* was published.[1] He may not have regarded *Poems* as having reached in poetry the level of *Moby-Dick* in prose, but he was ready to propel himself from the company of Tennyson and the Brownings, small or smallish poets of his own time, into the company of Spenser and Milton, ready to think about writing not just a long poem like *The Excursion* but a still more ambitious poem like *The Faerie Queene,* whether it was technically a tragic dramatic poem or an epic. The evidence for thinking so is in his selection of reading material for his voyage and in his annotations in books he took.

Captain Thomas Melville had sailed the *Meteor* to Manila as early as 1855. When the family last heard from him, in 1859, he had been in Manila prepared to sail with his cargo to Calcutta before returning home. Now, the captain's brother had packed carefully, thinking that he would sail to Manila and thence he hardly knew where, he told Duyckinck—perhaps onward around the world. Indeed, the *Berkshire*

County Eagle announced that the *Meteor* "sails direct for San Francisco, and thence across the Pacific," making a year-long "voyage round the world." Always packing light, like his Ishmael, Melville could arrive at Southport in 1856 with a nightshirt and a toothbrush and then abandon his trunk to a storeroom in Liverpool.[2] Now able to indulge himself, since his brother could see to the stowing and retrieving of luggage and since he intended to stay in the same cabin for many months without transferring to another ship or to a shore lodging, Melville packed heavier yet managed to practice the *multum in parvo* principle, which always appealed to him, whether in tomahawks, Sheffield knives, or books. Freshly in the habit of borrowing old British magazines from Duyckinck for winter reading, on April 10, 1860, he consulted three of the 1834 volumes of the London *Quarterly Review* in the Astor Library (Olsen-Smith and Sealts 414a). Now he packed some old quarterlies—"lazy reading for lazy latitudes," he called it in his May 28 letter to Duyckinck, by which he meant thought-provoking reading. More directly to his purpose as a poet, he packed a small (or perhaps a middling large) library of great poetry— classical epic poetry in English translation, early modern European poetry in translation, and much English poetry, with an emphasis on the epic or very long poem.

On the *Meteor* he did not read much, apparently, until sailing up the western coast of South America. Then, acutely conscious of the grandeur of this episode in his life, which might include a circumnavigation of the globe, he began locating himself as he read—"Cape Horn," "Pacific Ocean," by convention designating this voyage "Cape Horn 2" although he was rounding the cape for the third time. In his Spenser he wrote "C. H. 2." He wrote "C. H. 2" in Thomas Duer Broughton's *Selections from the Popular Poetry of the Hindoos* (London: Martin, 1814; Sealts 87a)—an appropriate book to carry to Manila and perhaps on to Calcutta. Some of the surviving annotations establish at least a rough sequence of his reading. In Béranger's *Songs* (Philadelphia: Carey & Hart, 1844; Sealts 58) he wrote: "Pacific Ocean / Sep 4th 1860 / 19 S.L." In his Wordsworth he wrote, "Pacific Ocean, Sep. 14th 1860 / 5° 60″ N.L." In his Milton he wrote "C. Horn 1860" and "Pacific Ocean / N. L. 15° / Sep. 21th 1860." In his Dante he wrote "Pacific Ocean / Sunday Afternoon / Sep 22 1860." In Schiller's *Poems and Ballads* beside the last stanza of "To Emma," he wrote: "Sept 25th 1860 / North Pacific." In George Chapman's translation of excerpts from Homer, Hesiod, Musaeus, and Juvenal (London: Smith,

1858; Sealts 276), he wrote "C. H. 2."; in Chapman's two volumes of the *Iliads* in the same set (London: Smith, 1857; Sealts 277) he inscribed "C. H. 2." in the first and "Cape Horn 2." in the second (along with an annotation indicating that he was near San Francisco). In Chapman's *Odysseys* (London: Smith, 1857; Sealts 278) he wrote "Pacific Ocean / Oct 3d 1860 / 700 miles from San Francisco / C H 2." On October 15, while he was in San Francisco, he wrote the date in his copy of *Songs of England. The Book of English Songs* (London: Houlston & Wright, 1857; Sealts 342), edited by Charles Mackay (which he may have brought with him or may have acquired there). Returning to his copy of Wordsworth's poems on his way home, he annotated it "Gulf of Mexico Nov 6th 1860 / Steamer 'North Star.'" He carried a blank-book in which he wrote a few journal entries or else he wrote a few entries onto pages previously torn from a blank-book. There is no indication that he carried with him any of the four notebooks which he had used for his longer journals in 1849–50 and 1856–57.

All these books carrying Cape Horn notations are books of poetry—strong indication that he carried with him (besides the old periodicals) mainly a library of poetry (although he took a going-away present from Sarah Morewood, Hawthorne's new *The Marble Faun*). Of the books known to survive with 1860 Cape Horn annotations, Melville gave two away (one of which, the Spenser, later went out of the family for about a century). Others, the Wordsworth and the Dante, were apparently dispersed after his death. The particular books we know of cannot be the only volumes of poetry he took with him. Others may have been destroyed, some may survive with no record that they went round the Horn, and others with Cape Horn designations may yet show up. One clue to additional books Melville carried is that he repeatedly made cross-references between writers we know he had with him, comparing Spenser and Milton, Spenser and Wordsworth. Melville may have packed Pope's Homer in the Harper's Classical Library; a second translation of Dante, by John Carlyle; his Classical Library copy of Dryden's translation of Virgil's *Aeneid;* perhaps translations of Tasso and Ariosto; Chaucer (perhaps in the 1835 expurgated, modernized edition he picked up at some time). He refers to all of these in his annotations in some of the volumes he demonstrably took (though it cannot be proved that he made all the annotations on this voyage). In other marginalia possibly dating from this voyage, Melville referred to Byron, Keats, and Poe. Broughton was pleasant to carry to the Far East, but on a great clipper ship commanded by his brother, a veteran of several mercantile voyages to the Orient, Melville would have been in the mood to appreciate more than ever Camoëns's epic poem about Vasco da Gama's 1497–98 voyage around Africa to India, a celebration of the birth of modern commerce. (The purchase date Melville put in his only known copy of Camoëns, 1867 [Sealts 116], makes it too late for this voyage.) Melville may have brought along his copy of Ossian, James Macpherson's *Fingal, An Ancient Epic Poem,* which he had bought in 1848 and still remembered well in March 1862, as he showed in markings in Hazlitt's *Lectures on the English Comic Writers* and *Lectures on the English Poets.* There he underlined Hazlitt's remark that Ossian "is even without God in the world" and wrote in the top margin: "True: no gods, I think, are mentioned in Ossian," and applauded a passage in which Hazlitt praised Ossian: "I am rejoiced to see Hazlitt speak for Ossian. There is nothing more contemptable in that contemptable man (tho' good poet, in his department) Wordsworth, than his contempt for Ossian. And nothing that more raises my idea of Napoleon than his great admiration for him.—The loneliness of the spirit of Ossian harmonized with the loneliness of the greatness of Napoleon."[3]

Planning to think about the shape a long serious American poem might take, Melville may have brought along some American epics, perhaps even the plodding *Fredoniad* that he mentioned in his essay on Hawthorne, or Barlow's *The Vision of Columbus* (1787) or *The Columbiad* (1807). Even more likely, he may have had with him John Quincy Adams's *Dermot MacMorrogh, or, The Conquest of Ireland: an historical tale of the 12th century: in four cantos* (Boston: Carter & Hendee, 1832). He knew that the four cantos of *Dermot MacMorrogh* might have been six, for the *Literary World* of March 18, 1848, had announced that among the unpublished works of the late former president were poems, "including two new cantos of Dermot Mac-Morrough," cantos which seem to have disappeared. Reading Milton's justification "Of that Sort of Dramatic Poem which is Called Tragedy," his preface to *Samson Agonistes,* Melville was struck by the passage on how men in the highest dignity had labored "not a little to be thought able to compose a tragedy," even Augustus Caesar having abandoned his tragedy of Ajax after being displeased with what he had written. Melville groused: "J. Q. A. might have followed his example," evidence enough that he was familiar with the former president's *Dermot MacMorrogh.* Adams seems to have been on his mind, for he copied out into his Dante a passage from *Dermot MacMorrogh* (or something else, now erased, which he identified by Adams's initials). It looks as if Melville was optimistically weighing his prospects for succeeding in composing the highest form of verse (that sort of dramatic poem which is called a tragedy) against the former president's chances.

In September and early October of 1860, by the time the *Meteor* reached the Pacific, Melville had every reason to assume that *Poems* had already been published and was being reviewed. A powerful consequence of his certainty that *Poems* then existed as a printed and bound book was that when he read poets in the Pacific, even more than in the first weeks of the voyage, he thought of himself as a poet reading *other* poets, Spenser, Milton, Wordsworth. Melville was not merely deluded in thinking that his next step, the way of achieving the greatest prestige as a poet, lay in writing a long, ambitious poem. He had, by now, thought about how to do it. George Chapman, according to Michael Drayton's poetic praise, by his translation of the *Georgics* of Hesiod and other classical works had brought ancient treasures to England (very much, the language implied, as Drake and other great Elizabethan seamen had brought home new wealth). Reading this, Melville marked Drayton's assertion that by his toil Chapman had strongly expressed the "large dimensions of the English tongue." He was identifying a hope for himself as a poet, though he could never be a translator. Melville was also impressed by Richard Hooper's praise of Chapman in the introduction to the *Iliad,* especially this sentence: "When we consider the subtile influence of poetry upon the rising spirits of the age, it tempts me to hazard the speculation that, if Chapman's noble paraphrase had been read instead of Pope's enervating monotony, and as extensively, the present class of general readers would not only have been a more poetical class—as the fountain-head from the rock is above the artificial cascade in a pleasure-ground— but a finer order of human beings in respect of energy, love of nature at first-hand, and faith in their own impulses and aspirations." Melville drew three vertical lines along "subtile influence of poetry upon the rising spirits of the age" and underlined those words, and he underlined from "but a finer order" on through the rest of the sentence. Far from remaining in his state of alienation from the contemporary world, Melville was now thinking of how through poetry he might arouse "a finer order of human beings," at least among the English-reading world. It was in this ambitious mood that he checked and underlined "To build with level of my lofty stile" in

Spenser's "The Ruins of Rome" and wrote at the foot of the page one of his characteristic notations of literary borrowing, "Build the lofty rhyme / Milton."

As they sailed up the coast of South America Melville was either luxuriating in remembering some pieces that would be in the book waiting for him in San Francisco, or else writing new poetry. He jocularly reminded Tom on May 25, 1862, of the time he had overflowed with his own poetry: "I cant help thinking what a luckless chap you were that voyage you had a poetaster with you. You remember the romantic moonlight night, when the conceited donkey repeated to you about three cables' length of his verses." He may have been writing a work—presumably a poem—based on a Hawaiian legend, for at some time between the late 1850s and 1862 he tried and felt he had "bungled" the attempt. Gorham D. Gilman, a Boston businessman who had been in Hawaii, in 1858 or earlier sent Melville some of his manuscripts of Hawaiian tales, thinking Melville might appreciate the literary material. Among these was "Umi: A Tale of Hawaii as Narrated by King Kamehameha III." In returning the material on November 29, 1862, Melville said he had been charmed by the traditional Hawaiian tale of Umi, in which an illegitimate son of the king ultimately inherits the throne, and had found it "graceful & Greekish." He may have been bemused as well as charmed, for the name "Umi" would have had complicated associations for him, since long before, he may have responded to Grace Greenwood's irresistible portrait of Clingy Lingy by introducing a poetaster named Yoomy into the manuscript of *Mardi*. The fun of writing Yoomy's verses in 1848 or so had helped prepare him to write real poetry, a decade later. In his 1858–59 lecture on the South Seas Melville alluded to a "traditional Polynesian legend" that might particularly appeal to the ladies in his audience, since it was a "love legend of Kamekamehaha, Tahiti, and Otaheite, that was told by a king of one of these islands, and which has much of the grace, strangeness, and audacity of the Grecian fables." This was an allusion to Gilman's material, for the editor of the Milwaukee *Daily Wisconsin*, William Cramer, a family friend of the Melvilles, specified that Melville had mentioned "a manuscript tradition he had seen that was told by a King of one of those Islands."[4] When Melville at last returned the documents to Gilman on November 29, 1862, he said that he had taken Gilman's suggestion seriously: "Some time ago I tried my hand at elaborating it, but found I bungled, and gave it up." A reasonable guess is that Melville tried to elaborate the Hawaiian legend on the *Meteor,* when he was expecting to sail across the Pacific.

In San Francisco in mid-October there was weighty news to catch up on about the momentous American election, the partial unification of Italy—everything but "a bloody battle in Affghanistan" (*Moby-Dick,* chap. 1). None of that meant much to Melville at the moment, for at the Harbormaster's there was no book-sized package for him, arrived ahead of him by the Panama route, and the letters awaiting him confirmed that his poems had not been published. Tom also received startling news at the Harbormaster's—that he was to return around the Horn after an indefinite wait in San Francisco. His self-image as a published poet shattered, Melville immediately decided to go home—by ship to the isthmus, then across on the Panama Railroad to another ship. On October 20, Tom had his brother's gear transferred onto the steamship *Cortes.* Without porters, Herman could not easily transport his old periodicals and books of poetry off the ship, onto the train, and onto a ship again for the voyage to New York, but his annotations show that he kept at least the Wordsworth and the Schiller, which he read in the Caribbean. He may have left some of the bulkier and heavier volumes for Tom to carry home on his ship, for his need to have Homer and Milton and other epic volumes at hand would have evaporated when *Poems* was not awaiting him in San Francisco. A year and a half later Melville recalled the voyage as the time Captain Melville had "a poetaster" as passenger. The hard truth is that what distinguishes a real poet (even an Alfred Street) from an amateur is that his verses get published. Even an author of many published prose books cannot call himself a poet if he cannot publish his poetry. Melville had thought himself a published poet while on the *Meteor* in the Pacific, but he returned to New York City in November 1860 as a stalled poetaster, not the triumphant author of *Poems* and the author and planner of new, even more ambitious poetry.

If what he had written had been printed, we would know Melville as the man who published these volumes between 1846 and 1860: *Typee, Omoo, Mardi, Redburn, White-Jacket, Moby-Dick, Pierre, The Isle of the Cross, Israel Potter, The Piazza Tales, The Confidence-Man,* and *Poems.* We might now think of "Morning in Naples"—or "Afternoon in Naples"—in relation to "Benito Cereno" and to Melville's then-recent 1857 European observations rather than as a waif from Melville's last decade and a half, twinned with another waif, "At the Hostelry." The loss of *Poems,* like the loss of *The Isle of the Cross* (not to mention slighter losses like some of the prose tortoise pages[5] and the bungled attempt at writing a Hawaiian legend) has meant that we cannot see Melville's working life as a whole and cannot see the interrelationships of his works, between *The Isle of the Cross* and "Bartleby," for instance, or between anything in *Poems* and anything in *Battle-Pieces* (1866).

CHAPTER TEN

His Verse Still Unpublished, Melville Defines Himself as Poet, 1861–1862

MELVILLE SET FOOT IN MANHATTAN ON NOVEMBER 13, 1860, A WEEK after the election of Abraham Lincoln. The autumn was bleak as winter in his memory. In *Clarel* he recalled the next months of 1860–61: "That evil day, / Black in the New World's calendar— / The dolorous winter ere the war; / True Bridge of Sighs—so yet 'twill be / Esteemed in riper history— / Sad arch between contrasted eras" (4.5.74–79). A little surprisingly, not all his family and friends had been focused on the present American crisis. Some had preferred, as he phrased it at an agitated time in 1851, to look after Hungary—now to look after Italy, to take sides in a foreign struggle. His brother-in-law John C. Hoadley and his old friend Henry T. Tuckerman had been championing Garibaldi's campaign to unify Italy, Hoadley out of his passionate, erratic enthusiasm for a cause, Tuckerman on the basis of long close knowledge of Italy, Italian literature, and Garibaldi the man. American agitation for Greek freedom in the 1820s and the hysteria over Kossuth and Hungarian freedom late in 1851 had set a recognizable pattern: Americans tended to fixate on foreign crises during greater crises at home. What Tuckerman called "the sacred cause of Italian nationality" had come home to the educated classes in the northern United States as a feel-good liberal topic easier to talk about at the dinner table than, say, John Brown's raid on Harper's Ferry in October 1859. At a meeting in Newport (as reported in the Boston *Daily Transcript* on August 1, 1860), Tuckerman had offered the resolution that it was the "sacred duty" of Americans, "as citizens of a prosperous republic," to contribute money "to furnish arms and ammunition to Garibaldi in his holy crusade to free the oppressed and establish Italian independence." No one mentioned any impropriety in arming revolutionaries in a foreign land—certainly not in the Holy Land of Art. Early in 1861 in Lawrence, Massachusetts, Hoadley, chairman of a committee charged with congratulating Italy upon its unification, wrote resolutions out "most beautifully" in the French language for the Secretary of State to forward to their destination. By then, Tuckerman had published the definitive American article on Garibaldi in the January 1861 *North American Review.*

For months many members of Melville's family and their friends had been attempting to prevent an American war, doing all they could to placate the South in the face of a likely Republican victory. Before the election, Melville's father-in-law, Lemuel Shaw, retired as Chief Justice of the Commonwealth of Massachusetts, had been importuned to become an elector of the Constitutional Union Party, whose members hoped to prevent secession, and, failing that, to prevent war between the states. At Thanksgiving, while Melville was in the Shaw house, Shaw joined with Massachusetts unionists who urged conciliation toward the South. In December in New York City Melville's brother Allan's first wife's brother-in-law, Richard Lathers (treated as a brother-in-law of Herman's still), was working with John A. Dix and other men Melville knew, trying to stave off secession through a breathtakingly tardy plan for black colonization to Africa. In February 1861 Lathers attended a Peace Convention in Washington presided over by former president John Tyler (who had boarded at the Melvill house in Pittsfield in 1848), then set out with his wife, the aunt of Melville's brother Allan's daughters, on a quixotic, heroic mission to the South. Bewildered by unreal hopes and unpredictable realities after months away, Melville may have felt he had not grasped the subtleties of people's positions, and years later decided he needed to perform a little historical research if he were to grasp some of the issues. On June 30, 1866, at the Astor Library in New York he consulted the 626-page *A Report of the Debates and Proceedings in the Secret Sessions of the Conference Convention, for Proposing Amendments to the Constitution of the United States, held at Washington, D.C., in February, A.D. 1861* (New York: D. Appleton & Co., 1864), compiled by L. E. Chittenden (Olsen-Smith and Sealts 143.2). He wanted to have the history freshly in mind as he worked on the "Supplement" to his volume of Civil War poetry.

Despite the momentousness of the national crisis and despite his own uncharacteristic visits to his now-scattered family, Melville may have laid in some of his habitually weighty reading for that winter, one which proved brutally harsh as well as historically dolorous. Although he was humiliated that *Poems* was not on his work table (bound any way but blue and gold), he may have kept on writing poetry: it was now what he did. The year 1860 is the most likely for his composing a little poem for the captain of the *Meteor,* who was keeping his Christmas "Lonesome on the torrid deep":

> Thou that, duty-led, dost roam
> Far from thy shepherd-brother's home—
> Shearer of the ocean-foam!
> To whom one Christmas may not come,—
> Of thee I think
> Till on its brink
> The glass shows tears, beloved Tom!

This compliment to Tom looks like a poem for the specific occasion, a poetical toast offered amid other thoughtfully constructed Christmas toasts traditionally given by the males of the family (see *Log* 631). The next week, in the Dutch tradition of New Year's Day gift-giving, he inscribed to Lizzie his now-lost copy of *The Works of the Late Edgar Allan Poe* (New York: Blakeman & Mason, 1859; Sealts 404a). He had bought it in 1860, perhaps to carry round Cape Horn, and now had absorbed it to the point that it could be given away, though not to the point that he was willing to send it out of the house.

With his hopes dashed that he could become accepted at home as an American poet, Melville took seriously the possibility of becoming the American consul at Florence. In late March 1861, himself "duty-led," he agreed to go to Washington to seek the assistance of Thurlow Weed and Charles Sumner, a friend of Hoadley's. Called back urgently by word of Shaw's illness, Melville arrived in Boston too late to see his father-in-law alive but in time to participate in the momentous public mourning and state funeral. With her inheritance coming, Lizzie and Herman could more easily give up the idea of uprooting themselves as the Hawthornes had done and instead could consider how to keep their capital (the first they had possessed) from dwindling away before Herman was able to find some new way of making money. Even without a job, Herman felt he could afford to begin buying books again, for, a week after Shaw's funeral, he put the date April 9 in the two-volume *The Poetical Works of Shelley* (Boston: Little, Brown, 1857; Sealts 469) and a recent set of *The Poetical Works of Edmund Spenser* in five volumes (Boston: Little, Brown, 1855; Sealts 483). Presumably he bought them in Boston, where there were real bookstores, although he wrote "Pittsfield" after the date each time. Odd memories of the dead were at work in the purchase of each of these books, the Shelley reminding him of the artist William Edward West, who had told vivid stories of the living Shelley and Byron at Dr. Francis's house in Bond Street, the Spenser inevitably reminding him of his poring over his father's set, which he may already have promised to give to Augusta once he had found a suitable replacement.

Going to a bookstore on April 9, 1861, was a persistence of the quotidian amid extraordinary circumstances. The state funeral for Judge Shaw on April 2 had been followed four days later by news that Lincoln was sending a relief expedition to Fort Sumter, in the harbor of Charleston, since February in the Confederate state of South Carolina. Melville's life did not change immediately because of the war. He continued to visit scattered members of the family, and he continued to buy poetry. On July 3 he bought *The Poetical Works of James Thomson* (Boston: Little, Brown, 1854; Sealts 516), which contained poems familiar to him from his youth, perhaps picking up the volume on his way to New Rochelle, which he visited that day. On August 14 during a layover in Albany after visiting his mother in Gansevoort, he bought the two-volume *The Poetical Works of Alfred Tennyson* (Boston: Ticknor & Fields, 1861; Sealts 508). Later, in 1864 or afterward, he pasted in a newspaper clipping about William Brighty Rands's *Tangled Talk: An Essayist's Holiday* (London: A. Strahan & Co., 1864), a passage where Rands expressed disdain for "The Charge of the Light Brigade." Defending Tennyson, as mentioned earlier, Melville wrote "Stuff by a small man," drawing his version of a printer's fist pointing at the clipping. In October in New York near Central Park, at a yet-unidentified "Cedar Home," Melville bought Leigh Hunt's *Rimini and Other Poems* (Boston: Ticknor & Fields, 1844; Sealts 290a), much of which he must have been familiar with already.

On October 27, 1861, Melville made a momentous purchase, as far as we know the most important purchase of the year: Henry Taylor's *Notes from Life in Seven Essays* (Boston: Ticknor, Reed, & Fields, 1853; Sealts 290a). In Taylor he found a kindred spirit—a man equally familiar with the wisdom of Solomon as recorded in Ecclesiastes and the wisdom of Jesus the Son of Sirach as recorded in Ecclesiasticus. Another point of kinship for the erratically educated Melville was that Taylor, unlike many British writers, was not fluent in foreign languages. Yet Taylor was an intensely literary man, steeped like

Melville in centuries of English poetry, so that his field of reading was near Melville's own. Throughout his book Taylor quoted much poetry, some of it his own, some of it yet unidentified. He quoted George Herbert's "The Church Porch"; Chaucer's "Clerke's Tale"; Francis Quarles's lines on prodigality beginning "Thrice happy he whose nobler thoughts despise / To make an object of so easy gains" (from *Emblems, Divine and Moral*, 1.4); lines from his own *A Sicilian Summer* ("In many a vigil of her last sick bed"); *Hamlet; As You Like It; Coriolanus; As You Like It,* again; *Othello.* He quoted from Aubrey De Vere's *Waldenses, and Other Poems; Twelfth Night;* Crabbe's "The Parish Register"; *Julius Caesar;* Sir Walter Raleigh; Milton (*Paradise Lost*); Southey (*Oliver Newman*); Christopher Hervie (*The Synagogue*); the book of Job; *Hamlet,* again; John Fletcher ("Melancholy"); *Othello;* Cowley ("Ode upon Liberty"); Tennyson's "The Gardener's Daughter"; Coleridge's "The Night-Scene: A Dramatic Fragment"; William Wordsworth's "Malham Cove"; Shakespeare's sonnet 111; Southey's "My days among the dead are past"; Milton's sonnet "How soon hath Time"; Wordsworth's sonnet to B. R. Haydon; *Paradise Lost,* again; *King Lear;* Walter Savage Landor; *Coriolanus,* again ("a most inherent baseness"); Goethe's *Faust;* and Landor's "Imaginary Conversations." Of the quotations listed above, those from Fletcher to the last one by Milton were in the long essay "The Life Poetic," which Melville read meticulously, most likely late in 1861.

According to Taylor in "The Life Poetic," the "man of genius" (the poet) should lean "towards retirement," meaning removal from the bustle of cities. (The Duyckincks had referred to Melville's life at Arrowhead as "comparative retirement." In 1862, in his set of Cowley [see pp. 179–80 below], Melville marked T. Sprat's reproach of Cowley for showing a too earnest "Affection for Obscurity and Retirement.") Still, for cultivation of "the highest order of poetry" the poet should "be conversant with life and nature at large," should be "to a moderate extent, mixed up with the affairs of life." Melville marked this sentence: "He is but a child in knowledge, however versed in meditation, who has not to act, to suffer, and to teach, as well as to inquire and to learn." Taylor recognized the difficulty of achieving balance between the "contemplative life" and "the inordinate activities of the age." How a poet was to earn money was always a problem. The professions were too demanding for a poet to undertake; commercial life forced men into competition unsuited to a poet; political life was "too violent a diversion from poetic pursuits." If a poet failed to find a

field for "external activity, which would admit also of leisure and retirement," he nevertheless needed to lead a disciplined life. He needed
the "regimen of external circumstances and of obligations contracted
to others"—the sort of regimen Melville finally achieved at the end of
1866 in the Custom House. A poet with no occupation might find
himself "prey to many demands for small services, attentions, and ci-
vilities, such as will neither exercise his faculties, add to his knowledge, nor leave him to his thoughts." Cousin Elizabeth Gansevoort
long ago, in 1840, had identified Herman as the brother who had
nothing to do and therefore could escort Augusta across the width of
the Empire State to Bath, New York. Melville had done an inordinate
amount of visiting after his return from San Francisco. If the family
learned that he was no longer farming Arrowhead, what demands
would be made on him, now that he was plainly not publishing anything regularly? Melville marked this passage on the dangers of being
imposed on, and checked the conclusion that a poet in the midst of
the "bustling crowds of this present world" would find himself "in a
position of oppugnancy to those around him," so that he "must struggle in order to stand still."

The ideal life of the poet was one of "semi-seclusion" such as Tennyson described, Taylor said. Thinking of Samuel Rogers, probably,
and the excitement of city life, Melville marked this passage in Taylor:
"In London, in the present times, an eminent man is beset with a mul-
tiplicity of social enjoyments and excitements, the very waste-pipes of
genial sensibility; and the poet's imagination, instead of forming a
fund to be continually deepened and widened by influx from secret
sources, is diffused and spread abroad and speedily dried up." Melville
marked other passages on the poet's need for "an adequate unpopular-
ity" to constitute self-protection, and a line on "the perils of social
popularity." He boxed a line Taylor quoted from Coleridge's "The
Night-Scene: A Dramatic Fragment": "Deep self-possession, an intense repose"—part of the argument that a poet is by temperament so
excitable that he should avoid stimulation. Melville underlined this
assertion: "To the poet, solitude itself is an excitement." The poet
should look to the future for his reward, cherishing "some more or less
conscious anticipation of sympathy to come," Taylor advised, and,
agreeing, Melville marked the passage on the poet's not being granted
"contemporaneous and immediate admiration." Taylor said bluntly, "I
doubt whether any high endeavor of poetic art ever has been or ever
will be promoted by the stimulation of popular applause." Even the

greatest poets had found that their popularity during most if not all of their lives was "still a popularity which extends only to the cultivated, as distinguished from the merely educated classes, and does not bring with it any very profitable sale." Brooding on this, Melville underlined the distinction between the merely educated and the cultivated.

Acknowledging that poets cannot subsist by writing poetry, Taylor asked if they might "subsist by the aid of prose." But prose, Taylor realized, "will fail to return a profit, unless it be written for the market." (Melville marked all this.) Taylor held up Southey as a poet who wrote prose for the market ("marketable literature," a phrase Melville underlined) and wrote with "unrivalled industry, infinite stores of knowledge, extraordinary talents, and a delightful style," and yet merely subsisted in the most frugal manner and died leaving planned poetic works unfinished for lack of time. The last "marketable literature" Melville had published was *Israel Potter;* apparently unlike Southey, he had felt pulled apart by the need to write what he wanted to write and the conflicting need to write what would sell. In 1861 writing marketable prose was not an option to be considered. Illustrating the poignancy of Southey's leaving works unfinished, Taylor printed three lines from "Wordsworth": "Things incomplete, and purposes betrayed, / Make sadder transits o'er Truth's mystic glass, / Than noblest objects utterly decayed." (Melville may have remembered the words from the sonnet "Malham Cove," unmarked in his copy of Wordsworth's *Complete Poetical Works,* where it occurs a few pages after the sonnet to Haydon, which he annotated.) From 1876 until his death Melville would struggle to salvage old works and to complete new ones, and fail, notably in the biggest thing he left unfinished, the manuscript of *Billy Budd.* Taylor had no patience with a "spendthrift poet" or "one who is incompetent to the management of his affairs," words that may have stung Melville, whom the entire family in 1856 had recognized to be incapable of making financial decisions. Ideally, poets should not have to earn all the money they need for living, for "pecuniary difficulties" almost always impair men of "character and content." Ideally, there would be some "needful protection" for men of genius. His wife's inheritance had relieved Melville of the obligation to earn money, at the moment. What allowed Melville the leisure to read about the poetic life and to prepare to write more poetry rather than to go out looking for work seems to have been a sense of the entitlements due to genius, especially now that his long struggle to write marketable prose had ended in failure. Melville underlined

Taylor's observation that poetry "is the fruit of the whole moral, spiritual, intellectual, and practical being" and would be weakened if the poet lacked a frugal competence. At the end of this almost page-long sentence, Melville underlined and marked a passage on the gifts of the poet which were too often dimmed by imperfections of humanity. At best, on a poet with "a pure and unspotted life" God might bestow the "gifts of high reason, ardent imagination, efflorescence of fancy and intrepidity of impulse," so that he might write great poetry. "Out of the heart are the issues of life, and out of the life are the issues of poetry," Taylor declared. Melville underlined "intrepidity of impulse" and drew a line along the remaining part of the passage. Coolly as he expressed himself, Taylor allowed all along for the boldness of true genius.

Turning to how poets train themselves, Taylor recommended (in a passage Melville marked) "*select* reading," chiefly the literature of the seventeenth century because "the diction and the movement of that literature," both prose and poetry, is best fitted "to be used for the training of the mind for poetry." The complexity of that century's prose and poetry detained the reader "over what was pregnant and profound" and trained "the ear and utterance" of a would-be poet. This rang true to Melville, the lover of Robert Burton, Jeremy Taylor, Abraham Cowley, and John Dryden. Taylor celebrated a style difficult enough that a reader would be forced to suspend in mind complex thought as it was embodied in many phrases and clauses and then, at the end of the sentence, would comprehend in its entirety the whole of the complex meaning. Taylor continued: "For if we look at the long-suspended sentences of those days, with all their convolutions and intertextures—the many parts waiting for the ultimate wholeness—we shall perceive that without distinctive movement and rhythmical significance of a very high order, it would be impossible that they could be sustained in any sort of clearness" (Melville did the underlining). Under discussion was prose such as Melville had mastered in *Moby-Dick,* even more so in *Pierre,* and yet more so, to the detriment of popularity, in *The Confidence-Man.*

Taylor advised that the poet abstain from reading books plainly directed at the current popular reading audience, the sort of books which one may read on the run, and instead become familiar with "elder models in the matter of diction." (Melville marked the part on avoiding books "written *in* these times and *for* these times, to catch the fugacious or stimulate the sluggish reader.") Then, Taylor said, the poet would be able to employ as his own "that slightly archaistic coloring of language" (underlined and marked by Melville) which Spenser and others had thought "the best costume in which poetry can be clothed, combining what is common to other ages with what is characteristic of its own." Yet the true poet would be "choice and chary, as well as moderate, in the use of archaisms," shunning old forms which deserve to be forgotten while acting as a conservator of language. By "observing with a keener insight the latent metaphorical fitness or unfitness by which all language is pervaded," the poet would find himself "remanding to their more derivative significations, words which are beginning to go astray." Melville marked the passage on the precision of language required of the poet: "And though this peculiar aptitude will escape many of the poet's readers, (if he have many,) and much of it will not be recognised at once even by the more skilful few, yet in this, as in other matters of art, it is what can be fully appreciated only by continual study, that will lay the strongest foundations of fame." Alerted here, in the next months Melville marked many passages about poets' continual study and painstaking effort.

Melville marked Taylor's long footnote on Crabbe Robinson's testifying that Schiller had told him he read foreign writers in German lest he "lose his nicer perceptions" of what belonged to his own language. As a poet who knew only English, Melville could take consolation from Taylor's conclusion that Milton, whose "store of poetical images and material" was "greatly enriched" by his knowledge of the Latin and Greek classics and by Italian, yet had been damaged by letting Latin pervert his diction away from English. Melville marked Taylor's claim that a poet should not "deem himself to be prepared for the exercise of his vocation on a large scale" until he had reached middle age. (Milton himself had thought that he was maturing slowly, at twenty-three; and Melville in his Milton marked the section on Milton's age when he wrote *Paradise Lost* and his seasonal and daily working habits.) Melville marked "sixty-seventh year"—the age at which, according to Taylor, Dryden wrote "Alexander's Feast." Even the best "amorous poetry," Taylor thought, was apt to be the product of the "richer vein" available to a man well past his youth. More important, Taylor reflected: "The sense of proportion, which is required equally in the lighter as in the graver kinds of poetry, is naturally imperfect in youth, through undue ardor in particulars; and no very young poet will be content to sacrifice special felicities to general effect" (Melville's underlining). Taylor continued on the difficulty of attaining proper equilibrium in youth: "Nor can there well exist, at an early period of life, that rare and peculiar balance of all the faculties, which, even more perhaps than a peculiar force in any, constitutes a great poet:—the balance of reason with imagination, passion with self-possession, abundance with reserve, and inventive conception with executive ability" (that last meaning the ability to execute, to carry out). Melville underlined "peculiar balance of all the faculties" and sidelined all the rest of the sentence. That balance was something he could look for in himself now, long past his youth, when he could acknowledge that during the completion of *Moby-Dick* he had possessed everything Taylor described except a balanced judgment in matters financial.

Taylor advised that a youthful poet publish at once, freeing himself to move on to a work with "an ambition sufficiently long-sighted" (words Melville underlined). Taylor said that "early failure in those in whom there is genuine poetic genius, and what commonly accompanies it— 'Faith in the whispers of the lonely Muse'—acts as a sort of narcotic stimulant, allaying impatience, but quickening the deeper mind." Melville underlined "Faith" through "Muse," which (even without the footnoted "Wordsworth") he may have identified as from Wordsworth's "Sonnet to B. R. Haydon." Melville also carefully read Taylor's advice that poets should stop writing new poetry at seventy or so and set themselves to putting their earlier work in order, but not revising it obsessively, since by that time the poet might have lost his "clearness and decisiveness of choice" (words Melville underlined). The presumption, Taylor insisted, "should be in favor of the first draft." All in all, Melville found *Notes from Life* exceptionally thought-provoking, Taylor confirming much that he had already experienced and justifying him in courses he was prepared to continue. The essay "The Life Poetic," judging by his markings, came as a momentous help in Melville's defining his present condition as an unrecognized poet living on his wife's money and projecting cautiously how the rest of his life as a poet might work itself out. Nothing Taylor described was alien to his experience.

On April 11, 1860, while he was finishing *Poems,* Melville had visited the Astor Library in Lafayette Place to consult the two volumes of Moore's biography of Byron, a book long familiar to him (Olsen-Smith and Sealts 369a). In December 1861, probably a few weeks after he read *Notes from Life,* Melville put the address 103 East Tenth Street in a set of Byron (Boston: Little, Brown, 1853; Sealts 112). Beside *Don Juan,* canto 11, stanzas five and six (an ironic passage on growing more orthodox with every new push of an illness), Melville wrote: "this is excellent—the practical abandonment of good-humored devil-may-care. Byron is a better man in Don Juan than in his serious poems." He reminded himself to "learn by heart" ten lines of section three of the third canto of *The Island: or Christian and His Comrades:*

> A little stream came tumbling from the height,
> And straggling into ocean as it might,
> Its bounding crystal frolick'd in the ray,
> And gush'd from cliff to crag with saltless spray;
> Close on the wild, wide ocean, yet as pure
> And fresh as innocence, and more secure,
> Its silver torrent glitter'd o'er the deep,
> As the shy chamois' eye o'erlooks the steep,
> While far below the vast and sullen swell
> Of ocean's alpine azure rose and fell.

He may have wanted to get these particular lines by heart because they reminded him of the Marquesas or Tahiti, but, whatever his motive, this "learn by heart" shows that in his forties Melville was still memorizing poetry, and not merely purple passages or commonly quoted passages. From his instant recognition of poetic echoes, even in books where he could hardly have been prompted by critical commentaries or editorial footnotes, we have to conclude that he knew many hundreds, probably thousands of lines of poetry "by heart." When he encountered allusions, borrowings, and echoes as he read poems, he took pleasure in footnoting the interdebtedness of poets, putting an X by the passage and another X at the foot of the page, typically, along with the line borrowed from an earlier poet or influencing a later poet. Part of the pleasure of reading, for Melville, was recognizing and appreciating the debts that poets, especially great poets, owed to their predecessors.

While living in that rented space on East Tenth Street Melville walked a few steps over to call on Henry T. Tuckerman at 15 West Tenth Street, the Tenth Street Studio Building where many artists set up their studios. He missed his man, and Tuckerman could not return his call because he was laid up "with a severe neuralgic attack" (Parker 2:484). Talk had to wait into the next year. In late January 1862 Melville was back in New York, renting at 150 East Eighteenth Street. Tuckerman got his address through Evert Duyckinck, and they met as valetudinarians after their slightly farcical failures to connect.

Melville had experienced many failures to connect, perhaps most recently when he reported ruefully to his uncle Peter on March 21, 1861, that one political bird he tried to find, Thurlow Weed, had flown "back to its perch—Albany." Given Melville's intense interest in Italy and especially given the likelihood that he had already written his "Naples" poem in 1858 or 1859, Garibaldi must have been a topic of conversation between Melville and Tuckerman early in 1862, however large the American war loomed in their thoughts. As Melville had prepared to sail with Tom on the *Meteor*, Garibaldi had been preparing to sail from Genoa with his thousand Red Shirts. At the end of May 1860, just as Melville sailed, Garibaldi took Palermo, and in August he crossed the Strait of Messina. In early September he entered Naples, claiming Sicily and Naples for Victor Emmanuel II of Savoia. In early 1861 Italy was united, except what the Austrians held in the north and, most rankling, except for Rome. Melville could have seen many old articles printed during his absence at sea, for he caught up with some of the news in San Francisco, but Tuckerman's long essay in the *North American Review* of January 1861 by itself contained most of the details he used when he wrote a new hundred lines or so devoted to Garibaldi's liberation of Sicily and his crossing the strait to free Naples from "King Fanny, Bomba's heir." He may have written the new lines thinking he could fit them into the end of his poem about a drive through Naples, even though the poem was about what one form of the title stressed, Naples in the time of Bomba, before the brief reign of "King Fanny" (Francis II). Later he updated some of the lines (such as those that refer to Venice and Rome as both liberated and as part of Italy, which happened to Venice in 1866 and Rome in 1871). Whenever Melville gave renewed attention to Garibaldi, very possibly in 1861–62, he echoed Tuckerman's language. Much later, probably in the late 1870s, Melville revised the lines on Garibaldi and attached them to "At the Hostelry," but he never revised out of them some references that must have been put there in the early 1860s, such as the allusion to Turin as the capital of the new kingdom of Italy, which was true only until 1865.

On the first of February 1862, ready to make up a deficiency in his reading, Melville asked Evert Duyckinck for some volumes by dramatists contemporary with Shakespeare. Marlowe he knew, but he was ready to read Thomas Dekker and John Webster if Duyckinck had their plays. Either Melville borrowed the books and read them quickly or else he postponed that reading until very late in his life, when volumes in the Mermaid series became available. Instead of pursuing the Elizabethan dramatists and instead of writing more poetry, in the middle of February 1862 Melville embarked on what became an intense course of reading. With some of Lizzie's money in hand, he began buying books, week after week or even day after day, apparently pretty much for immediate sampling or thorough reading. After his purchases in London at the end of 1849 Melville never again bought books in bulk knowing that for the most part his delectation would be postponed. During his work on *Moby-Dick* (starting early in 1850) and his work on *Clarel* (starting early in 1870) he bought several books as source material, but never in such bulk in the long interval between those two projects. The single intense period of book-buying we know of, after his acquisitions in London, is that of early 1862. These books were not bought as source material for a projected book or a work in progress. Melville may not have started with a clear purpose in mind, but his book-buying rather quickly became focused. He bought volumes of poetry, usually by neglected or not-yet-established poets (he already owned most standard poets, though he added Cowley on March 21, 1862). He also bought books of literary history and criticism, and, toward the end, one major multivolume art history, the Vasari, which he had read in 1859 in Evert Duyckinck's copy (read carefully enough that he remembered a slight detail on shipboard in 1860). In all likelihood, in these months, February through April, Melville also bought books we know nothing about, for two of the most important, the Vasari and the Hazlitt, described below, were discovered late in the twentieth century. Furthermore, he was almost certainly borrowing some books, from Duyckinck or Tuckerman, most likely, for it was probably at this time that he took notes in his new Hazlitt from an article in the *Edinburgh Review* and took notes in his new Vasari from the third volume of Ruskin's *Modern Painters,* a book Melville did not yet own.

The following account of Melville's reading in early 1862 proceeds roughly in the sequence of his book-buying, skewed by his sometimes writing down only the month of purchase, not the day. The sequence in which Melville read his new books did not, of course, correspond precisely with the order in which he bought them, but most of his markings and annotations in them seem to have dated from this February through April period. To a great extent he was reading or at least looking over what he bought soon after buying it. Melville's annotations as well as his underlinings, marginal scorings, and other symbols in the texts and in the margins are obvious evidence of his engagement with what he read, but he did not always make any mark by passages that struck him powerfully. Building this chapter on some of Melville's markings in his books is not meant to foreclose the study of other markings and of these markings in relation to the whole texts.

At the outset of this extraordinary period of book-buying and reading, Melville was freshly prompted by his study of Taylor's *Notes from Life* to refine his efforts to place his own experience as prose writer and as poet in relation to what he could learn of other poets, particularly British poets of the previous three hundred years, both the long-famous and the obscure. He was alert to compare his sense of his own abilities and achievements with what others defined as the qualities that constituted literary greatness. Rather quickly he began actively marking recurrent topics, as when he focused repeatedly on the "pains" that writers had taken in their composition, on how "painstaking" they had been (even if others thought they had dashed their poems off). What he marked in writer after writer confirmed his own conviction that he too had taken infinite pains, even if his books had been "botches,"[1] and would always take such pains with his more ambitious poetry. Writing good poetry, in particular, took painstaking labor which often went unrewarded in the poet's lifetime, as it conspicuously had done in his own life, in 1860. Melville was enthralled by accounts of other writer's work habits in general. He became fascinated by the question of how much of poetic genius is innate and how much can be developed. He developed a rueful sense of himself as a perfectly ordinary genius, acting according to the well-established peculiarities of the class, not the unreasonably demanding fellow he had sometimes seemed to members of his family. Geniuses really were different from normal people although sometimes surprisingly like each other. After scanning some of his purchases he found himself wanting to study rhetoric in literature, to pick up, very likely, from about where he had dropped the great textbooks in 1839, when he left the Lansingburgh Academy. Now he took conscientious notes on literary techniques, most elaborately from Francis Jeffrey's review-essay on the Italian dramatist Victor Alfieri (writing down the notes in Hazlitt's *Lectures*). By the end of his course of reading and notetaking the autodidact was ready to articulate an aesthetic credo of his own.

On February 14, 1862, Melville bought *The Poetical Works of Thomas Hood* (Boston: Little, Brown, 1860; Sealts 279). In Richard Monckton Milnes's memoir Melville marked a section on the poet's excessive facility: "[I]f Mr. Hood had been able to place under some restraint the curious and complex machinery of words and syllables which his fancy was incessantly producing, his style would have been a great gainer." Among many other poems, Melville marked the entirety of "The Poet's Fate" ("What is a modern Poet's fate? / To write his thoughts upon a slate; — / The Critic spits on what is done,— / Gives it a wipe,—and all is gone"). In the first volume he did not bother to mark "The Haunted House," but he apparently noticed Hood's saying, in quotation marks, that wild birds fed near the deserted mansion with "shocking tameness." Melville knew this as an allusion to Cowper's "The Solitude of Alexander Selkirk," a poem he had quoted from memory in his journal in London, in late November 1849 ("Oh Solitude! where are thy charms"). As will become clear below, Melville had paid close attention to this passage even though he did not mark it.

On February 15, 1862, Melville bought *Poems of James Clarence Mangan* (New York: Haverty, 1859; Sealts 347). As he frequently did, Melville jotted down an essential biographical date: "Died about 1848." The introduction by John Mitchel began with something sure to arouse an ironic smile in Melville, an apology for daring to call the attention of the literary world to a poet not included in *Poets of the Nineteenth Century,* edited by the Reverend Robert Aris Willmot and (in its American edition) Evert A. Duyckinck. The volume was divided into four sections: "German Anthology," "Irish Anthology," "Apocrypha," and "Miscellaneous." Many pages in the first section consisted of translations from Schiller, who had long been of interest to Melville. One of the many poems by Schiller that Melville triple-checked was "The Words of Delusion" (Triumph, Treasure, and Truth), where the delusion is the hope that worth will be rewarded by "Triumph and Treasure" and the dream that the "noonbeams of Truth" will ever shine on human clay. Early in the introduction Melville marked the account of Mangan's being an outsider: "Mangan was not only an Irishman,—not only an Irish papist,—not only an Irish papist rebel;—but throughout his whole literary life of twenty years, he never deigned to attorn to English criticism," never "seemed to be aware that there was a British public to please." (Melville did not query "attorn," which meant "to pay homage to.") This description defined some of Mangan's appeal beyond his translating German poets. He was an obscure outsider, theologically suspect, oblivious to the judgments of the literary elite. On back flyleaves Melville noted (from p. 156) "at whiles" (which he underlined in the text), "aneath," the foreign word "Franquistán," the rhymes "e'ening – meaning," "sternest – earnest" (these two in reverse order of occurrence), and "lonely – only." Then he noted: "shorn & cowled" (also on 156). Melville plainly found a highly self-conscious use of "archaisms" in form and diction to be attractive in Mangan, as a little later he did in the Pre-Raphaelites.

Also on February 15, 1862, Melville bought *The Poetical Works of Thomas Moore* (Boston: Little, Brown, 1856 [1854?]; Sealts 370). He may have read in this book at once, in mid-February, but if so he returned to it in October 1862. Probably he knew already many of the "Poems Relating to America." Certainly he already knew many of Moore's songs and Moore's life of Byron. He knew *Lalla Rookh* (dedicated to Samuel Rogers), and he knew enough of literary history to identify the people referred to in "The 'Living Dog' and 'The Dead Lion'" as Leigh Hunt and Byron. Now he was struck by Moore's portrayal of himself as being, "at all times, a far more slow and painstaking workman than would ever be guessed, I fear, from the result." In the preface to *Lalla Rookh* Moore went farther, in words Melville partially underlined: "Having thus laid open the secrets of the workshop to account for the time expended in writing this work, I must also, in justice to my own industry, notice the pains I took in long and laboriously reading for it" (that is, historical research for *Lalla Rookh*). Whatever pains in "time and trouble" Moore took in his "preparatory process," he felt repaid by the result. Moore's account of beginning verse tales and progressing hundreds of lines into them before abandoning them would have struck home to Melville, who had apparently tried to write the tale of Umi, very likely in verse, in the late 1850s or 1860.

On February 17, 1862, Melville bought *The Works of Robert Fergusson* (London: Fullarton, 1857; Sealts 215). Melville was interested in some passages that had nothing to do with poetry (on seagoing, on men disappearing). In all likelihood he saw poignant parallels from his own life. In Gansevoort's vein is the letter from Robert Fergusson's brother Henry requesting him to take more care with his verses: "I desire it as a favour, [that] you would often examine your poetical pieces before you commit them to the press: this advice I hope you'll the more readily take, as most young authors are apt to be more criticized than those who have had a little experience. Pope himself was one of the most careful in this respect, and none yet has ever surpass'd him."

Melville marked a contrast of a "poor, down-crushed lad" with the rich man who writes "as a recreation" in his study, "surrounded with all the delicacies, and comforts, and securities of life." He was struck by dialect words (though he did not mark the Scottish glossary) and by the stated influence of Fergusson's "Farmer's Ingle" on Burns's "The Cotter's Saturday Night."

On February 26, 1862, Melville bought four volumes by Isaac Disraeli. *Amenities of Literature, Consisting of Sketches and Characters of English Literature* (London: Routledge, 1859; Sealts 184) was a very solid literary history, scholarship packaged for the educated general reader. Melville was interested in what Disraeli said about "many beautiful archaisms, scattered remnants of our language, which explain those obscurities of our more ancient writers, singularities of phrase, or lingual peculiarities, which have so often bewildered the most acute of our commentators." Disraeli went on to say that modern editors have corrected in error, not knowing the original provincial idiom. The second volume was Disraeli's *The Calamities and Quarrels of Authors, with Some Inquiries Respecting their Moral and Literary Characters, and Memoirs for our Literary History* (London: Routledge, 1860; Sealts 185). Melville found himself justified as he read on. He heavily marked and underlined this: "No man is the wiser for his learning: it may administer matter to work in, or objects to work upon; but wit and wisdom are born with a man." Isaac Disraeli's *Curiosities of Literature* (London: Routledge, 1859; Sealts 186) proved to be a richly gossipy three-volume work containing many items on poetry, including Plato's description of the feelings of the poet in the *Phaedon.* Melville found confirmation for one of his deep convictions in a passage he marked and partly underlined: "Faultless mediocrity industry can preserve in one continued degree; but excellence, the daring and the happy, can only be attained, by human faculties, by starts." He found stories that may have aroused ugly memories or else have given him precedent for future actions, conspicuously an account of the poet Baron Haller's burning his manuscripts. The last Disraeli purchase from February 26, 1862, was *The Literary Character; or, The History of Men of Genius, Drawn from Their own Feelings and Confessions* (London: Routledge, 1859; Sealts 187). This richly anecdotal book, perhaps more than any other, confirmed for Melville that he was not an abnormal genius at all but on the contrary a perfectly normal literary genius. His reclusiveness was normal, for geniuses, because "prolonged solitary work" was necessary if great literary works were to be produced.

Even his unbroken industry in writing *Redburn, White-Jacket,* and the short version of *Pierre* was normal, he found, in a passage he marked heavily: "If there are not periods when they shall allow their days to melt harmoniously into each other, if they do not pass whole weeks together in their study, without intervening absences, they will not be admitted into the last recess of the Muses. Whether their glory come from researches, or from enthusiasm, time, with not a feather ruffled on his wings, time alone opens discoveries and kindles meditation. This desert of solitude, so vast and so dreary to the man of the world, to the man of genius is the magical garden of Armida, whose enchantments arose amidst solitude, while solitude was everywhere among those enchantments." Melville found here an anatomy of genius and a palliation of every domestic offense he had committed, including his neglecting "family affairs." The Disraeli volumes provided massive, infinitely varied histories of creative writers both obscure and famous, all of whom Melville could identify with one way or another. These Disraeli volumes, perhaps more than any others he ever read, allowed him to situate himself confidently in a thick context of writers. His volume of poetry had gone unpublished and unread, but he was not alone.

On March 1, 1862, Melville bought Giorgio Vasari's *Lives of the Most Eminent Painters, Sculptors, and Architects* in five volumes (London: Bohn, 1849–52; Sealts 534a). He had read Vasari earlier, in a set borrowed from Evert Duyckinck, but reread this five-volume set. Melville's notes throughout the volumes of Vasari do not reveal much about poetry directly, given Vasari's subject matter, but indirectly they reveal much, for at times he quickly applied to the art of poetry what he read about painting and sculpture. Notably, Vasari helped clarify for him the distinction between expression and form, or design. Melville was struck by Leonardo da Vinci's deliberately not manifesting the greatest "clearness of forms" but emphasizing "the great foundation of all, design" (5:385); clarity of design he saw as more important than coloring (the painterly equivalent of literary "expression"). In the third volume (23) Melville marked a passage on Raphael's imitating Michelangelo and commented: "The inimitable imitator. Good deal of the Virgil about Raphael." He may already have made the association of Virgil and Tennyson as imitators, and of course may have taken note of this passage already in 1859 in Duyckinck's copy. That is, Vasari may have influenced the passage he wrote on Tennyson and Virgil as part of the Naples poem, even if he wrote it in 1859 or early 1860. In his lives of working artists, or the working lives of artists, Vasari was fascinated by the proportion of genius to industry and of genius and industry in contrast to laziness and self-indulgence and also alert when an artist was content with less than the highest art. There was no substitute for genius, for an artist (4:65) could work "with infinite difficulty and most laborious pains-taking" without ever having the facility with which Nature and study sometimes reward those who labor and who have genius. (Reading notes Melville made in the first volume of the Vasari are discussed below.)

On March 4, 1862, Melville bought Anne Louise Germaine (Necker), Baronne de Staël's *Germany* (New York: Derby & Jackson, 1859; Sealts 487), annotating the first volume with that date but annotating the second April 1862, presumably when he got round to it. The first volume had two parts: "Of Germany, and the Manners of Germans" and "Of Literature and the Arts" (which dealt with particular writers and salient works, including separate essays on Goethe and on different works by him). The second volume concluded the section "On Literature and the Arts" and included a section on "Philosophy and Ethics" and another on "Religion and Enthusiasm." Melville read and marked parts of all four sections. Staël interested him and challenged him on philosophical and particularly on ethical issues, but she also challenged him about literary techniques and on distinctions among literary genres. Staël confirmed again what he had recognized in Disraeli, ways of accounting for his role in his family, where his legitimate artistic demands were or were not recognized and where his writerly crotchets might not be cheerfully tolerated. Like Disraeli, she helped him see his own place as a working writer. Throughout the volumes he marked sections on writers (the importance of having one's mind "developed in solitude"); on men of genius; on style; on attitudes toward art (particularly the importance of taking talent seriously and working at art painstakingly). He underlined the assertion that rhyme "is the image of hope and of memory" (the earlier sound making one hope for another, the latter making one remember the earlier). In the chapter "Of Poetry" Melville boxed this sentence: "Poetic genius is an internal disposition, of the same nature with that which renders us capable of a generous sacrifice." Staël saw Schiller's earliest works as over-fervid: "The education of life depraves the frivolous, but perfects the reflecting mind," a judgment which confirmed what Melville had read in Taylor's *Notes from Life*. In the chapter on "Wallenstein and Mary Stuart" Melville paid attention to this assertion about achieving unity: "Nothing is so easy as to compose what are called brilliant verses; there are moulds ready made for the purpose; but what is very difficult, is to render every detail subordinate to the whole, and to find every part united in the whole, as well as the reflection of the whole in every part." In "Of Style, and of Versification in the German Language" he triple-lined and checked her statement that "the effects of poetry depend still more on the melody of words than on the ideas which they serve to express," and commented: "This is measurably true of all but dramatic poetry and, perhaps, narrative verse." Melville was profoundly sympathetic with Staël's "Of Ignorance and Frivolity of Spirit in Their Relation to Ethics," where he marked this passage: "The ignorance of our days is contemptuous, and endeavors to turn into ridicule the labors and the meditations of enlightened men. The philosophical spirit has spread over almost all classes a facility of reasoning, which is used to depreciate every thing that is great and serious in human nature, and we are at that epoch of civilization in which all the beauties of the soul are mouldering into dust." He took balm from her denunciation of "our civilized barbarians" who "only instruct themselves just enough to ridicule, by a few set phrases, the meditations of a whole life." At some time Melville put these closing lines to his "Hostelry" poem: "But sprinkle, do, some drops of grace, / Nor polish us all into commonplace."[2] In *Clarel* Melville would similarly inveigh against culture debased into commonplace (e.g., at 1.34 and 4.21).

Interested throughout in generic distinctions, Melville focused on this formulation by Staël: "Lyric poetry is expressed in the name of the author himself; he no longer assumes a character, but experiences in his own person, the various emotions he describes." This presumably was what Melville had done in his "Naples" poem. Melville followed with great interest Staël's distinction between Epic and Romance. "Events like those of the Iliad interest of themselves, and the less the author's own sentiments are brought forward, the greater is the impression made by the picture; but if we set ourselves to describe romantic situations with the impartial calmness of Homer, the result would not be very alluring." Melville commented: "Admirable distinction. In the 'Idylls of the King' (Tennyson) we see the Homeric, or rather Odyssean manner pervading *romantic* stories, and the result is a kind of 'shocking tameness.'" Melville saw in Tennyson's attempt at the epic a startling, almost ludicrous sentimentalizing, romanticizing, and trivializing of characters that ought to have been mighty pageant

creatures. Tennyson in his *Idylls* was building in an aesthetic and intellectual anomaly that would shock and ultimately repel the wiser
readers. (Here Melville's writing down "shocking tameness" rather
than Cowper's "Their tameness is shocking to me" suggests that he
was remembering Thomas Hood's rewording of Cowper in "The
Haunted House" from his reading a few weeks earlier.)

Sometime in March 1862 Melville bought William Hazlitt's *Lec-
tures on the English Comic Writers* and *Lectures on the English Poets,* the two
volumes bound as one. The first volume contained these lectures: "On
Shakespeare and Ben Jonson," "On Cowley, Butler, Suckling,
Etherege, &c.," "On Wycherley, Congreve, Vanbrugh, and Farquhar,"
"On the Periodical Essayists," "On the English Novelists," "On the
Works of Hogarth," and "On the Comic Writers of the Last Century."
Melville made annotations about poetry even in the first volume, for
some of the comic writers Hazlitt treated there were poets and Hazlitt
at times expatiated explicitly on poetry. In the first lecture, "On Wit
and Humour," Melville read a passage on "the intrinsic superiority of
poetry or imagination to wit" and both marked and checked the cul-
mination of the discussion about how easy it is to mar an effect: "The
slightest want of unity of impression is an infallible ground to rest the
ludicrous upon. But in serious poetry, which aims at rivetting our af-
fections, every blow must tell home. The missing a single time is fa-
tal, and undoes the spell." In the second lecture Melville marked
quotations from John Donne and some of Hazlitt's judgments ("His
satires are too clerical. He shows, if I may so speak, too much disgust,
and, at the same time, too much contempt for vice"). Melville marked
the quotation from Cowley's "The Grasshopper" as well as this judgment: "Cowley's Essays are among the most agreeable prose compositions in our language, being equally recommended by sense, wit,
learning, and interesting personal history, and written in a style quite
free from the faults of his poetry." In the lecture on the English novelists Melville marked long sections on the *"instinct of the imagination"*
which Hazlitt said was what "stamps the character of genius on the
productions of art more than any other circumstance: for it works un-
consciously, like nature, and receives its impressions from a kind of inspiration."

Lectures on the English Poets consisted of eight lectures: "Introductory.—On Poetry in general," "On Chaucer and Spenser," "On Shakspeare and Milton," "On Dryden and Pope," "On Thomson and
Cowper," "On Swift, Young, Gray, Collins, &c.," "On Burns, and the

old English Ballads," "On the Living Poets"; and four appendices: "On Milton's Lycidas," "On the Character of Milton's Eve," "On Mr. Wordsworth's Poem, 'The Excursion,'" and "Pope, Lord Byron, and Mr. Bowles" (the Reverend W. L. Bowles, author of *Strictures on the Life and Writings of Pope*). In the introductory essay Hazlitt recurred to the lecture "On Wit and Humour" to emphasize that he was concerned with "serious" poetry. Melville marked this: "It [poetry] is not a mere frivolous accomplishment (as some persons have been led to imagine,) the trifling amusement of a few idle readers or leisure hours—it has been the study and delight of mankind in all ages." He bracketed what Hazlitt called Milton's idea of poetry, "Thoughts that voluntary move / Harmonious numbers," and underlined the word "voluntary." He checked and underlined the assertion that "Nothing is a subject for poetry that admits of a dispute." In an excursus by Hazlitt in "On Shakspeare and Milton," Melville marked this:

> The great fault of a modern school of poetry is that it is an experiment to reduce poetry to a mere effusion of natural sensibility; or, what is worse, to divest it both of imaginary splendour and human passion, to surround the meanest objects with the morbid feelings and devouring egotism of the writers' own minds. Milton and Shakspeare did not so understand poetry. They gave a more liberal interpretation both to nature and art. They did not do all they could to get rid of the one and the other, to fill up the dreary void with the Moods of their own Minds. . . . But to the men I speak of there is nothing interesting, nothing heroical, but themselves. To them the fall of gods or of great men is the same. They do not enter into the feeling. . . . They are even debarred from the last poor, paltry consolation of an unmanly triumph over fallen greatness; for their minds reject, with a convulsive effort and intolerable loathing, the very idea that there ever was, or was thought to be, anything superior to themselves.

Melville marked the whole passage, but at this point he noted: "Wordsworth was in the writer's mind here, very likely." He was beginning to define himself as a poet against Wordsworth, not against any of his younger, lesser contemporaries such as Tennyson.

Later in this third lecture Hazlitt, without identifying his source, quoted at length from "Reason of Church Government Urged Against Prelaty" Milton's early hope that he "might perhaps leave something so written to after-times as they should not willingly let it die." Melville marked the whole of Milton's magnificent passage, perhaps the greatest statement of literary ambition by any writer in the English language, and marked the subsequent quotation from Spenser on the same topic: "The noble heart that harbours virtuous thought, / And is with child of glorious great intent, / Can never rest until it forth have brought / The eternal brood of glory excellent." Milton, Hazlitt said in comment on these lines, "did not write from casual impulse, but after a severe examination of his own strength, and with a resolution to leave nothing undone which it was in his power to do. He always labours, and almost always succeeds." Shakespeare was greater: "In Milton, there is always an appearance of effort: in Shakspeare, scarcely any." Melville marked, without comment, what Hazlitt said about Milton's "spirit of partisanship" and Donne's also being "a political partisan." Melville's own firm rejection of partisanship in poetry (in his note on "Lycidas") may have been written before or after he read this passage.

In the chapter "On Thomson and Cowper" Melville triple-lined the following passage, which follows a discussion of the pleasing but humble efforts of the poet Robert Bloomfield: "It should seem from this and other instances that have occurred within the last century, that we cannot expect from original genius alone, without education, in modern and more artificial periods, the same bold and independent results as in former periods." He marked the lengthy discussion of the difficulty a modern writer, even a writer marked by original genius, has in achieving the highest excellence. In "On Swift, Young, Gray, Collins, &c.," Melville marked the passage where Hazlitt quoted someone's mockery of *Candide* (a book Melville had admiringly alluded to in *The Confidence-Man* and casually referred to in "At the Hostelry") as "the dull product of a scoffer's pen." Recognizing the source, the pugnacious passage disparaging *Candide* in the second book of *The Excursion,* Melville noted: "Wordsworth so called it." In the seventh lecture, "On Burns, and the Old English Ballads," Hazlitt condemned Wordsworth for muffing his great chance to defend the "moral character" of Burns and "the moral tendency of his writings." In "On the Living Poets," as mentioned in chapter 4 above, Melville took exception to Hazlitt's characterization of Rogers in *Pleasures of Memory* as a "a very lady-like poet," elegant but feeble, and reflected on the source: "In Hazlitt you have at times to allow for indigestion." Melville was ready to make allowances, particularly when he approved Hazlitt's judgments on Wordsworth, such as his saying that the poem of Ruth "shows little power, or power enervated by extreme fastidiousness." He approvingly underlined and triple-checked this conclusion about the weakness of Thomas Moore: "Fortitude of mind is the first requisite of a tragic or epic writer." He marked Hazlitt's characterization of Wordsworth: "the only person from whom I ever learnt anything." Melville heavily marked the last half of the stanza Hazlitt quoted from the "Ode— Intimations of Immortality" ("I do not grieve, but rather find / Strength in what remains behind; / In the primal sympathy, / Which having been, must ever be; / In the soothing thoughts that spring / Out of human suffering; / In years that bring the philosophic mind!"). For the lines "In the soothing thoughts that spring / Out of human suffering" Melville had recourse to an unusual symbol instead of his simple X in the margin—an X with each space dotted, and he wrote this note at the foot of the page: "A rigid analysis would make this sentiment appear in a different light from the one in which it is, probably, generally received. Its vagueness makes it susceptible of many interpretations; but Truth is susceptible of but one." Its vagueness made it easy for the superficial to use in sentimental and pious reassurances, made it especially useful to some of the Unitarians of Melville's acquaintance who did not take other people's suffering very seriously. Having probed deeper into the nature of human suffering than most, Melville may have felt skeptical that deeply soothing thoughts were likely to spring out of profound human suffering.

Melville may or may not have read much in this two-in-one book before making revealing notations that had nothing to do with Hazlitt.[3] Starting on the page opposite the beginning of the text in *Lectures on the English Comic Writers,* Melville entered notes on Francis Jeffrey's January 1810 *Edinburgh Review* essay on Victor Alfieri. Profoundly interested in what Jeffrey said about how Alfieri conceived a literary work, developed it, versified it, then polished, corrected, and revised it, Melville filled the page with notes from Jeffrey, then added three lines on the top of the next page, above the start of the first lecture. In his notes, reminders to himself, not exact quotations, Melville was not intent on improving his knowledge of Alfieri so much as using Jeffrey's comments to fix in his mind what he might eschew and what he might employ in his own style.

In his review-essay Jeffrey had written:

> As they [Alfieri's dramas] have not adopted the choral songs of the Greek stage . . . they are, on the whole, less poetical than those ancient compositions; although they are worked throughout with a

fine and careful hand, and diligently purified from every thing ig-
noble or feeble in the expression. The author's anxiety to keep clear
of figures of mere ostentation, and to exclude all showpieces of fine
writing in a dialogue of deep interest or impetuous passion, has betrayed him, on some occasions, into too sententious and strained a
diction, and given an air of labour and heaviness to many parts of
his composition. He has felt, perhaps a little too constantly, that the
cardinal virtue of a dramatic writer is to keep his personages to the
business and the concerns that lye before them; and by no means to
let them turn to moral philosophers, or rhetorical describers of their
own emotions. But, in his zealous adherence to this good maxim, he
seems sometime to have forgotten, that certain passions are declam-
atory in nature as well as on the stage; and that, at any rate, they do
not all vent themselves in concise and pithy sayings, but run occasionally into hyperbole and amplification. As it is the great excellence, so it is occasionally the chief fault of Alfieri's dialogue, that
every word is honestly employed to help forward the action of the
play, in serious argument, necessary narrative, or the direct expression of natural emotion. There are no excursions or digressions,—no
episodical conversations,—and none but the most brief moraliz-
ings. This gives a certain air of solidity to the whole structure of the
piece, that is apt to prove oppressive to an ordinary reader, and re-
duces the entire drama to too great uniformity.

Glancing back and forth at Jeffrey, perhaps struggling with small
type, Melville made these summary notes in his Hazlitt: "Worked
throughout with a fine and careful hand. Figures of mere ostentation.
Show-pieces of fine writing. Nature is not confined to conciseness, but
at times amplifies. Too sententious & strained a diction. The solidity
of the structure is apt to prove oppressive to the *ordinary* reader. Too
great uniformity."
Jeffrey had said this about Alfieri's dramas:

With regard to the diction of these pieces, it is not for *tramontane*
critics to presume to offer any opinion. They are considered, in Italy,
we believe, as the purest specimens of the *favella Toscana* that late
ages have produced. To us they certainly seem to want something of
that flow and sweetness to which we have been accustomed in Italian poetry, and to be formed rather upon the model of Dante than of
Petrarca. At all events, it is obvious that the style is highly elaborate
and artificial; and that the author is constantly striving to give it a
sort of factitious force and energy, by the use of condensed and em-
phatic expressions, interrogatories, antitheses, and short and inverted

sentences. In all these respects, as well as in the chastized gravity of the sentiments, and the temperance and propriety of all the delineations of passion, these pieces are exactly the reverse of what we should have expected from the fiery, fickle and impatient character of the author. From all that Alfieri has told us of himself, we should have expected to find in his plays great vehemence and irregular eloquence—sublime and extravagant sentiments—passions rising to frenzy—and poetry swelling into bombast. Instead of this, we have a subdued and concise representation of energetic discourses— passions, not loud but deep—and a style so severely correct and scrupulously pure, as to indicate, even to unskilful eyes, the great labour which must have been bestowed on its purification.

Melville extracted from that passage these notes: "Wanting flow & sweetness. Strives to give a fictitious force & energy by condensation & emphasis & inversion. Chastened [possibly "Chastized"] quality. Temperance and propriety of delineation of the passions." The use of "fictitious" is bothersome. Perhaps it was only a slip in copying, but perhaps Melville's eyes were so weak that they did not read the word right (particularly if the text he was reading was in small print, as *Modern British Essayists* was and American reprints of the *Edinburgh Review* typically were). We have to assume that he knew the word "factitious." "Chastened" is another problem because of the difficulty of being sure what Melville wrote down; perhaps he read "Chastized" correctly and copied down "Chastized." Over on the next page, Melville continued his notes: "Discerning, with a mind that has refined [this word looks more like "reposed"] from the subject the best thoughts & rejecting the dross." In Jeffrey's essay no close parallel has been found beyond the two passages on purification already quoted.

Perhaps examination of the books Melville was reading or perhaps the emergence of other documentary evidence will yet identify the point, presumably early in 1862, when Melville was reminded of Jeffrey's essay on Alfieri. If he had brought his Jeffrey volume in *Modern British Essayists* to New York City Melville would probably have made his notes in the Alfieri essay in that volume, despite its intimidatingly small margins. Melville could easily have borrowed the Jeffrey essay in a collection or in a reprint of the *Edinburgh Review.* The American authority on Alfieri was Henry T. Tuckerman, whom Melville had called on late in 1861, who had been trying to get hold of him early in the year, and who in all likelihood found his way to Melville early in 1862, soon after Melville settled into the rented house. A parallel example of making notes on one volume in another volume is Melville's elaborate notes in the seventh volume of his Shakespeare from an article in the July 1823 London *Quarterly Review* on the persecution of witches. He took those notes sometime before finishing *Moby-Dick* and presumably wrote them down in his Shakespeare because he could not keep possession of the copy of the magazine he was using. Another close parallel is his taking detailed notes from the third volume of Ruskin's *Modern Painters* in his Vasari (see below).

On March 17, 1862, Melville bought Heinrich Heine's *The Poems of Heine* (London: Bohn, 1861; Sealts 268). Later, apparently, perhaps after he read Swinburne's *Mary Stuart* (1881), Melville made a note on Heine's "Clarissa": "Swinburne's inspiration is tracable distantly in some of these things,—Especially in Queen Mary."

Reminded of Abraham Cowley by Taylor, Hazlitt, and other writers, on March 21, 1862, Melville bought an early three-volume set of Cowley (London: Tonson, 1707, and Charles Harper, 1711; Sealts 160a). In the preface to the first volume he marked a passage on men becoming poets for life and on the times (civil war or peace), moods, conditions, in which men may write poetry. Melville triple-checked "On the Death of Mr. Crashaw," the "Poet and Saint," and marked the tolerant passage on how Richard Crashaw (who became a Catholic) may harmlessly have diverged from Cowley's *"Mother Church"*: "His *Faith* perhaps in some nice Tenets might / Be wrong; his *Life,* I'm sure, was *in the right*" (1:44). Melville footnoted: " 'He can't be wrong whose life is in the right.' Pope," recognizing that Pope had borrowed from Cowley in the *Essay on Man,* epistle 3, section 6, where Pope had decried religious partisanship and concluded that one's particular modes of faith "can't be wrong whose life is in the right." In *The Mistress,* the subsection on "The Prophet" (1:113), Melville marked what Cowley boasted that he would teach the God of Love: "I'll teach him things he never knew before; / I'll teach him a *Receipt* to make / *Words* that *weep,* and *Tears* that *speak.*" Melville noted: "Thoughts that breathe and words that burn," having recognized Thomas Gray's borrowing in "The Progress of Poesy." Melville regularly paid close attention to English poets when they wrote about poems about poetry. By "The Inconstant" (1:153) Melville wrote "Sheridan's Song," meaning "Here's to the maiden of bashful fifteen," a song from *School for Scandal* (3.1) plainly suggested by this Cowley poem. In stanza 6 of the "Second Olympique Ode of Pindar" (1:189), Melville marked a passage on a topic he was brooding about: "Greatness of *Mind* and *Fortune* too / Th'

Olympique Trophies shew. / Both their several Parts must do / In the noble *Chase* of *Fame*, / This without that is *blind,* that without this is
lame." In "Destiny" (1:228) he marked the Muse's injunction to Cowley that he should be content "with the small *barren Praise* / That neglected *Verse* does raise." In the ode "To Dr. Scarborough" (1:237) he
triple-checked "When all's done, *Life is an Incurable Disease*" and wrote
"Pope"—reminded of "long disease, my life" in "An Epistle to Dr. Ar-
buthnot." (Later, in the prose discourse "Of Liberty" [2:682], Melville
marked Cowley's "the Epidemical Disease of Life" without mention-
ing Pope.) In the long "Davideis, A Sacred Poem of the Troubles of
David," taking music as involving song, or poetry, Melville marked a
passage in the first book (1:305–6) on the power of music to soothe
Saul. As in Collins's later ode, the singer of verses was a creator imitating God the Creator: "As first a various unform'd *Hint* we
find / Rise in some god-like *Poet*'s fertile *Mind,* / 'Till all the Parts and
Words their Places take, / And with just Marches *Verse* and *Musick*
make; / Such was *God's Poem,* this *World*'s new *Essay;* / So wild and rude
in its first Draught it lay; / Th'ungovern'd Parts no *Correspondence*
knew, / An artless *War* from thwarting *Motions* grew; / 'Till they to
Number and fixt Rules were brought / By the *eternal Mind's Poetick
Thought.*" In the discourse "Of Agriculture" (2:714) Cowley described
Virgil's portrayal of Evander's welcoming Aeneas into his "rustick
Court." Recognizing the passage, Melville noted: " 'Dare to be poor'
Dryden's Æneid." (The reference is in book 8 of the *Aeneid.*) In the essay "Of My Self" (2:782) Melville double-checked passages about the
importance of Cowley's reading Spenser early—reading all of
Spenser's poetry before he was twelve years old. Twelve, as it happens,
may have been Herman's age when he first read Spenser (see Parker
1:72–73). Melville marked much of the last portion of the preface to
"Cutter of Coleman-Street." At the end (2:[800]) he drew a box
around this assertion of Cowley's: *"That from all which I have written I
never receiv'd the least Benefit, or the least Advantage, but, on the contrary,
have felt sometimes the Effects of Malice and Misfortune."* He footnoted:
"How few will credit this; nevertheless how true, one doubts not, said
by a man like Cowley."

On March 22, 1862, Melville bought Ralph Waldo Emerson's
Essays, Second Series (Boston: Munroe, 1844; Sealts 205). He already
knew some of Emerson's essays from his reading at the Hawthorne
cottage in 1850, and his young brother-in-law Sam Shaw on a visit to
Arrowhead in the summer of 1859 had brought him a copy of the

1858 edition of Emerson's *Poems*. Now in 1862 in reading Emerson's essays Melville raged against the Unitarian coldness toward human suffering which he recognized in the Transcendentalist, the former Unitarian minister. When he came upon Emerson's assertion that the poet "disposes very easily of the most disagreeable facts," Melville retorted sarcastically, "So it would seem. In this sense Mr E. is a great poet." Melville could never relax for long with Emerson: some dunderheaded blindness to human suffering would jolt him out of his admiration. He marked the passage in "The Poet" where Emerson described the low and plain way in which the poet should live ("the air should suffice for his inspiration, and he should be tipsy with water") and footnoted his partial agreement: "This makes the Wordsworthian poet—not the Shakespearian." As he read during these weeks in New York City, Wordsworth was more and more the great modern poet against whom he was steadily defining himself.

In April 1862 Melville bought Charles Churchill's *The Poetical Works . . . With Copious Notes and a Life of the Author* (Boston: Little, Brown, 1854; Sealts 144). In Churchill's "Gotham" he could have seen many mentions of the pains poets must take, a recurrent subject in this season's reading. In "The Author" Melville marked these bitter lines: "Much are the precious hours of youth misspent / In climbing learning's rugged steep ascent; / When to the top the bold adventurer's got, / He reigns vain monarch o'er a barren spot, / Whilst in the vale of ignorance below / Folly and vice to rank luxuriance grow; / Honours and wealth pour in on every side, / And proud preferment rolls her golden tide." Melville wrote: "Wordsworth."

During all the time he read in these early months of 1862, Wordsworth was the poet most prominent in Melville's mind as his modern predecessor, the one he envied for his tenure as poet laureate and other honors and was contemptuous of for Wordsworth's own contempt for ordinary people (ironic in view of the subject matter of much of his poetry). Chances are that Melville, as surmised above, knew the interview with Wordsworth in 1833 which Orville Dewey had recorded in his *Old World and the New* (New York: Harper & Brothers, 1836). Dewey had lectured the poet, but allowed him a few phrases: "He thought there could be no independence in legislators who were dependant for their places upon the ever wavering breath of popular opinion." Acknowledging Dewey's declaration that there was no stopping "political liberty," that in the civilized world "the course of opinion was irresistibly setting towards universal education and popular forms of government," Wordsworth had seen "nothing but darkness, disorder, and misery in the immediate prospect," so that "all he could do was to cast himself on Providence." Melville himself could be ironically contemptuous of the "independent electors" in the infant United States, but he was repulsed by the disdain shown by the elderly Wordsworth. Melville's introduction to criticism on Wordsworth had come in the massive Carey and Hart compendium, *Modern British Essayists,* and he had kept on reading about Wordsworth, if not often rereading the poems in his volume of Wordsworth or seeking out late-published volumes. At some time he read the prose supplements in his Wordsworth with some care, and in 1869 or later he marked lines quoted from *The Prelude* in Matthew Arnold's *Essays in Criticism* (Boston: Ticknor & Fields, 1865; Sealts 17): "The marble index of a mind forever / Voyaging through strange seas of Thought, alone." Even in 1862, Melville never failed to acknowledge the grandeur of Wordsworth's early achievements, but he never warmed to the man as he did to so many other poets.

On April 3, 1862, Melville bought Henry Kirke White's *The Poetical Works and Remains* (New York: Appleton, 1857; Sealts 556). Melville marked a passage in "Warton: Remarks on the English Poets" on the damage Pope and his imitators had done by introducing

> a species of refinement into our language, which has banished that nerve and pathos for which Milton had rendered it eminent. Harmonious modulations, and unvarying exactness of measure, totally precluding sublimity and fire, have reduced our fashionable poetry to mere singsong. But Thomas Warton, whose taste was unvitiated by the frivolities of the day, immediately saw the intrinsic worth of what the world then slighted. He saw that the ancient poets contained a fund of strength, and beauty of imagery as well as diction, which in the hands of genius would shine forth with redoubled lustre. Entirely rejecting, therefore, modern niceties, he extracted the honied sweets from these beautiful, though neglected flowers. Every grace of sentiment, every poetical term, which a false taste had rendered obsolete, was by him revived and made to grace his own ideas; and though many will condemn him as guilty of plagiarism, yet few will be able to withhold the tribute of their praise.

Once again Melville was rejecting mere excellence of technique, mere polish. Nothing he attempted would preclude "sublimity and fire" any more than it would eschew what Henry Taylor called "intrepidity of impulse."

According to Merton M. Sealts Jr. (1988, 168), Raymond Weaver reported seeing Melville's copy of *The Poetical Works of William Collins* (dated April 1862), in the 1854 Boston: Little, Brown edition (Sealts 156). On May 19, 1862, Melville gave a copy of Collins's poetry, bound with some Shakespeare (London: Cooke, 17—; Sealts 464), to his sister Fanny, along with the Cooke edition of Shenstone and Thomson. He must have known, long before 1862, the odes, including the "Ode on the Poetical Character" with its echo of Cowley on God and the poet as creators.

On April 6, 1862, Melville made one of the most important of his 1862 purchases, Matthew Arnold's *Poems* (Boston: Ticknor & Fields, 1856; Sealts 21). Reading Arnold, like reading Hazlitt, helped focus Melville's feelings about Wordsworth. He read Arnold's "Obermann" in the light of Wordsworth and Goethe. Asking if Obermann is unpopular because of a pain too sharp that underlies his calm, Arnold looks at the two greatest poets of his time—Wordsworth still living as he writes, Goethe buried at Weimar—and identifies their failures: "Wordsworth's eyes avert their ken / From half of human fate; / And Goethe's course few sons of men / May think to emulate." Melville noted: "True as to Wordsworth. Of Goethe it might also be said that he averted his eyes from everything except Nature, Intellect, & Beauty." Having read enough of "The Youth of Nature" to understand what the subject was, Melville rejoiced at the aptness of Arnold's opening, "Rais'd are the dripping oars— / Silent the boat." The oars are raised above the waters of Windermere (unnamed) in tribute to Wordsworth. Melville at once saw the literary allusions. In "Ode on the Death of Thomson. The Scene on the Thames near Richmond" (1749), Collins had written words that Melville now wrote down: "and oft suspend the dashing oar / to bid his gentle spirit rest." This poem had been particularly mentioned on page xiv of the 1854 edition of Collins Melville owned, in the "Memoir" composed from the researches of Alexander Dyce. Then Wordsworth in "Remembrance of Collins. Composed upon the Thames near Richmond" (1798), a poem unmarked in Melville's copy of Wordsworth's *Poetical Works,* had returned the compliment: "Now let us, as we float along / For *him* suspend the dashing oar." Melville commented: "How beautifully appropriate therefor this reminiscent prelude of Arnold concerning Wordsworth," a clear example of Melville's alertness to literary echoes and re-echoes. By now he was about as close as one could get to being an ideal reader of poetry.

Arnold's preface, which had first appeared in the 1853 edition, as
an aesthetic document was taken seriously by Arnold's and Melville's
contemporaries, and within a generation was ranked with some of
Dryden's and Wordsworth's theoretical treatises. Among Victorian
aesthetic documents, it was almost on a par with the third, 1856 volume of Ruskin's *Modern Painters,* which may have been indebted to it,
although what is similar in them may be their mutual indebtedness to
Aristotle. Whatever Melville thought of Arnold's poems, he recognized the writer of the "Preface" as a thinker worth grappling with, although at moments showing an ameliorative spirit too near to
Emerson's. When Arnold quoted Schiller as saying that all Art is
"'dedicated to Joy',," Melville retorted: "The 'Laocoon' is not dedicated to Joy, neither is 'Hamlet.' Yet there is a degree of truth in this,
only it don't imply that the subjects of true Art must be joyful
subjects.—Schiller was at once helped & hurt by Goethe. This saying
is a Schillerized Goethecism." Melville marked and underlined
Arnold's insistence on "the all-importance of the choice of a subject,"
scored what Arnold said about "one moral impression left by a great
action treated as a whole," marked the qualities Arnold praised in
classical works ("their intense significance, their noble simplicity, and
their calm pathos"), underlined the warning against "the jargon of
modern criticism," and heavily checked and marked this sentence: "If
they are endeavoring to practise any art, they remember the plain and
simple proceedings of the old artists, who attained their grand results
by penetrating themselves with some noble and significant action, not
by inflating themselves with a belief in the preëminent importance
and greatness of their own times." Melville also marked a passage
quoting Goethe on two kinds of dilettanti in poetry: "he who neglects
the indispensable mechanical part, and thinks he has done enough if
he show spirituality and feeling; and he who seeks to arrive at poetry
merely by mechanism . . . without soul and matter."

Melville took Arnold as a friendly interpreter of Greek theories of
tragedy, paying attention to what Arnold said about greater actions
and nobler personages, as in this passage: "For what reason was the
Greek tragic poet confined to so limited a range of subjects? Because
there are so few actions which unite in themselves, in the highest degree, the conditions of excellence. . . . A few actions, therefore, eminently adapted for tragedy, maintained almost exclusive possession of
the Greek tragic stage." Arnold quoted from Aristotle, "All depends
upon the subject." The ancients had subordinated expression to ac-

tion; the moderns did the reverse, to the detriment of their art. Throughout the essay Melville also focused upon Arnold's allusions to "expression"—"a certain baldness of expression in Greek tragedy"; Shakespeare's "wonderful gift of expression," particularly in a summation of three things for a modern writer to learn from the ancients: "the all-importance of the choice of a subject; the necessity of accurate construction; and the subordinate character of expression." Melville responded profoundly to the peroration, in which Arnold discounted modern chauvinism and argued that serious poets, steeped in the past, will not "talk of their mission, nor of interpreting their age, nor of the coming Poet."

Reading Arnold's "Preface" brought Melville toward the end of his prolonged phase of gathering and testing ideas on aesthetics and particularly on what constitutes literary greatness. At last he was ready to begin distilling what he had been learning for months and to integrate those ideas with his own long-held convictions based on his own experience as a reader and writer. The sequence is in doubt, as with so much of Melville's reading and annotating during early 1862, but at some time, probably while he was in New York City, away from his own bookshelves so that he had to buy or borrow books or consult them in a library (the Astor Library shows no use by him for this period), he got hands on Ruskin's *Modern Painters.* The likelihood is that Melville used a borrowed copy of Ruskin rather than the set which he acquired no earlier than 1865, since he made notes on it in the Vasari he had acquired on March 1 (see below). In the later set which he is known to have owned he did not mark the passages he took notes on in the Vasari, having, it may be, already absorbed those passages. Quite possibly Melville had found Arnold's ideas stimulating enough to be discussed with his friend Tuckerman, who then loaned him the Ruskin. Tuckerman in 1862 had a good run of Ruskin. Four volumes of the 1856–60 edition of *Modern Painters,* including the third volume published in 1856, were auctioned from his estate in June 1872 along with these volumes: *Unto this last; Four essays on the first principles of political economy* (1866); *Sesame and lilies* (1866); *The stones of Venice, with illustrations on wood* (1860); *The mystery of life and its arts* (1869); *Lectures on architecture and painting* (1854?); *The political economy of art* (1858); *The queen of the air; being a study of the Greek myths of cloud and storm* (1869); *The two paths; being lectures on art, and its application to decoration and manufacture* (1859); and *The ethics of the dust* (1866).[4]

It would seem likely that Melville read Arnold before Ruskin because if he had read Ruskin first he would have marked similar phrasing when he found it in the Arnold, his 1862 copy of which survives. There could be other reasons for Melville's making his notes from Ruskin in his Vasari, and nothing ties the notes to 1862 except the fact that the subject matter of the earlier notes are very close to the subject matter of the Arnold preface and the topics in the latter notes in the Vasari are quite close to other topics Melville was reading and annotating in this intense session of reading in early 1862.

As Scott Norsworthy discovered in 2006,[5] most of Melville's notes on the flyleaf of his Vasari are from Ruskin's *Modern Painters* (mainly in the 1856 third volume). Wanting to make notes on literary greatness where he could consult them over and over again, Melville turned to a work he had bought in March. On the recto of the front flyleaf of the first volume of his set of Vasari he wrote: "Attain the highest result.—" He was quoting verbatim from a footnote in Ruskin's second volume of *Modern Painters*. The next note is verbatim from the third volume of *Modern Painters,* "A quality of Grasp.—" After reading Ruskin's section on "Choice of Noble Subject" (where he wrote of "the habitual choice of subjects" and the "habitual choice of sacred subjects"), Melville jotted down in the Vasari: "The habitual choice of noble subjects.—" In the Vasari Melville wrote down the single word "Expression," probably having in mind Ruskin's emphasis on the "perfect unison of expression" with "the full and natural exertion" of a painter's pictorial power in the details of a work. He apparently was not referring to "expression" as Arnold used it, as a weaker quality than action. Some of Arnold's 1853 phrases may have suggested some of Ruskin's 1856 phrases: "great human action"; "a noble action"; "the all-importance of the choice of a subject"; the fact that the old artists "attained their grand results by penetrating themselves with some noble and significant action." In any case, phrases Melville read (and sometimes marked) in Arnold were close to phrases he copied down from Ruskin—close enough to suggest that there was some connection between his buying and reading Arnold and his getting hold of a copy of Ruskin.

After "Expression" Melville wrote: "Get in as much as you can.— / Finish is completeness, fulness, not polish.—" There is "a meritorious finish," Ruskin had said, "but that finish does not consist in smoothing or polishing, but in the *completeness of the expression of ideas.*" Melville continued, drawing on Ruskin's "On the Real Nature of Greatness of Style," section 18: "Greatness is a matter of scale,—/ Clearness

& firmness.— / The greatest number of the greatest ideas.—" Next Melville focused on Ruskin's saying that "the greatness or smallness of a man is, in the most conclusive sense, determined for him at his birth." Education, Ruskin said, and "favourable circumstances, resolution, and industry can do much," but could never make "great man out of small." The idea that aesthetic finish was fullness and not polish had been held by Melville for many years (witness in chap. 32 of *Moby-Dick* his tribute to the builders of the cathedral of Cologne). At this point Melville stopped making verbatim or near-verbatim notes and began paraphrasing more loosely and elaborating what he had been learning, and not only from Ruskin: "Greatness is determined for a man at his birth. There is no *making* oneself great, in any act or art. But there is such a thing as the development of greatness— prolonged, painful, and painstaking." Earlier Melville had marked in Disraeli's *Calumnies and Quarrels* that learning made no man wiser: "[W]it and wisdom are born with a man." Greatness was determined at birth. Melville had also, for months now, been marking terms like pains and painstaking as he tried to weigh the significance of hard application in the production of art, such as Thomas Moore's self-description, and was using such terms, as in his defense of Samuel Rogers against William Hazlitt as "a painstaking man of talent." In the Vasari itself Melville may already have noticed passages such as one he marked in the fourth volume on Sebastiano's performing "all that he did with infinite difficulty and most laborious pains-taking." Now at last Melville was summing up the disparate injunctions and admonitions he had been absorbing (and had been testing against his own experience) and was able to jot down, in a place where he could keep it, an integrated aesthetic credo.

If indeed he made his notes from Jeffrey in his Hazlitt and his notes from Ruskin in his Vasari during his session of study in New York City in 1862, then Melville's aesthetic investigations of the previous months came to a satisfying conclusion: he had done his winter's research and reflection, and was ready to go home to Arrowhead. In "At the Hostelry" he said that Claude Lorraine wisely refused to waver in aesthetic theory's "wildering maze"; instead, he haunted the hazy Arcadian woods, pursuing Beauty. This winter Melville was not wavering in theory's wildering maze: he had distilled practical advice from people who had thought seriously about aesthetic issues, and at the end of his quest he had defined his own aesthetic credo.

CHAPTER ELEVEN

Battle-Pieces and Aspects of the War: Melville's Second Volume of Poems

AFTER HE RETURNED TO ARROWHEAD IN THE LAST WEEK OF APRIL 1862, laden with his fresh plunder from the New York booksellers, Melville gave away some of his books of poetry. On May 15 he inscribed to his sister Helen the five-volume set of Spenser he had procured only a year earlier. Uniquely, she took the trouble to start copying into it his marginalia from their father's eight-in-four set of Spenser, which Melville at some point gave Augusta.[1] On May 19 Melville gave his sister Fanny his Cooke editions of Shakespeare and Collins (bound together) and of Shenstone and of Thomson. He was not depriving himself: he kept his beloved 1849 set of Shakespeare and his newly purchased edition of Collins; he kept the Thomson he purchased in 1861, and in various collections he probably had all the Shenstone he needed. Now that he had found a satisfying aesthetic credo and had identified historical precedents for his status as a literary genius living in obscurity, Melville's giving away some duplicate books of poetry may have been a way of clearing the deck for a new stage in his creative life.

Judging from a letter he wrote his brother Tom on May 25, 1862, Melville was not only giving away books of poetry but also putting away some of his own poetic manuscripts. Counting on Tom to know the difference between Byron's *Don Juan* and the Bible, he humorously advised corporal punishment for hapless lads on the *Meteor:* "Strap them, I beseech you. You remember what the Bible says: 'Oh ye who teach the children of the nations,/Holland, France, England, Germany or Spain,/I pray ye *strap* them upon all occasions,/It mends their morals; never mind the pain.'" Melville went on, in a passage mentioned earlier:

Since I have quoted poetry above, it puts me in mind of my own doggerel. You will be pleased to learn that I have disposed of a lot of it at a great bargain. In fact, a trunk-maker took the whole stock off my hands at ten cents the pound. So, when you buy a new trunk again, just peep at the lining & perhaps you may be rewarded by some glorious stanza stareing you in the face & claiming admiration. If you were not such a devel of a ways off, I would send you a trunk, by way of presentation-copy. I cant help thinking what a luckless chap you were that voyage you had a poetaster with you. You remember the romantic moonlight night, when the conceited donkey repeated to you about three cables' length of his verses. But you bore it like a hero. I cant in fact recall so much as a single *wince.* [Melville was punning on a sailor-pronunciation of *wince,* or windlass, which could make light work of long cables.] To be sure, you went to bed immediately upon the conclusion of the entertainment; but this much I am sure of, whatever were your sufferings, you never gave them utterance. Tom, my boy, I admire you. I say again, you are a hero.—By the way, I hope in God's name, that rumor which reached your owners (C & P.) a few weeks since—that dreadful rumor is not true. They heard that you had begun to take to—— drink?—Oh no, but worse——to sonnet-writing. That off Cape Horn instead of being on deck about your business, you devoted your time to writing a sonnet on your mistress' eyebrow, & another upon her "tournure".—"I'll be damned" says Curtis (he was very profane) "if I'll have a sonneteer among my Captains."—"Well, if he has taken to poetizing," says Peabody—["]God help the ship!"—I have written them contradicting the rumor in your name. What villian & secret enemy of yours set this cursed report afloat, I cant imagine.

After this loving self-mockery and teasing, Melville posed a new question—"Do you want to hear about the war?"—and followed it with a few lines of ironic extravaganza similar to what he wrote to Gansevoort in 1846, at the outbreak of the war against Mexico. In the tall tale of his selling his manuscripts to a trunk-maker Melville was putting an end to the first phase of his career as a poet, but giving no sign that his next poetry would be about the war.

No one familiar with literary conventions would take this letter to Tom as a literal announcement that Melville had sold his poetic manuscripts to a trunk-maker, but it may be an oblique fashion of announcing that he was destroying some of his poetic manuscripts. More likely, he was putting away manuscripts, including the poems that had been in the rejected volume and any he had written on the voyage with Tom or later, such as the lines on Garibaldi that he added to the Naples poem and later moved to "At the Hostelry." Melville may simply have put his poetic manuscripts so far out of sight that he did not begin to sort through them again until a decade and a half later. Early in 1877 he sent "The Age of the Antonines" to Hoadley with the disclaimer "I send you something I found the other day—came across it—in a lot of papers. I remember that the lines were suggested by a passage in Gibbon (Decline & Fall)." (In this usage a "lot" is a discrete batch, like an auctioneer's lot, not necessarily a large batch.) When he wrote Hoadley, months after the humiliating failure of *Clarel,* Melville was pulling himself together to continue his career as a poet. Within a few more weeks, he published some poetry which has never been identified and is known only by his sister Fanny's query to their cousin Kate Gansevoort Lansing (Mrs. Abraham Lansing): "Ever so much love for Abe. Did he receive the paper containing those lines by Herman?" (Parker 2:816). (In the family correspondence, "lines" meant lines of poetry and, as used here, "paper" meant a newspaper, postal regulations and cheap rates allowing one member of the family to send an issue of a newspaper to another when it contained something of special interest.) Recently retrieved from a pile of old manuscripts, and then recently copied out once already for Hoadley, the poetry Melville published in 1877 could well have been "The Age of the Antonines." It may yet be found in a newspaper, printed there perhaps around two decades after it was written and a decade and a half before it appeared in *Timoleon.*

In the middle of 1862, when the war was continuing far longer than anyone had predicted, Melville seems to have hesitated before moving on to the next phase of his career as a poet. Fanny on April 1, 1862, had written their cousin Kate Gansevoort about Kate's younger brother, Henry, wanting to know what company he was in so she could follow him in the papers as he moved about.[2] Nothing suggests that Melville followed the fortunes of his friends and kinsmen as assiduously as Fanny was prepared to do with Cousin Henry, but the war was inescapable. His brother-in-law Sam Shaw described his and Melville's driving and walking in the Berkshires as being interspersed with much news of the war. Later in 1862, when Melville's first cousin Guert Gansevoort was court-martialed for being drunk and wrecking his ship, Allan was one of Guert's comforters, so everyone in the family must have had private information to supplement what they read in the papers. The other Gansevoort cousin, Henry, was not taking a role in the war comparable to those the Hero of the Tea Party (Herman's Melvill grandfather) and the Hero of Fort Stanwix (Herman and Henry's Gansevoort grandfather) had taken in the Revolutionary War. If no grandson of the Heroes would equal or surpass their military exploits, might their quieter cousin record the war in poetry? Arnold had insisted on the importance of a poet's choosing a great action and Ruskin had directed him to noble subjects, but Melville may not have been ready to take up the present "noble and significant action" in his own time and his own country.

A bit of evidence that Melville may have been thinking of writing war poetry is his possible purchase of a book hastily written and hastily published by an old acquaintance, Richard Grant White: *National Hymns. How They Are Written and How They are Not Written: A Lyric and National Study for the Times.* White dated the preface September 16, 1861, just before the book was printed, so Melville could have bought it during his stay in New York City later that year or his longer stay in 1862. In 1922, when forging a Melville item was hardly worthwhile (although forgers had been at work on Melville even earlier), the reputable Anderson Galleries sold what purported to be a presentation copy of *National Hymns* from him to the musician Fanny M. Raymond (Sealts 556.1b). No one has reported seeing this book since 1922, and there is no other record of Melville's knowing this woman, who moved, as far as we know, in Manhattan circles that did not overlap with his own narrow circuit. If Melville in fact bought this book, he may have been misled by the title, for it was about what White, in curmudgeonly mode, saw as the necessity, after the outbreak of war, to choose a national song because, according to White's prolonged, contradictory rant, the extremely popular "Star Spangled Banner" had proved "almost useless" as "a patriotic song for the people at large." The book was not about putting the war into poetry.

People Melville knew were writing about the war very early, in prose. One of his closest literary friends, Henry T. Tuckerman, put the date July 1861 on the introduction to his *The Rebellion: Its Latent Causes and True Significance. In Letters to a Friend Abroad* (New York: James G. Gregory, 1861). A few months later, Tuckerman was seeking Melville out; and Melville, given a look at the *Rebellion* pamphlet, would have found much to stir him, not least the reference to an event that transpired while he was in Pittsfield—New Yorkers' hearing "the bugle charge which proclaimed Garibaldi's invincible forays under the

walls of Rome, wake the peaceful echoes of the Astor Library."
Garibaldi's own flag, fresh from the siege of Rome, had been "presented to the Garibaldi Guard, in Lafayette Place, New York, when
the regiment marched to the bugle charge of their Italian hero." Situ-
ated on Lafayette Place, the Astor Library, visited by Melville and
members of his family before, during, and after the war, had rever-
berated with martial music. Melville would have found many of
Tuckerman's arguments worth pondering and discussing, and the
wide-ranging pamphlet gives a good idea of some topics of their conversations, although, always, art and literature would have been on
both their minds. Still, his imperfect health and stressful family life
would have postponed any literary response to his friend's pamphlet.

After mid-fall of 1862 any thought Melville had of putting the
war into a book (whether consisting of "doggerel" or lofty new poetry)
would have been hampered if not thwarted by domestic disruptions.
Tacitly admitting that he was now unable to run the farm successfully,
Melville moved his family into a rented house on South Street in
Pittsfield, all but emptying Arrowhead. His severe injury in a carriage
accident in November 1862, at the end of the move, put a halt to his
creative life for a considerable duration. Over the next months he
made a slow recovery but his body was never again as strong as it had
been. Weak or not, Melville in 1863 witnessed war preparations in
Pittsfield and in visits to New York City, and went out at night to
witness one great public demonstration, the celebration of the victo-
ries at Gettysburg and Vicksburg. Besides enduring physical pain
from the accident and confusion in his living space, Melville experienced a series of private traumas, great or small. The negotiations and
sale of Arrowhead to Allan in May 1863, on terms distinctly in Allan's
favor, may have been severely traumatic, for Melville was raiding
Lizzie's inheritance to purchase Allan's now-shabby Twenty-sixth
Street house. In 1863, also, his friends David Davidson and George L.
Duyckinck died a day apart in March, and throughout the early fall
Sarah Morewood fought to stay active but at last collapsed and died.
Late in the year, in October, Melville himself was uncharacteristically
"busy with his house" (Allan's former house on Twenty-sixth Street)
while his wife was living in the chaos of South Street.[3]

Another writer might not necessarily have needed access to his library for planning a book of war poems, but Melville liked to have his
books around him and needed a writing desk (to the point of wiping
off one speckled with chicken droppings, so he could dash off an essay

on Hawthorne). From late 1862, when he moved to South Street, Melville most likely did not have anything like normal access to his library. Late in 1863 the Melvilles not only moved to New York but moved again in New York, after their possessions had to be left temporarily at Allan's new house before being moved to Twenty-sixth Street, where most of the Civil War poems were presumably written. When Duyckinck sent him a book to review in December 1863, just as the family was becoming settled, Melville replied (December 31): "As for scribbling anything about it, tho' I would like to please you, I have not spirit enough." The successive moves had been traumatic, not having all his books at hand had been disrupting and frustrating, and Melville was damaged physically and psychologically all through 1863. Tempting as it is to think that he must have been writing war poems all along, there is no hard evidence that Melville wrote any of his Civil War poems in 1861, 1862, or 1863.

Yet by early 1864, at the latest, Melville was writing about the war, even if he had still not set himself the grander role of putting the war into a book of poetry. The evidence comes only several weeks after his refusing to scribble anything for Duyckinck. In a printed circular dated February 5, 1864, Alexander Bliss and John P. Kennedy asked many writers to contribute a manuscript for a volume benefiting union hospital work, *Autograph Leaves of our Country's Authors.* It is not known if Melville received the invitation in February or not until several weeks later, so it is impossible to tell how soon he acted on the request. Presumably following directions in a lost personal note accompanying the printed request, Melville around mid-March submitted to Bliss a poetic manuscript, "Inscription / For the Slain / At Fredericksburgh." On March 22 he wrote again, apologizing for having blundered "the other day" by sending "an uncorrected draught— in fact, the *wrong sheet.*" Copies of the book, printed from the "uncorrected draught," were available by April 9, 1864. Except for the verses in *Mardi* and perhaps some verses in other prose works, this was Melville's first appearance in print as a poet.

In *Battle-Pieces* Melville did not republish the poem from *Autograph Leaves,* in any version, although he recast a line ("Death to the brave's a starry night") for the last lines of "Chattanooga" ("Life was to these a dream fulfilled, / And death a starry night"). He did include in the book sixteen other "Verses Inscriptive and Memorial." Several of these memorialize the slain and battlefields of 1861–63, so by early 1864 Melville may have already composed a number of such "Inscriptions."

Being brief by their nature and taking only a matter of minutes or hours to compose after reading newspaper or magazine accounts, the inscriptions might naturally have been among those written while Melville's living situation was unsettled and before he had a fuller sense of what kinds of war poems he might write. His placing the group to the back of *Battle-Pieces* ("relegating" may be more appropriate than "placing") could reflect his awareness that some of them were somewhat older than poems in the body of the book.

By April 8, 1864, Allan Melville, at least, was behaving as if he thought Herman would write about the war. Seeking a pass for him and Herman to visit their cousin Henry Gansevoort in camp in Virginia, Allan asked Richard Lathers to write Secretary of War Edwin M. Stanton "introducing Herman & stating his wish, as a literary man he might be favored." Allan specified, "such men should have opportunities to see that they may describe" (Parker 2:562–63). Stanton issued the pass, and Melville made his visit, during which he took part in a raid against the great guerrilla fighter John S. Mosby. Overtired and overexposed to the cold nights, Melville did not write about his experience immediately, but within a few weeks or months he may have made the best of his opportunity by writing his longest war poem, "The Scout toward Aldie."

In the prefatory note to *Battle-Pieces* Melville made this flat statement about when he wrote the poems: "With few exceptions, the Pieces in this volume originated in an impulse imparted by the fall of Richmond"—which occurred on April 3, 1865. By December 1865 or January 1866 Melville had enough poems in hand for him to arrange for their publication in a book, if in fact the anonymous publication of "The March to the Sea" on two full pages of the February issue of *Harper's New Monthly Magazine* (out in late January) means that Melville had already arranged that poems be published in the magazine before the book was brought out. In the March issue the Harpers published "The Cumberland"; in the April issue, "Philip"; in the June issue, "Chattanooga"; and in the July issue "Gettysburg." At least one poem, "Lee in the Capitol," had not been thought of when Melville arranged for book publication. It is based on Robert E. Lee's testimony before the Reconstruction Committee of Congress on February 17, 1866. Publication of the testimony was long delayed, and only after the Washington *National Intelligencer* printed it on March 28 was it rapidly picked up by New York papers. Two or three months after finishing the Lee poem, by early summer of 1866, appalled at the fury of Radical Republicans intent on punishing the South, Melville decided he had to add a prose "Supplement." On June 30, 1866, at the Astor Library he consulted a book identified by a staff member in the library's "Daily Record" as "Secret Debate" (that is, Chittenden's *A Report of . . . the Secret Sessions,* mentioned earlier) to get back in mind some of the arguments used by people he knew and others who hoped to appease the South (Olsen-Smith and Sealts 143.2). In August 1865 *Harper's* had reviewed John W. Draper's *Thoughts on the Future Civil Policy of America* (New York: Harper, [1865]; Sealts 190), but Melville waited a year, until July 11, 1866, to buy it. Going by the title, or perhaps attracted by Draper's mention of Machiavelli, who was on his own mind, Melville may have hoped it would help him with the "Supplement," but much of it had been delivered as lectures early in 1865, before Reconstruction was under way, and he probably found little use for it.

Printed sources tell little or nothing about the chronology of the composition of Melville's war poems. While he consulted some books toward the end, it was newspaper reports which provided the basis for many of the poems. Through much of 1861, the second half of 1862, and almost all of 1863 Melville had only irregular access to a range of New York and Boston papers, mainly during his stays in New York and his briefer visits to Allan. Throughout the war Allan subscribed to several newspapers, but nothing indicates that Melville ever borrowed any of them. Surviving stacks of Allan's Civil War–era papers which surfaced in the 1990s were not mutilated, as might have happened if sources for *Battle-Pieces* poems had been cut out. Whenever he was in New York, however, Melville could visit reading rooms where current and back files of many newspapers were available. Toward the end of the war, while living in New York City, Melville seems indeed to have clipped some newspaper items for use in his poetry, judging from his notes to "The Stone Fleet" and "The Frenzy in the Wake." Still, lack of access to his own library or other libraries and to big city newspapers early in the war would not necessarily have kept Melville from writing poems that went into *Battle-Pieces,* for compilations of war reporting were available for sale starting late in 1861.

Melville's old friend Robert Tomes, who had made himself into an American military historian, issued three volumes on *The War with the South: A History of the Great American Rebellion,* the last ready in 1865; some of the many engravings were from drawings that Melville's illustrator friend Felix Darley had made for the volume. During the war years Melville stayed in contact with Evert A. Duyckinck, who was collecting documents for what turned out to be another three-volume *National History of the War for the Union, Civil, Military and Naval, Founded on Official and Other Authentic Documents* (copyrighted in 1861 by Johnson, Fry & Co. of 27 Beekman Street, published beginning in 1862). That first volume (1862) ends in November 1861; the second (dated 1865) covers October 1861 to November 1862; and the third (also dated 1865) covers December 1862 to April 1865. As Duyckinck's title pages explained, the volumes were illustrated with highly finished steel engravings, including battle scenes by sea and land, and full-length portraits of naval and military heroes, engraved from original paintings by Alonzo Chappel (a phenomenally speedy brushman) and by the young Thomas Nast, not yet known as a political satirist. Melville may never have owned a set, although John C. Hoadley bought the three volumes and had them bound in half calf, gilt. Still, Melville might have had access at need to documents that went into the *National History of the War* as well as the rest of the massive array of documents which Duyckinck gathered before ultimately rejecting many of them from the compilation. Nothing has been adduced to show that anything in Duyckinck's volumes was irrefutably the *specific* source for anything in *Battle-Pieces*, but supplementary information was available to Melville, in abundance, in Duyckinck's working files. Whether Melville knew the volumes or not is not known, but in his search for documents he would naturally have consulted works his friends had compiled. Melville also had access all through the war to *Harper's Weekly*, a lavish source of news and engravings made from on-the-scene photographs and sketches. Once he began writing, Melville could find in compilations documenting the war anything he had missed in current newspapers.

The greatest compilation, the volumes of the *Rebellion Record* (consisting of, as the subtitle said, *A Diary of American Events, with Documents, Narratives, Illustrative Incidents, Poetry, Etc.*), became Melville's source for many newspaper reports of battles. Separate numbers of the *Record* were issued roughly every month, before being collected into the folio volumes, the first of which was published late in 1861. In engaging to publish the *Rebellion Record* George P. Putnam had expected the documentary history to be completed in a single volume or at most two, according to *Putnam's Monthly Magazine* (January 1868), when the eleventh volume was published, before the series was cut short at twelve volumes. Even if scholars were to establish the precise chronology of the publication of volumes and individual numbers of the *Rebellion Record,* that information might not tell much about the sequence of Melville's composing in relation to the reporting of military events. In view of all the uncertainties, it is no wonder that Stanton Garner in his *Civil War World of Herman Melville* decided the simple and elegant strategy was to discuss the poems in *Battle-Pieces* in the chronology of the events they depict, whenever that was possible.

When Melville wrote the prefatory note to *Battle-Pieces* has not been established—perhaps after writing all but the "Supplement." This note consists of three paragraphs:

> With few exceptions, the Pieces in this volume originated in an impulse imparted by the fall of Richmond. They were composed without reference to collective arrangement, but, being brought together in review, naturally fall into the order assumed.
>
> The events and incidents of the conflict—making up a whole, in varied amplitude, corresponding with the geographical area covered by the war—from these but a few themes have been taken, such as for any cause chanced to imprint themselves upon the mind.
>
> The aspects which the strife as a memory assumes are as manifold as are the moods of involuntary meditation—moods variable, and at times widely at variance. Yielding instinctively, one after another, to feelings not inspired from any one source exclusively, and unmindful, without purposing to be, of consistency, I seem, in most of these verses, to have but placed a harp in a window, and noted the contrasted airs which wayward winds have played upon the strings.

This note plainly was written after the basic order of the book had been created, even if the body of the book had not yet been set in type.

In the second sentence, Melville may have been commenting about two phases, of separate composition and subsequent ordering. By saying "collective arrangement" he could have meant collection into a book of poems, as opposed to some other publication, but the subsequent phrasing seems to indicate that he meant arrangement in particular order *within* his book of war poems. Aware that his prefatory notes are seldom notable for strictest clarity and veracity, critics have tended to discount the possibility that Melville may have composed many of the poems without intending to put them into a book of war poems. As far as the rapidity of composition is concerned, critics have also been skeptical, but, allowing some leeway for the phrase "few exceptions," Melville may have been speaking accurately. It is not necessary to assume that for some occult reason he was misrepresenting himself when he denied what his readers might otherwise have taken for granted, that he had been writing poems all through the war, as events portrayed in the poems occurred. Melville was a practiced poet, author of a complete book of poems that should have been published in 1860, and he was, after all, the man who had written *Redburn* in two months, then in the next two months wrote *White-Jacket*. Without further evidence, dates of composition of individual poems remain speculative, limited mainly by the dates of the events described, starting with the stated initiatory date (for most of the poems) of April 1865, and ending with the date assigned to "Lee in the Capitol" (April 1866), and the publication of *Battle-Pieces* in mid-August 1866.

The main title *Battle-Pieces,* Melville expected his readers to know, was borrowed from the sister art of painting, particular Dutch and English paintings which depicted sea-battles, but also from the sister art of music, where popular battle-pieces included the bagpipers' favorite, "The Battle of Waterloo." Set-pieces in poems by Scott and others were known in Melville's time as "battle-pieces." The subtitle, "Aspects of the War," allowed for poems that did not deal specifically with battles. Melville made it clear that the prose "Supplement" was written after the poems and the notes: "Were I fastidiously anxious for the symmetry of this book, it would close with the notes. But the times are such that patriotism—not free from solicitude—urges a claim overriding all literary scruple." He dated his writing as "more than a year since the memorable surrender," and further dated it by alluding to recent histories and biographies written by Southerners and already "freely published at the North by loyal houses," and widely read. He also alluded to the "mourners who this summer bear flowers to the mounds of the Virginian and Georgian dead"—a strong indication that he wrote the "Supplement" some weeks after the actual anniversary of the surrender, and in response to the excessively punitive mood of the Radical Republicans.

As far as we know, Melville seems not to have been influenced by any of the war poems which peppered collections like the *Rebellion Record* and appeared in newspapers and magazines (such as *Harper's Weekly,* to which he subscribed). There is no evidence that he paid attention to other poets' volumes of Civil War poems such as Henry Howard Brownell's *Lyrics of a Day; or, Newspaper-Poetry* (New York: Carleton, 1864). Nor, with the possible but unlikely exception of "Donelson," does he show the influence of the recent war poets of Britain such as Sydney Dobell, whose poems in *England in Time of War*

(1856) focus on a home front rather than distant battles. As we have seen, Melville knew Tennyson's "The Charge of the Light Brigade," which anticipated *Battle-Pieces* in its newspaper origins, but he seems not to have been influenced by the poet laureate's major response to the Crimean War, in *Maud.* Older British poets such as Milton, Scott, and Wordsworth demonstrably did influence Melville in *Battle-Pieces.* For all of his self-conscious violation of "literary scruples" as to "the symmetry of this book" (by including the "Supplement"), *Battle-Pieces* was very much in British literary traditions, very obviously the product of a man steeped not only in British poetry of the previous three and a half centuries but also in their writings about that poetry in "supplementary" essays.

The poem sent to Bliss, like the sixteen poems printed in the back of *Battle-Pieces* under the subtitle "Verses Inscriptive and Memorial" (for example, "Inscription for Graves at Pea Ridge, Arkansas"), demonstrates how closely Melville was working in a British literary tradition. At least one of the poems in this group, "A Requiem for Soldiers lost in Ocean Transports," reflected his painstaking metrical analysis of "Lycidas," but the inspiration for using the genre of "Inscriptions" was mainly eighteenth century and modern. Such "inscriptions" were familiar to Melville from Southey's *The Doctor,* where he had found the idea of "extracts" for *Moby-Dick.* He also knew the group of "Inscriptions" in his edition of Wordsworth, the appendix called "Essay Upon Epitaphs," and the end of the fifth book of *The Excursion.* He was familiar with at least some of these: Shenstone's "Inscription: On a Tablet Against a Root-House," Burns's "Inscription on a Goblet," Coleridge's "Inscription for a Fountain on a Heath," and Bryant's "Inscription for the Entrance to a Wood."

Melville had marked and taken to heart this passage in Wordsworth's "Essay Supplementary to the Preface":

> The appropriate business of poetry, (which, nevertheless, if genuine, is as permanent as pure science,) her appropriate employment, her privilege and her *duty,* is to treat of things not as they *are,* but as they *appear;* not as they exist in themselves, but as they *seem* to exist to the *senses* and to the *passions.* What a world of delusion does this acknowledged principle prepare for the inexperienced! what temptations to go astray are here held forth for them whose thoughts have been little disciplined by the understanding, and whose feelings revolt from the sway of reason!

Melville had made it his business to witness war at first hand, but he emphasized in the prefatory note that he was capturing in the poems the aspects which episodes of the strife took on in his informed memory, his variable moods coloring the way he recalled the battles. Like Wordsworth, he was attempting to do the proper business of poetry by treating of things as they appeared to him, as they *seemed* to exist to his senses and passions. Melville's decision in many of his poems not to aim for what was then being called Dutch realism or Pre-Raphaelite realism was not designed to win him the widest audience, but it was a conscious literary choice made under the influence of the former poet laureate, dead only a decade and a half.

As one would expect, Melville's poetic strategies in *Battle-Pieces* reflect his note-taking in 1862, Francis Jeffrey's description of Victor Alfieri's avoiding "Figures of mere ostentation.—Show-pieces of fine writing." Like Alfieri, Melville was prepared in some poems to sacrifice "flow & sweetness" in striving to give "force & energy by condensation & emphasis & inversion." Alfieri had achieved, Jeffrey said, a chastened gravity, and had displayed "Temperance and propriety of delineation of the passions." Ruskin's aesthetic tenets which Melville had written down in his Vasari were also in his mind as he wrote his war poems. He would value "completeness, fullness," even in a short poem, over "fine writing" and high polish. *Battle-Pieces* was a more literary book than the reviewers realized—in his immersion in the genre of inscriptions; in his choice of Wordsworth for authority on poetic distance from subject; in his choice of Milton (along with Alfieri as interpreted by Jeffrey) as authority for a spareness in rhyme and diction; and in his choice of Arnold and Ruskin for contemporary applications of Aristotelian principles involving the choice of noble actions.

Earnestly trying not to idealize military glory, especially in this modern war where impersonal mechanical power often seemed to overwhelm any personal heroism, Melville recollected one of Milton's pronouncements. These opening lines from "A Utilitarian View of the Monitor's Fight" are fitted to its speaker, who is not to be identified with the poet:

> Plain be the phrase, yet apt the verse,
>   More ponderous than nimble;
> For since grimed War here laid aside
> His Orient pomp, 'twould ill befit
>   Overmuch to ply
>   The rhyme's barbaric cymbal.

Here Melville was acknowledging "The Verse" section preceding *Paradise Lost,* where Milton declared that "Rime" was "no necessary Adjunct or true Ornament of Poem or good Verse, <u>in longer Works especially</u>, but the Invention of a barbarous Age, to set off wretched matter and lame Meeter" (see Mathieu; the underlining is Melville's in his copy). True "musical delight," Milton declared, "<u>consists only in apt Numbers, fit quantity of Syllables, and the sense variously drawn out from one verse into another</u>, not in the jingling sound of like endings" (Melville's underlining). In *The Poetical Works and Remains of Henry Kirke White,* which Melville bought during his quest for an aesthetic credo in 1862, he had read the comment that "Harmonious modulations, and <u>unvarying exactness of measure</u>, totally precluding sublimity and fire, have reduced our fashionable poetry to mere singsong"—and he underlined the indicated words as a good modern affirmation of Milton's principles. Melville was not abjuring rhyme for his war poems but moving toward flexible rhyme schemes such as those in battle-pieces by Thomas Campbell and Sir Walter Scott.

Basing "Lee in the Capitol" on newspaper articles, Melville mythologized the man who had endured a public renunciation of military glory—something parallel to the grandeur of his own renunciation, for years now, of literary glory: informing the poem is Melville's profound though covert identification with Lee. Even his depiction of Lee's choosing not "coldly to endure his doom" (line 93) is infused with the determination he mustered in order to write and publish *Battle-Pieces.* In its form, an imaginary oration by a real historical figure, "Lee in the Capitol" follows hallowed rhetorical precedent, classical and Shakespearean, as well as American classroom exercises.

Just as the "Inscriptions" were conventional, however odd-looking to twenty-first-century readers without a grounding in eighteenth-century British poetry, so was the "Supplement" part of a literary convention as honorable, almost, as a "l'envoy." In particular, Melville had pored over Wordsworth's "Essay Supplementary to the Preface" from the 1815 edition of *Poems* (which he possessed in his 1839 *Poetical Works* along with the more famous preface to the second edition of *Lyrical Ballads*). His own "Supplement" shows that Melville was brooding over British parallels, not over the unresolved issues of the War of the Roses and Cromwell's regime but over the more recent Stuart-Hanoverian parallels, especially George IV's rearing a monument "over the remains of the enemy of his dynasty, Charles Edward, the invader of England and victor in the rout at Preston Pans"—a gesture that mitigated against the ugly possibility that Grant's descendants might "pursue with rancor, or slur by sour neglect, the memory of Stonewall Jackson." The course of events was controlled by Northern politicians who had not yet learned to act like statesmen, but Melville dared to hope that the South could be defeated without being shamed:

> Supposing a happy issue out of present perplexities, then, in the generation next to come, Southerners there will be yielding allegiance to the Union, feeling all their interests bound up in it, and yet cherishing unrebuked that kind of feeling for the memory of the soldiers of the fallen Confederacy that Burns, Scott, and the Ettrick Shepherd felt for the memory of the gallant clansmen ruined through their fidelity to the Stuarts—a feeling whose passion was tempered by the poetry imbuing it, and which in no wise affected their loyalty to the Georges, and which, it may be added, indirectly contributed excellent things to literature.

Melville saw himself like Robert Burns, like Sir Walter Scott, and like James Hogg (the Ettrick Shepherd, that powerful presence in the Albany of Melville's youth)—a poet daring to be fair to defeated rebels while contributing to the poetic record of the victors. As he looked over the accumulating postwar histories and biographies, Melville recognized his own battle-pieces as constituting a parallel "poetic record" of the war.

IN THE INTRODUCTION I CHALLENGED ALFRED KAZIN'S CLAIM THAT poetry was only a sideline for Melville. On the contrary, I insisted, for many years poetry was obsessively important to him. Despite the looming (and tentatively explored) significance of the mass of Melville's marginalia in books of poetry and in writings about poetry, I was staggered by what I found once I began writing this book. All his life Melville saturated himself in poetry, especially British poetry. He read omnivorously, nicely distinguishing between great poetry and pleasant, readable lower tiers of poetry. Trained to memorize, in his forties and probably beyond he still set himself to "get by heart" passages of poetry that pleased him. He was blessed with a capacious, retentive memory that allowed him to carry great swatches of poetry in his head, so that he could identify influences and borrowings when he encountered them. While reading poetry perhaps nothing delighted him more than imagining the joy one great poet had in playing with the conceits and words of another. Conscientiously he set himself to understanding critical treatises on aesthetics and tried to embody his findings in his own poetry. He knew his own worth. By the early 1860s, he had identified his own rank and fate as poet by studying the lives of poets in the best literary histories as well as literary and artistic biographies from the Renaissance to his own time.

While recognizing that profound knowledge of poetry and poetics could not guarantee that Melville himself would achieve greatness in poetry, I have not directly challenged the other part of Kazin's judgment, that Melville was never "good" at writing poetry. Nowhere have I attempted to make the case for the lasting value of Melville's poetry as literature. Seeing that the making of Melville the poet was territory almost unexplored, I set myself to chart the terrain, not to hold a pointer to its various beauties. Earlier, in the second volume of my biography of Melville, I also avoided championing Melville as a poet, never holding his poetry up alongside the best by other poets, never casting about for quotable praise by reputable critics of poetry, although such praise was available, and not only from those known primarily as Melville critics. My strategy then and now has been to make the case tacitly by setting Melville's work in the context of poets like the Brownings and Tennyson (rather than poets like Stoddard and Stedman). I trust it will be clear that I rank many of the short poems with great poems by Whitman and Dickinson, his only equals among American poets of the nineteenth century. Despite my reticence, any careful reader of the chapters on *Clarel* in my biography would conclude rightly that I rank it as the greatest long poem in American literature, unless one puts "Song of Myself" in the same category. Melville wrestled strenuously, even nobly, with the angel, Art—and often won. Heroic wrestling almost surely occurred in the years just before he finished his first volume of poetry in 1860. During at least one prolonged period, 1870 through 1875, he wrestled with the angel daily, weekly, monthly. This book stops at the time Melville went public as a poet, and it stops, as my biography did, without defending Melville's poetry. Kazin proved (in phrasing from *Pierre*) exhilarative and provocative to me. With any luck *Melville: The Making of the Poet* will prove equally challenging to young Melvilleans willing to absorb and augment the evidence presented in this book and eager to champion particular poems and to make their own attempts to confirm Melville's high status as poet. *Melville the Poet* and *Melville as Poet* may not long remain unwritten.

INTRODUCTION

1. See, e.g., *Correspondence,* the entry for May 22, 1860 (343–45). Unless otherwise specified, all quotations of letters to or from Melville are from this volume; citations are by date. References to dates, events, or documents that are not otherwise documented here are based on my biography (cited by volume and page, e.g., Parker 1:883), my ongoing *The New Melville Log* (the revised and greatly expanded edition of Jay Leyda's *The Melville Log*), the various published volumes of the Northwestern-Newberry Edition of the writings of Herman Melville (hereafter NN), and the publications listed in the Works Cited.

2. *The Confidence-Man,* chap. 1. Unless otherwise noted, all quotations of Melville's works follow the NN Edition. Because the chapters in Melville's works are short, citations are by chapter to allow location in other editions.

3. *Battle-Pieces, John Marr,* and *Timoleon* make up the *Published Poems* volume (11) of the NN Edition; *Clarel* is volume 12 in the edition (1991).

4. The manuscripts variously titled "Naples" and "At the Hostelry," like the other poetic and prose manuscripts preserved by his widow after Melville's death, including "House of the Tragic Poet," *Billy Budd, Sailor,* and the near-final *Weeds and Wildings Chiefly,* are in the Houghton Library of Harvard University and are published in the final NN volume (15). Facts about the dates of composition of Melville's poetry are based on the second volume of my biography, Robert Sandberg's 1989 Northwestern University dissertation, and on work reported in the *Published Poems* volume.

5. The memoir was published in Smith, *History of Pittsfield* (1876). See *Log* 63–64 and, for a reprint of the full text, Sealts, "Thomas Melvill, Jr." (1987).

6. Melville made the comment in a letter to Leonard G. Sanford, June 22, 1886.

7. The "Augusta Papers" are those of Melville's sister Augusta, now in the Gansevoort-Lansing Collection, Rare Books and Manuscript Division, The New York Public Library, Astor, Lenox, and Tilden Foundations; quotations from her correspondence and other materials in this collection (cited as NYPL-GL) are my transcriptions from the originals, unless otherwise specified. For books Melville owned, see chap. 3, note 2 below.

CHAPTER ONE

1. Reviews are quoted from Higgins and Parker, *Herman Melville: The Contemporary Reviews* (1995), which preserves any unusual spelling and punctuation. Later in this chapter, the review of *Mardi* in the New Bedford *Mercury* is a more recent discovery communicated to me by Mark Wojnar.

2. The publisher was Ticknor, Reed, and Fields, who were already promising a new work by Nathaniel Hawthorne, one not yet named as *The Scarlet Letter.*

3. *Log* is used throughout to refer to Jay Leyda's *The Melville Log* (1951; reprinted with a Supplement, 1969), which is arranged chronologically. *New Log* refers to my ongoing version of *The New Melville Log.*

4. Since the only known copy of the *Daily News* is defective, the quotation beginning "Buy this Book" is eked out from the passage as quoted in the advertisement in the New York *Tribune* for May 31, 1856.

CHAPTER TWO

1. The sixteen known surviving manuscript leaves from the first draft of *Typee* are in NYPL-GL; the transcription is mine.

2. *Life in a Man-of-War or Scenes in "Old Ironsides" During her Cruise in the Pacific. By a Fore-Top-Man* (Philadelphia: Lydia R. Bailey, Printer, 1841).

3. Evert A. Duyckinck to his wife, August 9, 1851 (*New Log*). From an 1896 text we know at least roughly what Melville read aloud.

4. Reconstructed texts of the lectures Melville delivered in 1857–58 ("Statues in Rome"), 1858–59 ("The South Seas"), and 1859–60 ("Travel") are included in *The Piazza Tales and Other Prose Pieces, 1839–1860,* volume 9 of the NN Edition, pp. 398–423.

5. Quotations from *Weeds and Wildings Chiefly, With a Rose or Two,* follow the text in Robert C. Ryan's 1967 Northwestern University dissertation.

CHAPTER THREE

1. The family surname was usually spelled Melvill in Allan's lifetime; after his death in 1832 Maria Gansevoort Melvill and her children normally used the spelling Melville. Allan's letter to Shaw is in the Houghton Library of Harvard University, bMS Am 188 (68); it is quoted here with permission.

2. Books Melville is known to have owned or consulted are identified by the number assigned by Merton M. Sealts Jr. in his *Melville's Reading* and its supplements (including Sealts 1990 and Olsen-Smith and Sealts 2004). The Spenser owned by Allan Melvill and later Herman Melville was *The Poetical Works of Edmund Spenser* (London: J. Bell, 1787–88), 8 v. in 4; Sealts 483a. It was a New Year's gift to Allan from his friend Obadiah Rich Jr. (1783–1850—born in Truro, Massachusetts, and later the great London dealer in Americana). It is now in the Melville Collection of the Houghton Library of Harvard University, donated by Melville's great-granddaughter Priscilla Osborne Ambrose and her children Will and Catherine.

3. Jay Leyda included much of Melville's marginalia in *The Melville Log,* in remarkably reliable transcriptions, and Walker Cowen put more in his dissertation and book, *Melville's Marginalia,* in sometimes shaky transcriptions. Many books containing important marginalia (for example, the Wordsworth, the Milton, Hazlitt's *Lectures,* the Vasari, and the Spenser) surfaced too late for Cowen to see them. Transcriptions throughout of Melville's markings and marginalia in his books are mine unless otherwise noted.

4. Woodbridge's other pieces in the *Zodiac* are indicative of the allusive poetry of the time. "The Last Day of Summer" (August 1835) was subtitled "Imitated from Moore" (whose "The Last Rose of Summer" was already world famous). Billed as expressly written "For the Zodiac" were "To My Little Nephew Willy" and "Genius" (both December 1835); "The New-Year's Book" (January 1836); and "Scenes on the Ocean" (February 1836), with the epigraph "Likeness of heaven! / Agent of power, / Man is thy victim, / Shipwreck thy dower." Also "for the *Zodiac*" (April 1836) was an untitled poem by Woodbridge introduced as "written for and sung at the opening of a Literary Institution" as well as an "Impromptu—to Eliza." For the May 1836 magazine she contributed "Not All a Dream," with an epigraph from Byron: "I had a dream, which was not all a dream" (the opening of "Darkness"), followed below by "My Brain!" Others were "The Gentle Nurse" and "I've Strung my Lyre" (June 1836); "The Ocean Dirge" (September 1836); and "Gertrude" (November 1836). The January 1837 issue contained "Night Scene Upon Kirauea," the epigraph of which reads: "Péle abode in Kirauea, / In the pit, ever feeding the fires," footnoted to *"Polynesian Researches"* as "Goddess of Volcanoes"—that is, William Ellis's *Polynesian Researches,* later a source for Herman Melville.

5. *M'Fingal* (in the 1782 or the 1826 edition) may have been in the Boston house on Green Street during Herman and Gansevoort's visits to their Melvill grandparents because it depicted an event in which Major Thomas Melvill had participated—as one of those who "In shape of Indians, drown'd the tea."

6. In his 1837 *Index Rerum* (see note 8 below), Gansevoort noted under "Bleecker": "some notice of Mrs. Ann Eliza, one of our early poets—her Memoirs & works were published but are now not to be found—see Stone's Life of Brant v1, c9. p206-207—note."

7. Melville's awareness of the Boston Common concessionaire and his Bunker Hill speeches (there was one in 1827 and perhaps others) and poem might explain how he formed the false impression (recorded in his 1850 essay on Hawthorne) that "Pop" Emmons was also the epic poet, the author of *The Fredoniad* (which in fact was by his brother Richard Emmons). Melville, however, was not alone in this confusion; Park Benjamin in the New York *New World* of July 18, 1840, wrote: "The Fredoniad is an epic poem—a great epic in five books or cantos, by the illustrious Emmons, some times called 'Pop'—a monosyllable worthy of his genius."

8. Gansevoort Melville's surviving volumes of the *Index Rerum,* along with his letters and other documents quoted in this chapter, are in the Melville Collection of the Berkshire Athenaeum.

9. The *Mosses* essay is collected in the NN *Piazza Tales* volume, 239–53.

10. See *Correspondence* 10–19 and 551–64.

11. Gansevoort Melville's letters and other documents quoted in this paragraph and the following one are transcribed from the originals in the Melville Collection of the Berkshire Athenaeum.

12. See Parker 1:320–21, where I had not identified this poetry as by Byron.

13. Fanny Melville's "Myself" and Augusta Melville's *Orient Pearls* are in NYPL-GL. Other poems Augusta entered into her book include "The Rights of Women" (1849, by Mrs. E. Little—"'The rights of women,' what are they?/The right to labor and to pray;/The right to watch while others sleep,/The right o'er others' woes to weep;/The right to succor in distress"); "When I am Old" ("Copied from Fanny's book"); "The Love of Later Years" (1849, "Copied from Lizzie's book"); "We are Growing Old" (1849, by the blind poet of Stranolar, Ireland, Frances Browne, 1816–79); "I Think of Thee in the Night" (1850, by T. K. Hervey, 1799–1859); "The Virgin's Grave" (1850, by William Gilmore Simms); "The Crown of Amaranth" (1851, by "L. S."—Lydia Sigourney); "Lines Written on Leaving New Rochelle" (1851, by Joseph Rodman Drake—just as Allan Melville's brother-in-law Richard

Lathers was building an Italianate villa there); "And his victor crown of ama-ranth, / Shall never fade away" (1851, a reference to 1 Peter 5:4); "Jesus of Nazareth passeth by" (1851, by Lydia H. Sigourney, a reference to Luke 18:37); "Woman's Faith" (1851; probably Sir Walter Scott's "The Truth of Woman," which begins "Woman's faith, and woman's trust"); "Sadly we Mourn Each Vanished Grace" (1851, by Barry Cornwall); "My Last Resting Place" (1851, by A. D. V. S.); "Yield Not to Despair" (1851, by the English physician Nathaniel Cotton, 1705–88, from "The Fireside"); and "To be Re-signed when Ills Betide" (1852, also by Cotton). Inside the front cover of her commonplace book Augusta pasted a newspaper printing of Longfellow's "Endymion," which she dated September 19, 1853, the day of George Griggs's engagement to her sister Helen. The women in his household may have shared very few of their favorite poems with the author in their midst, but into the house came the sources of the poems they copied into their "books," and the commonplace books themselves were cherished for many years.

14. Melville commented that this poem was "Hafiz Englished," and added: "Ah, Will was a trump." I examined Melville's copy of Davenant's *Works* (London: Printed by T. N. for Henry Herringman, 1673; Sealts 176) at the Howard S. Mott Bookstore in Sheffield, Massachusetts, on June 8, 1990.

15. George L. Duyckinck repeated the story about Lockhart as a cold fish to Joann Miller in his letter of December 11, 1849 (in the Duyckinck Collec-tion, Rare Books and Manuscript Division, The New York Public Library, Astor, Lenox, and Tilden Foundations [hereafter NYPL-D]).

16. Melville's Dante was the Cary translation entitled *The Vision; or Hell, Purga-tory, and Paradise* (London: Bohn, 1847; Sealts 174).

17. See *Piazza Tales* 669 and *Correspondence* 150–51.

18. In July 1850 Evert Duyckinck sent Augusta the prose *The Vale of Cedars,* by Grace Aguilar, and *In Memoriam* (see also chap. 4 below). In November 1852 Duyckinck sent Augusta the Reverend R. A. Willmott's *Summer Time in the Country,* a sort of summer diary of Willmott's promiscuous reading and out-ings and thoughts about literary and artistic subjects in which the pages are strewn with carefully selected quotations from poetry relevant to esoteric topics, descriptions of birds, then of bird calls, or descriptions of gardens— real ones and ones in poems. One entry is a disquisition on how lucky Waller has been in his critics; another gives a snippet of Cowley's verse letter to Eve-lyn, quoted at length in Leigh Hunt's *Book for a Corner,* which Duyckinck had given Augusta earlier. Among the poets repeatedly cited by Willmott are Spenser, Shakespeare, Milton, Thomson, Shenstone, Cowper, on through Wordsworth, Coleridge, Byron, and some Keats. The Willmott book displays

a mind so saturated with British poetry that it could be retrieved topically. *Summer Time in the Country* was at Arrowhead for several years, available to Melville, whose own mind was equally saturated with the same poetry. (In 1853 John C. Hoadley, engaged to Melville's sister Catherine, gave their sister Helen the new volume by Whittier, *The Chapel of the Hermits.*) As a more special gift than a mere book, Cornelius Mathews in the summer of 1850 sent Elizabeth Shaw Melville "The Cry of the Human" in Elizabeth Barrett Browning's own hand, a gift to him from the poet years before (*Log* 388–89). In January 1854, under pressure to welcome his new brother-in-law into the family, Melville gave Hoadley the volumes of Chatterton he had bought in London in 1849 (Sealts 137). In 1859 Melville's brother-in-law Sam Shaw gave him the new (1858) volume of *Poems* by Judge Shaw's old acquaintance Ralph Waldo Emerson. Melville gave many of his books of poetry to his sisters (books that he did not feel he needed any more, but also books that he felt he had no exclusive claim to, such as his father's set of Spenser); to his daughters, including some that he seems to have wanted to have around the house); and to his wife (for instance, his copy of Poe's poems, and, late in life, an occasion-specific gift—the poems of Thomas Bailey Aldrich, bestowed because Aldrich had bought a house on Mount Vernon Street near the Shaw house on Beacon Hill).

19. Melville's copy of *The Poetical Works of John Milton* (2 vols., Boston: Hilliard, Gray, 1836; Sealts 358b) first surfaced in 1983.

CHAPTER FOUR

1. "Gad-fly" as a mock title for a literary magazine was used by Poe in the "Thingum Bob" skit printed in the *Southern Literary Messenger* in December 1844 and reprinted in the *Broadway Journal* in July 1845; that piece begins by facetiously naming two great poets, Shakespeare and Emmons, a collocation that hints at a humorous contemporary context for Melville's pairing of Emmons and Homer in his 1850 essay on Hawthorne's *Mosses,* where Shakespeare figures largely, though not in the short passage about Pop Emmons.

2. The present Houghton Library number for this account statement from Wiley is bMS Am 188 (524). (Sealts's location of the document as in Harvard College Library-Wiley Collection was erroneous: it is in what Sealts referred to elsewhere as HCL-M, the Melville family papers at Harvard.)

3. For this annotation in Melville's copy of Shakespeare see *Log* 291.

4. Powell's May(?) 1849 letter to Evert A. Duyckinck (Parker 1:646).

5. This quotation and ones later in this paragraph are from the journals Melville kept during his trips, printed in the NN *Journals* volume; citations are to the date of the entry.

6. Ironically, late in 1851, after the excursion to Mount Saddleback (or Greylock), George Duyckinck and surely Evert Duyckinck (from whom his brother kept no secrets) were distressingly reminded that poetry in America could embody dangerous impulses. Augusta Melville as a confidante of Sarah Morewood was entrusted with the "heart poetry" she had written in August on Greylock in the first frenzy of her infatuation with George, to whom she recklessly sent copies of the verses. Sarah Morewood's letters to George Duyckinck are in NYPL-D, carefully preserved by Evert Duyckinck. Augusta's consoling letter (see Parker 2:46) exists in a draft in NYPL-GL.

7. The chapter on Wordsworth had been printed as early as February 1841, in the *Southern Literary Messenger* of February 1841, long before Tuckerman collected it in *Thoughts on the Poets*.

8. In chapter 9 below, see Melville's 1862 annotation in Hazlitt's *Lectures on the English Poets* about "that contemptible man" Wordsworth.

9. For Allan Melvill's copy of Spenser, see chap. 3, n. 2 above.

10. For Melville's copy of Hazlitt (New York: Derby & Jackson, 1859), see Olsen-Smith and Sealts 263b.

11. See *Reading Melville's "Pierre; or, The Ambiguities,"* by Brian Higgins and Hershel Parker (Baton Rouge: Louisiana State University Press, 2006).

12. For *The Isle of the Cross* see the introduction above and Parker 2:136–61.

CHAPTER FIVE

1. Melville made this comment in annotating his copy of Chatterton; see chapter 4 above.

CHAPTER SIX

1. The Campbell allusion ("the deadly space between"), first identified by Stanton Garner (1977), occurs in chapter 11; the Tennyson allusion is in chapter 4 (see also chap. 8 below). Citations for *Billy Budd, Sailor,* are to the text by Hayford and Sealts 1962.

2. See Melville's journal entry for April 5, 1857 (*Journals* 120).

3. See Melville's letter to Hawthorne, July 22, 1851 (*Correspondence* 199).

4. These comments are from Tuckerman's January 1861 article in the *North American Review.*

5. Because it was written as a letter inviting Shepherd to visit, the poem appears in the NN *Correspondence* volume (337–39).

CHAPTER SEVEN

1. George Duyckinck to Rosalie Baker, July 26, 1858 (see *Log* 594; Parker 2:379).

2. The letter is in NYPL-D (Box 12); most of it is transcribed in *Log* 618.

3. The letter is in NYPL-D (Box 12); it is partially transcribed in *Log* 618.

4. The letter is in NYPL-D (Box 12); it is partially transcribed in *Log* 620.

5. Private communication to Parker, February 21, 2003.

CHAPTER EIGHT

1. For the pilgrimage by Coan and Gulick, see Parker 2:397–400. Melville referred to the superiority of classical times at the end of "Statues in Rome" (*Piazza Tales* 408–9).

2. When I found the description in the *Log* (642) unclear, Deborah Norsworthy kindly examined the clipping as Melville had placed it in his edition of Tennyson's poetry and showed that in his contemptuous comment Melville was defending Tennyson against the writer of the piece he had pasted in. The "stuff" was not Tennyson's.

3. This transcription is mine, with the assistance of Dennis Marnon, from the manuscript in the Houghton Library of Harvard University (HCL-M), but I consulted Robert A. Sandberg's dissertation, as I did regularly in working with the "Naples" poem and "At the Hostelry."

4. Presumably by the late 1850s Virgil was linked with Tennyson in Melville's mind not only as melancholy laureates but also as fellow imitators. In 1862, reading in his set of Vasari, Melville marked a passage on Raphael's imitating Michelangelo (3.23) and commented: "The inimitable imitator. Good deal of the Virgil about Raphael—." In the *Mosses* essay Melville had cried, "Let us boldly contemn all imitation, though it comes to us graceful and fragrant as the morning."

CHAPTER NINE

1. The reference to Krakens occurs in Melville's letter to Hawthorne, November 17, 1851.

2. See *Journals* 628, 633.

3. Transcriptions of Melville's marginalia in his edition of Hazlitt's *Lectures* (New York: Derby & Jackson, 1859; Olsen-Smith and Sealts 263b) are mine throughout.

4. See *Piazza Tales* 779–80.

5. In 1854 Melville supplied the Harpers with now lost sections of a "tortoise-hunting" book that did not duplicate anything in "The Encantadas" (Parker 2:216–23).

CHAPTER TEN

1. See Parker 1:840–42 for my redating of the letter to Hawthorne dated [June 1?], 1851, in *Correspondence* (191), on evidence in a letter from Augusta Melville to Allan Melville dated May 16, 1851, and deposited at Arrowhead by Anna Morewood in the early 1990s. The *Correspondence* volume was already in print when I made the redating. When I went over the evidence with him, Hayford approved the redating.

2. This is Sandberg's transcription from the surviving manuscript in HCL-M.

3. We know little about Melville's note-taking. Blank-books were available at stationers and he used them for journals but we do not yet have evidence for his using them for note-taking while we do have evidence for his using library slips and for his using pages in other books which he was sure he would keep.

4. See Parker 2:745. The sale of Tuckerman's books is documented in the Leavitt auction catalogue in the American Antiquarian Society; most of the books were sold on the first day of the auction, June 10, 1872.

5. Scott Norsworthy communicated this information to me privately.

CHAPTER ELEVEN

1. In the twentieth century the annotations Helen transcribed into the 1855 Little, Brown set were known decades before the eight-in-four set surfaced, and her handwriting was mistaken for Melville's own.

2. Fanny's letter is in NYPL-GL (Box 215).

3. The phrase is Allan's, writing to Augusta on October 12, 1863 (Parker 2:552).

WORKS CITED

Arnold, Matthew. *Essays in Criticism.* Boston: Ticknor & Fields, 1865.

————. *Poems.* Boston: Ticknor & Fields, 1856.

Battenfeld, David H. "The Source for the Hymn in *Moby-Dick.*" In *Moby-Dick,* ed. Hershel Parker and Harrison Hayford, 574–77. New York: W. W. Norton, 2001. Originally published in *American Literature* 27 (November 1955): 393–96.

Baym, Nina. "Melville's Quarrel with Fiction." *PMLA* 94 (October 1979): 909–23.

Berthold, Dennis. "Melville and Dutch Genre Painting." In *Savage Eye: Melville and the Visual Arts,* ed. Christopher Sten, 218–45. Kent, Ohio: Kent State University Press, 1991.

————. "Melville, Garibaldi, and the Medusa of Revolution." *American Literary History* 9 (1997): 425–59.

Bezanson, Walter. "Melville's Reading of Arnold's Poetry." *PMLA* 69 (June 1954): 365–69.

Bezanson, Walter, ed. *Clarel.* New York: Hendricks House, 1960.

Blair, Hugh. *Lectures on Rhetoric and Belles Lettres.* New York: Duyckinck, 1817.

Brodhead, Richard H. "All in the Family." Review of *Herman Melville: A Biography,* by Hershel Parker. *New York Times Book Review,* June 23, 2002, 13.

Browning, Elizabeth Barrett. *Prometheus Bound, and other Poems; including Sonnets from the Portuguese, Casa Guidi Windows, etc.* New York: Francis & Co., 1851.

Buell, Lawrence. "Melville the Poet." In *The Cambridge Companion to Herman Melville,* ed. Robert S. Levine, 135–56. New York: Cambridge University Press, 1998.

Byron, George Gordon, Lord. *The Poetical Works.* Boston: Little, Brown, 1853.

Channing, William Ellery. *Poems.* Boston: J. Munroe, 1847.

Chapman, George, trans. *Homer's Batrachomyomachia . . . ,* ed. Richard Hooper. London: Smith, 1858.

————. *The Iliads of Homer,* ed. Richard Hooper. 2 vols. London: Smith 1857.

Charvat, William. "Melville." In *The Profession of Authorship in America: 1800–1870,* by William Charvat, ed. Matthew J. Bruccoli, 204–61. Columbus: Ohio State University Press, 1968.

Chatterton, Thomas. *Poetical Works.* Cambridge: Grant, 1842.

Churchill, Charles. *The Poetical Works . . . With Copious Notes and a Life of the Author.* Boston: Little, Brown, 1854.

Cowen, Walker. "Melville's Marginalia." Ph.D. diss., Harvard University, 1965. Reprint, New York: Garland, 1988.

Cowley, Abraham. *The Works of Abraham Cowley.* 3 vols. London: Tonson, 1707, and Charles Harper, 1711.

Currie, Janette. "From Altrive to Albany: James Hogg's Transatlantic Publication." *STAR-Project Archive* (February 2004), www.star.ac.uk/Archive/Publications.httm.

Dante Alighieri. *The Vision; or Hell, Purgatory, and Paradise,* trans. Henry Cary. London: Bohn, 1847.

Davenant, William. *Works.* London: Printed by T. N. for Henry Herringman, 1673.

Davis, Merrell R. *Melville's "Mardi": A Chartless Voyage.* New Haven: Yale University Press, 1952. Reprint, Hamden, Conn.: Archon Books, 1967.

Davis, Merrell R., and William H. Gilman. *The Letters of Herman Melville.* New Haven: Yale University Press, 1960.

Day, Frank L. *Melville's Use of "The Rebellion Record" in His Poetry.* Clemson, S.C.: Clemson University Press, 2002.

————. "Melville and Sherman March to the Sea." *American Notes & Queries* 2 (May 1964): 134–36.

Delbanco, Andrew. "The Great White Male." Review of *Herman Melville: A Biography,* by Hershel Parker. *New Republic,* September 30, 2002, 33–37.

————. *Herman Melville: His World and Work.* New York: Knopf, 2005.

Dewey, Orville. *Old World and the New.* New York: Harper & Brothers, 1836.

Dickens, Charles. *The Letters of Charles Dickens.* The Pilgrim Edition. Oxford: Clarendon. Vol. 4, 1844–1846, ed. Kathleen Tillotson, 1977. Vol. 5, 1847–1849, ed. Graham Storey and K. J. Fielding, 1981. Vol. 6, 1850–1852, ed. Graham Storey, Kathleen Tillotson, and Nina Burgis, 1988.

Disraeli, Isaac. *Amenities of Literature, Consisting of Sketches and Characters of English Literature.* London: Routledge, 1859.

————. *The Calamities and Quarrels of Authors, with Some Inquiries Respecting their Moral and Literary Characters, and Memoirs for our Literary History.* London: Routledge, 1860.

————. *Curiosities of Literature.* London: Routledge, 1859.

————. *The Literary Character; or, The History of Men of Genius, Drawn from Their own Feelings and Confessions.* London: Routledge, 1859.

Dwyer, J. H. *An Essay on Elocution; with Elucidatory Passages from Various Authors to which are added Remarks on Reading Prose and Verse, with Suggestions to Instructors of the Art.* 2nd ed. New York: G. & C. Carville, & E. Bliss, 1828.

Emerson, Ralph Waldo. *Essays, Second Series.* Boston: Munroe, 1844.

Emmons, Richard. *The Fredoniad: or, Independence Preserved. An Epick Poem of the Late War of 1812.* 4 vols. Boston: Published for the Author, by William Emmons, 1827.

Emmons, William. *The Battle of Bunker Hill, or The Temple of Liberty; an Historical Poem in Four Cantos.* New York: Printed by Sackett & Sargent, 1839.

Fergusson, Robert. *The Works of Robert Fergusson.* London: Fullarton, 1857.

Garner, Stanton. *The Civil War World of Herman Melville.* Lawrence: The University Press of Kansas, 1993.

———. "Melville and Thomas Campbell: The 'Deadly Space Between.' " *English Language Notes* 14 (1977): 289–90.

Gilman, William H. *Melville's Early Life and "Redburn."* New York: New York University Press, 1951.

Greenwood, Grace [Sarah Jane Clarke]. *Haps and Mishaps of a Tour in Europe.* Boston: Ticknor, Reed, & Fields, 1853.

Grey, Robin, and Douglas Robillard with Hershel Parker. "Melville's Milton: A Transcription of Melville's Marginalia in His Copy of *The Poetical Works of John Milton.*" *Leviathan* 4 (March and October 2002): 117–204.

Hayford, Harrison. "The Significance of Melville's 'Agatha' Letters." *ELH, A Journal of English Literary History* 13 (December 1946): 299–310.

Hayford, Harrison, and Merton M. Sealts Jr., eds. *Billy Budd, Sailor (An Inside Narrative),* by Herman Melville. Chicago: University of Chicago Press, 1962.

Hazlitt, William. *Lectures on the English Comic Writers* and *Lectures on the English Poets.* 2 vols. in one. New York: Derby & Jackson, 1859.

Heffernan, Thomas F. "Melville and Wordsworth." *American Literature* 49 (1977): 338–51.

Heflin, Wilson. "New Light on Herman Melville's Cruise in the *Charles and Henry.*" *Historic Nantucket* 22 (October 1974): 6–27.

Hemans, Felicia. *The Poetical Works.* Boston: Phillips, 1859.

Higgins, Brian, and Hershel Parker. *Herman Melville: The Contemporary Reviews.* Cambridge: Cambridge University Press, 1995.

Higgins, Brian, and Hershel Parker. *Reading Melville's "Pierre; or, The Ambiguities."* Baton Rouge: Louisiana State University Press, 2006.

Hood, Thomas. *The Poetical Works of Thomas Hood.* Boston: Little, Brown, 1860.

Howard, Leon. "Historical Note." In *Pierre; or, The Ambiguities,* ed. Harrison Hayford, Hershel Parker, and G. Thomas Tanselle, 365–79. Evanston and Chicago: Northwestern University Press and The Newberry Library, 1971.

Irving, Washington. *The Sketch-Book of Geoffrey Crayon, Gent.,* ed. Haskell Springer. Boston: Twayne, 1978.

Kames, Henry Home, Lord. *Elements of Criticism.* New York: Collins & Hannay, Collins & Co., and G. & C. Carvill, 1829.

Kelley, Philip, and Ronald Hudson, eds. *The Brownings' Correspondence.* Vol. 5. Winfield, Kansas: Wedgestone Press, 1987.

Kinter, Elvan, ed. *Letters of Robert Browning and Elizabeth Barrett Browning.* Cambridge: Harvard University Press, 1969.

Levine, Robert S. "Introduction." *The Cambridge Companion to Herman Melville,* ed. Levine, 1–11. Cambridge: Cambridge University Press, 1998.

Leyda, Jay. *The Melville Log: A Documentary Life of Herman Melville, 1819–1891.* 2 vols. New York: Harcourt, Brace, 1951. Reprinted with a Supplement, New York: Gordian Press, 1969.

Life in a Man-of-War or Scenes in "Old Ironsides" During her Cruise in the Pacific. By a Fore-Top-Man. Philadelphia: Lydia R. Bailey, Printer, 1841.

Mangan, James Clarence. *Poems of James Clarence Mangan.* New York: Haverty, 1859.

Mathieu, Bertrand. " 'Plain Mechanic Power': Melville's Earliest Poems, *Battle-Pieces and Aspects of the War.*" In "Symposium: Melville the Poet," ed. Douglas Robillard, special issue, *Essays in Arts and Sciences* 5, no. 2 (July 1976): 116–21.

McWilliams, John P. *The American Epic: Transforming a Genre, 1770–1860.* New York: Cambridge University Press, 1989.

Melville, Herman. *The Confidence-Man: His Masquerade.* Ed. Harrison Hayford, Hershel Parker, and G. Thomas Tanselle. The Writings of Herman Melville 10. Evanston and Chicago: Northwestern University Press and The Newberry Library, 1984.

———. *Correspondence.* Ed. Lynn Horth. The Writings of Herman Melville 14. Evanston and Chicago: Northwestern University Press and The Newberry Library, 1993.

———. *Journals.* Ed. Howard C. Horsford with Lynn Horth. The Writings of Herman Melville 15. Evanston and Chicago: Northwestern University Press and The Newberry Library, 1989.

———. *Mardi and A Voyage Thither.* Ed. Harrison Hayford, Hershel Parker, and G. Thomas Tanselle. The Writings of Herman Melville 3. Evanston and Chicago: Northwestern University Press and The Newberry Library, 1970.

———. "Memoir of Thomas Melvill Jr." In *The History of Pittsfield (Berkshire County,) Massachusetts, from the Year 1800 to the Year 1876,* by J. E. A. Smith, 399–400. Springfield, Mass.: Bryan, 1876.

———. *Moby-Dick, or, The Whale.* Ed. Harrison Hayford, Hershel Parker, and G. Thomas Tanselle. The Writings of Herman Melville 6. Evanston and Chicago: Northwestern University Press and The Newberry Library, 1988.

———. *Omoo: A Narrative of Adventures in the South Seas.* Ed. Harrison Hayford, Hershel Parker, and G. Thomas Tanselle. The Writings of Herman Melville 2. Evanston and Chicago: Northwestern University Press and The Newberry Library, 1968.

——. *The Piazza Tales and Other Prose Pieces, 1839–1860*. Ed. Harrison Hayford, Alma A. MacDougall, G. Thomas Tanselle, et al. The Writings of Herman Melville 9. Evanston and Chicago: Northwestern University Press and The Newberry Library, 1987.

——. *Pierre; or, The Ambiguities*. Ed. Harrison Hayford, Hershel Parker, and G. Thomas Tanselle. The Writings of Herman Melville 7. Evanston and Chicago: Northwestern University Press and The Newberry Library, 1971.

——. *Pierre; or, The Ambiguities: The Kraken Edition*. Ed. Hershel Parker, pictures by Maurice Sendak. New York: HarperCollins, 1995.

——. *Published Poems*. Ed. Robert C. Ryan, Harrison Hayford, Alma Mac-Dougall Reising, and G. Thomas Tanselle, with Historical Note by Hershel Parker. The Writings of Herman Melville 11. Evanston and Chicago: Northwestern University Press and The Newberry Library, in progress.

——. *Redburn: His First Voyage*. Ed. Harrison Hayford, Hershel Parker, and G. Thomas Tanselle. The Writings of Herman Melville 4. Evanston and Chicago: Northwestern University Press and The Newberry Library, 1969.

——. *"Weeds and Wildings Chiefly: With a Rose or Two:* Reading Text and Genetic Text." Ed. Robert C. Ryan. Ph.D. diss., Northwestern University, 1967.

——. *White-Jacket; or, The World in a Man-of-War*. Ed. Harrison Hayford, Hershel Parker, and G. Thomas Tanselle. The Writings of Herman Melville 5. Evanston and Chicago: Northwestern University Press and The Newberry Library, 1970.

Metcalf, Eleanor Melville. *Herman Melville: Cycle and Epicycle*. Cambridge, Mass.: Harvard University Press, 1953.

Milder, Robert. "Herman Melville 1819–1891: A Brief Biography." In *A Historical Guide to Herman Melville,* ed. Giles Gunn, 17–58. New York: Oxford University Press, 2005.

——. "Melville's 'Intentions' in *Pierre.*" *Studies in the Novel* 6 (Summer 1974): 186–99.

Milton, John. *The Poetical Works of John Milton*. 2 vols. Boston: Hilliard, Gray, 1836.

Minnigerode, Meade. *Some Personal Letters of Herman Melville and a Bibliography*. New York: The Brick Row Bookshop, 1922.

The Modern British Essayists. 8 vols. Philadelphia: Carey & Hart, 1847–48.

Moore, Thomas. *Life of Lord Byron*. Boston: Little, Brown, 1853[?].

——. *The Poetical Works of Thomas Moore*. Boston: Little, Brown, 1856 [1854?].

Moss, Sidney. *Poe's Literary Battles: The Critic in the Context of His Literary Milieu*. Durham, N.C.: Duke University Press, 1963.

Mumford, Lewis. *Herman Melville*. New York: Harcourt, Brace, 1929.

Murray, Henry A. "Introduction" and "Explanatory Notes." In *Pierre; or, The Ambiguities,* ed. Murray, xiii–ciii, 429–504. New York: Hendricks House, 1949.

Olsen-Smith, Steven, and Dennis C. Marnon. "Melville's Marginalia in *The Works of Sir William D'Avenant:* A Transcription." *Leviathan* 6 (March 2004): 79–102.

Olsen-Smith, Steven, and Merton M. Sealts Jr. "A Cumulative Supplement to *Melville's Reading.*" *Leviathan* 6 (March 2004): 55–77.

Parker, Hershel. *Herman Melville: A Biography, 1819–1851* and *Herman Melville: A Biography, 1851–1891.* 2 vols. Baltimore: Johns Hopkins University Press, 1996, 2002.

———. "Herman Melville's *The Isle of the Cross.*" *American Literature* 62 (March 1990): 1–16.

———. "Historical Note." In *Pierre; or, The Ambiguities,* ed. Harrison Hayford, Hershel Parker, and G. Thomas Tanselle, 379–401. Evanston and Chicago: Northwestern University Press and The Newberry Library, 1971.

———. "Melville and Politics." Ph.D. diss., Northwestern University, 1963.

Parker, Hershel, ed. *Gansevoort Melville's London Journal, and Letters from England, 1845.* New York: New York Public Library, 1966.

Poole, Gordon. "Naples in the Time of Melville: Italian Politics 1857." *Melville Society Extracts* 105 (June 1996): 8–9.

Poole, Gordon, ed. *"At the Hostelry" and "Naples in the Time of Bomba."* Naples: Istituto Universitario Orientale, 1989.

Pommer, Henry. *Milton and Melville.* Pittsburgh: University of Pittsburgh Press, 1950.

Powell, Thomas. *The Living Authors of America.* New York: Stringer & Townsend, 1850.

———. *The Living Authors of England.* New York: D. Appleton & Co., 1849.

Robillard, Douglas, ed. *Poems of Herman Melville.* New Haven, Conn.: College & University Press, 1976.

Ruskin, John. *Modern Painters. Of Many Things.* New York: Wiley & Halsted, 1856.

Sandberg, Robert A. " 'The Adjustment of Screens': Putative Narrators, Authors, and Editors in Melville's Unfinished *Burgundy Club* Book." *Texas Studies in Literature and Language* 31 (Fall 1989): 426–50.

———. "Melville's Unfinished *Burgundy Club* Book." Ph.D. diss., Northwestern University, 1989.

Schultz, Elizabeth. "Melville's Agony: After the Whale." Review of *Herman Melville: A Biography,* by Hershel Parker. *Common Review* 2 (Winter 2002): 40–46.

Sealts, Merton M., Jr. "Historical Note." In *The Piazza Tales and Other Prose Pieces, 1839–1860,* ed. Harrison Hayford, Hershel Parker, and G. Thomas Tanselle, 457–533. Evanston and Chicago: Northwestern University Press and The Newberry Library, 1987.

———. *Melville's Reading: Revised and Enlarged Edition.* Columbia: University of South Carolina Press, 1988.

———. "A Supplementary Note to *Melville's Reading* (1988)." *Melville Society Extracts* 80 (February 1990): 5–10.

———. "Thomas Melvill, Jr., in *The History of Pittsfield.*" *Harvard Library Bulletin* 35 (Spring 1987): 201–17.

Smith, J. E. A. *The History of Pittsfield, (Berkshire County,) Massachusetts, From the Year 1800 to the Year 1876.* Springfield, Mass.: C. W. Bryan & Co., 1876.

Spenser, Edmund. *The Poetical Works.* 8 vols. in 4. London: J. Bell, 1787–88.

Staël, Anne Louise Germaine (Necker), Baronne de. *Germany.* New York: Derby & Jackson, 1859.

Stoddard, Richard Henry, et al. *Poets' Homes: Pen and Pencil Sketches of American Poets and Their Homes.* Boston: D. Lothrop & Co., 1877.

Taylor, Henry. *Notes from Life in Seven Essays.* Boston: Ticknor, Reed, & Fields, 1853.

Tennant, William. *Anster Fair.* Edinburgh: Cockburn, 1812.

Tennyson, Alfred Lord. *The Princess.* New ed. Boston: Ticknor & Fields, 1855.

Thorp, Willard, ed. *Herman Melville: Representative Selections.* New York: American Book Co., 1938.

Tuckerman, Henry T. "Giuseppe Garibaldi." Review of William Arthur, *Italy in Transition. North American Review* 92 (January 1861): 15–56.

———. *The Rebellion: Its Latent Causes and True Significance. In Letters to a Friend Abroad.* New York: James G. Gregory, 1861.

———. *Thoughts on the Poets.* New York: C. S. Francis & Co., 1846.

Vasari, Giorgio. *Lives of the Most Eminent Painters, Sculptors, and Architects.* 5 vols. London: Bohn, 1849–52.

Wallace, Robert K. *Melville and Turner: Spheres of Love and Fright.* Athens: The University of Georgia Press, 1992.

———. "Melville's Prints and Engravings at the Berkshire Athenaeum." *Essays in Arts and Sciences* 15 (June 1986): 59–90.

Weaver, Raymond. *Herman Melville: Mariner and Mystic.* New York: Doran, 1921.

White, Henry Kirke. *The Poetical Works and Remains.* New York: Appleton, 1857.

Wordsworth, William. *The Complete Poetical Works of William Wordsworth,* ed. Henry Reed. Philadelphia: James Kay, Jun. & Brother, 1839.

INDEX

About the Author

Hershel Parker, H. Fletcher Brown Professor Emeritus at the University of Delaware, is General Editor of the final two volumes of the Northwestern-Newberry Edition of the writings of Herman Melville, succeeding Harrison Hayford. Parker's books include *Flawed Texts and Verbal Icons, Reading "Billy Budd,"* and the 1995 edition of Melville's *Pierre, or, The Ambiguities,* illustrated by Maurice Sendak. He is also the author of *Herman Melville: A Biography, 1819–1851* and *Herman Melville: A Biography, 1851–1891,* the first volume a Pulitzer finalist and each the winner of the highest award from the Association of American Publishers' Professional/Scholarly Publishing Division. He lives in Morro Bay, California.